MANAGING PEOPLE IN ENTREPRENEURIAL ORGANIZATIONS:

LEARNING FROM THE MERGER OF ENTREPRENEURSHIP AND HUMAN RESOURCE MANAGEMENT

ADVANCES IN ENTREPRENEURSHIP, FIRM EMERGENCE AND GROWTH

Series Editor: Jerome A. Katz

Volumes 3–4: Edited by Jerome A. Katz

ADVANCES IN ENTREPRENEURSHIP, FIRM EMERGENCE AND
GROWTH   VOLUME 5

MANAGING PEOPLE IN ENTREPRENEURIAL ORGANIZATIONS:

LEARNING FROM THE MERGER OF ENTREPRENEURSHIP AND HUMAN RESOURCE MANAGEMENT

EDITED BY

JEROME A. KATZ

Department of Management, School of Business,
Saint Louis University, USA

THERESA M. WELBOURNE

University of Michigan Business School, USA

2002

JAI
An Imprint of Elsevier Science

Amsterdam – Boston – London – New York – Oxford – Paris
San Diego – San Francisco – Singapore – Sydney – Tokyo

ELSEVIER SCIENCE Ltd
The Boulevard, Langford Lane
Kidlington, Oxford OX5 1GB, UK

First edition 2002

Library of Congress Cataloging in Publication Data
A catalog record from the Library of Congress has been applied for.

British Library Cataloguing in Publication Data
A catalogue record from the British Library has been applied for.

ISBN: 0-7623-0877-X
ISSN: 1074-7540 (Series)

⊗The paper used in this publication meets the requirements of ANSI/NISO Z39.48-1992 (Permanence of Paper).
Printed in The Netherlands.

CONTENTS

v

LIST OF CONTRIBUTORS

Howard E. Aldrich	University of North Carolina at Chapel Hill, Chapel Hill, USA
Linda Amuso	iQuantic, Inc., San Francisco, USA
Robert A. Baron	Lally School of Management and Technology, Troy, USA
Rosemary Batt	Cornell University, Ithaca, USA
Karen Bishop	University of Louisville, Louisville, USA
Daniel M. Cable	University of North Carolina at Chapel Hill, Chapel Hill, USA
Mary E. Graham	Clarkson University, Potsdam, USA
Robert L. Heneman	The Ohio State University, Columbus, USA
Diane E. Johnson	University of Alabama, Tuscaloosa, USA
Jerome A. Katz	Saint Louis University, St. Louis, USA
Gideon D. Markman	University of Georgia, Athens, Greece
Brian Murray	University of Dallas, Irving, USA
Judith W. Tansky	The Ohio State University, Columbus, USA
Theresa M. Welbourne	University of Michigan, Ann Arbor, USA
Ian O. Williamson	University of Maryland, College Park, USA

INTRODUCTION:
HUMAN RESOURCE MANAGEMENT
IN ENTREPRENEURIAL SETTINGS:
TOWARDS A RELATIONAL APPROACH

Remember just a few months ago – well, it seemed like just a few months ago at least:

- when every college in the United States seemed to be starting up a new curriculum in e-business;
- when endowed chairs were being given right and left to professors who understood the brave new world of the "e";
- when students would not even attend those recruiting fairs for large, established firms, and instead, started a new e-business or jumped into the hottest dot com they could find;
- when all the large businesses took one floor and devoted it to "e" – these companies forego the company dress code, bought pool tables, painted the "e" floors cool colors, and fought to keep their talent because the latest "dot com" down the street was trying to seduce their programmers to leave;
- when stock was worth a lot, but the company was not?

What did we learn in those days that seem so long ago?

First, most people did not really know what the "e" in e-business really meant. We tried to tell them that the "e" word has been around for ages. It stands for entrepreneurship. We, the people who study entrepreneurship, were not surprised by the rise and fall of the dot coms. We also will not be surprised by the steady growth in dot com businesses after the big bust. We saw the coming, fallout and subsequent real business growth resulting from telephones, biotechnology, computers, and more. The big "E" stands for entrepreneurship, and regardless of industry or hottest craze, entrepreneurship is a global phenomenon that spurs economic growth, prosperity, new ideas, technology, jobs, and education. Within each new industry that springs up, there are winners and losers. This special issue is interested in the one constant that drives companies to be successful or to fail. We think that one constant is how people are managed, and how the cycle of people management changes as a company faces the challenges of growth and survival.

The last years of the 20th Century may well have reflected a brief "golden age" for human resource management. In an economy where ideas and capital were plentiful, the critical facet for success increasingly became human resources. Having the people on hand, with the right skills to bring new products into existence with a first mover advantage became the definitive factor. Venture capital financing was plentiful. Entrepreneurs with ideas were plentiful, but ironically, organizational members, whether they were experienced managers, programmers, webmasters, or graphic artists, were in short supply. As a result, HRM policies and initiatives proliferated. Like the boom times that inspired them, some of these efforts, such as on-site masseuses and 24-hour pizza bars, defined what history will recall as indicative of the excesses of the period. On the other hand, the experimentation around, and even the desperation for human resources, no doubt will leave some aspects of HRM far better grounded and developed.

Building on these experiences, as well as a special issue of *Entrepreneurship: Theory & Practice*, that we published on the topic in 2000, we have developed a more in-depth, follow-on focused on *human resource management and entrepreneurship*. Given the importance of entrepreneurship to our economy, the criticality of human capital to assuring success, and the recent golden age of HRM during the Internet Boom, you would think that the combination of entrepreneurship and human resource management would draw a significant number of researchers. We were surprised to find that was not the case. There seems to be only a handful of individuals doing research that can be considered to be at the juncture of these two fields,[1] and the chapters in this special issue, we think, represent some of the best work being done on this topic. But given the limited number of researchers, being "best" in a new area takes on a unique meaning. Best means that ideas are being tried for the first time. This volume does not represent the conclusive moment for HR & entrepreneurship. Instead, it is at the beginning of what we hope will be a tidal wave of work that will help small and medium-size businesses grow in the brave new world ahead.

If you are used to thinking about traditional human resource management (HRM), then you probably expect chapters on selection, recruitment, training, compensation, labor relations, and performance appraisal. These are the tools of the trade that we call human resource management. In this book, you will find some papers that cover those topics. But you will also find research on leadership, firm growth, and the role of the CEO. The authors who wrote for this volume, along with the editors, think that the study of HRM and entrepreneurship must go beyond the traditional domain of HRM because people management in smaller, entrepreneurial firms is not dependent on an HR department.

Ironically, the approach that has been traditionally used in the field of HRM, finding the HRM department and describing what work it performed, has a strong parallel with early entrepreneurship research. In HRM research, it's not the existence of formal policies and procedures that will make or break a company, but because formal policies can more easily be measured and observed, those practices have tended to be the focus on much of the HRM research. And because in most large companies, the group that is in charge of these formal performance appraisal, selection and compensation practices is the HRM department, that's where researchers have focused the study of people issues within organizations.

Similarly, from its infancy in the 1950s through the mid-1990s, most researchers[2] studied entrepreneurs retrospectively, finding people who owned businesses and looking at what they did and how they started. The lessons of this approach to entrepreneurship research focused on the problem of generalizability. The retrospective approach systematically overlooked many key groups of entrepreneurs. For example, people who started short-lived businesses or seasonal businesses were overlooked. People who started businesses so "right" they were quickly bought up by their major customer or merged into another firm were similarly lost. The firm that went bankrupt and the firm that closed because of a successful harvest were both overlooked. The lesson of this was the need to look prospectively and broadly at the processes and people of entrepreneurship in order to truly understand what it means. With pioneering efforts like the Entrepreneurship Research Consortium (Reynolds, 2000), this became possible.

There *is* HRM going on in firms too small to have an HRM department, or even an HRM officer. But when the HRM department is not there, who does HRM? Like all other unassigned activities in the firm, it falls to the leadership team, the founder, the CEO, and the rest of the senior management team. Increasingly, the job of HRM also falls to the rest of the employees in the company. These fledgling efforts are critical to the development of the HRM capacity in the firm, because it has long been known that the organizational culture and norms are established by the actions of the founder, or founding team, in the firm's formative stages (Schein, 1983; Barron, Burton & Hannon, 1996; Boeker, 1989).

This means that these earliest HRM efforts are important in the here-and-now as an effort to manage the firm's relationships with its employees and in the future tense, as the basis for pointing out the direction, manner and historical context of future elaborations of the HRM function in the firm. In other words, to understand the HRM function of *any* firm in depth, it is essential to recognize, analyze and theorize about the HRM process for the firm's inception. And to know about the HRM practices of *all* firms, both large and small, requires using new approaches to theorizing about the HRM process. It may well require theories that permit the development of prospective versus retrospective methods of conceptualizing the HRM process.

Entrepreneurship's own method for moving from retrospective to prospective sampling methods is instructive in helping craft a definition of HRM that is more truly generalizable. We would like to suggest an answer to that question, and it is one that we think will intrigue scholars from not only the field of HRM, but from organization behavior, organization development, strategy, and entrepreneurship (and perhaps more). Unfortunately, formal HRM does not tend to be a 'construct' of interest to either CEOs or to academics studying entrepreneurship.

In entrepreneurial firms, securing and motivating employees is one of the key elements of the founder's job description. Whether these employees are family members contributing their work, or highly paid professionals with salary and stock options, the fundamental activities of HRM fall onto the entrepreneur. Hence, we would like to introduce an idea – that the "people" thing we need to study is the *relationship between an organization and its members*.

Looked at this way, the centrality of an entrepreneurial basis for HRM becomes readily apparent. When any organization is born, the founder does the relationship management, and the organization and the founder may be nearly isomorphic. In the parlance of Katz and Kahn's (1978) open systems theory, the founder and the firm are nearly fully included in one another at birth. As the company grows, the firm and the owner overlap less and less, reflecting the increasingly partial inclusion, with the organization coming to represent an open system in its own right. As this happens, the relation of the organization to the founder in issues such as compensation and managerial development become legitimate issues, and with the continued growth of the firm there is the greater institutionalization and delegation of HRM, replacing the founder's relationships with organizational members. As other open systems researchers demonstrated (Eden, 1973, p. 75), organizational membership begins with the addition of the first worker other than the owner, and shows a developmental progression in complexity as more members are added (Eden, 1975; Weick, 1969), and as levels of hierarchy grow, resulting in a loss of the direct relation between the founder and the members (Jaques, 1976; Kets deVries, 1977).

This definition also facilitates a demarcation among differing sets of relationships. Marketing reflects relationships with clients or customers. Finance reflects relationships with those holding debt or equity positions. R&D reflects the relationship to bodies of relevant intellectual properties or technologies, and HRM represents the company's relationships with its human resources, the organization's members.

Having these parallels based on segmentation of relationships is useful because it facilitates learning from the findings of the related fields. For example, success in IPO efforts depends on the integral involvement of the entrepreneur or the venture team (Cyr, Johnson & Welbourne, 2000). One implication of this is that a lack of top management involvement in any major relational function arguably results in poor performance of the function. This can come from a failure of top managers to spend enough time as the organization grows and the entrepreneur is spread increasingly thin. It can also be seen as a result of too great a degree of delegation.

Katz and Kahn (1978) identified the idea of the "leading subsystem" of an organization, an idea that suggests that any organization will tend to focus its attention on one of its key subsystems (what we call functions). Historically, research in entrepreneurial firms has shown that the CEO/founder usually describes the firm's leading subsystem or distinctive competency in terms of relationships with customers or investors or technologies, even though professionals are hired to manage those formal ties. In industries that are more dependent on its organizational members for success, whether because of the sales relationships or technological skills of its members, several lines of research are beginning to converge on the idea that those firms in which the CEO is integrally involved with managing employee relationships are likely to be more successful.

If indeed there *is* a general idea of relationship management in organizations, and relations with employees (alias HRM), relations with customers (alias Marketing), relations with competitors (alias Strategy) and relationships with sources of debt or equity (alias Finance) are all applications of this approach, it suggests that there might be some guiding principle of organizational relationship style (and its management). So far the overall coherent management of relationships in general has not been given a thought. If this general approach exists, then we begin to see that relationship management might not be best when contained in functional silos.

From the idea presented in this volume, we believe a case can be made that one can view relationships with people as a key "strategic" advantage for companies. Relationships are so central to firms. A case could be made that, perhaps, a growing company should consider hiring someone as their Chief Relationship Executive before they hire a HRM executive, or even a marketing executive. In that way, a growing company would be strategic in the way that it manages its relationships with employees, customers, suppliers, investors, and the general public.

Given the idea that relationship management is a key strategic variable, then the construct of interest in this volume may not necessarily be HRM, but relationship management in entrepreneurial firms, with the focus being the management of relationships with employees. This approach also suggests that the next step could be a research effort focused on relationships in general, which would require even more merging of disciplines. This could lead to an effort spanning how one enhances customer relationships, employee relationships, supplier relationships, public relations, and investor relations in entrepreneurial firms. Such an effort could serve as a topic of interest for either a special issue of a journal or a conference.

The chapters in this volume are organized along the lines of the life cycle of entrepreneurship from the nascent entrepreneur's initial considerations, through firm formation, its search for a HRM strategy and its first employees, and onto the handling of these employees within the organizational context.

In writing "Performance in Fast-growth firms: The behavioral and role demands of the founders throughout the firm's development," Johnson and Bishop offer a role-based view of the entrepreneurial firm through much of its life cycle. Building on a diverse literature, they offer a conceptualization of the roles founders play in the firm at different times, and then turn this view around to consider how the demands of life cycle stage and its attendant roles determine much of the time demands that entrepreneurs face. Their work provides a cogent multilevel appreciation of how organizational macro variables and individual micro variables mutually affect one another, paving the way for an active line of research and normative modeling in the future.

Markman and Baron's "Individual Differences And The Pursuit Of New Ventures: A Model Of Person- Entrepreneurship Fit" provides a visionary approach to the consideration of entrepreneurial entry. Building from the tradition of person-setting "fit" from motivational and vocational theory, they develop the entrepreneurial firm as a setting-to-be and then extend the model to account for the potential of fit, or misfit, between the entrepreneur and the firm the entrepreneur creates. In the tradition of person-setting fit, the goal is to explain the conditions leading to higher and lower levels of satisfaction as a way of explaining motivated action by individuals. Their chapter is a fresh application of a long-standing model in the work literature to an obvious, but previously largely overlooked setting.

"Human Resource Management Models for Entrepreneurial Opportunity: Existing Knowledge and New Directions" by Heneman and Tansky offers a detailed literature review on past efforts by entrepreneurship and other researchers to detail the nature of Human Resource Management practices in entrepreneurial firms. Offering coverage of universal, strategic and contingency approaches to organizing and explaining HRM practices, they offer a synthetic model grounded in the contingency approach but advanced through the inclusion of variables and relations found in universal and strategic models as a "best practice" approach to conceptualizing the HRM process in entrepreneurial firms.

If the relational idea that begins this introduction can be said to have sprung from any single piece in this volume, "Smaller But Not Necessarily Weaker: How Small Businesses Can Overcome Barriers To Recruitment" by Williamson, Cable and Aldrich would be that chapter. Aldrich has long championed a socially grounded approach to entrepreneurial processes, and in this chapter, Williamson, Cable and Aldrich demonstrate how social relationships underlie recruitment processes. Their choice of entrepreneurial firms as a setting in which to show this stems from the clarity of the interaction of social networks and recruitment in these smaller-scale settings. They offer a lesson on reframing what some see as the shortcomings of small firms in order to attract highly qualified recruits away from larger firms.

If the dot-com boom and bust is viewed as a naturally occurring experiment, then one of the most evident manipulations of that unique time was the use of stock as an inducement to join entrepreneurial firms. Graham, Murray, and Amuso, in "Stock-Related Rewards in Entrepreneurial Firms," provide an insightful and conceptually rich consideration of the role stock-related rewards paid in firms during the dot.com era. Beyond the review of the substantial literature on the topic, they are able to offer a unique empirical grounding through the use of survey data from iQuantic's own surveys of firms using stock-related rewards. This results in a chapter that melds concept and practice and offers one of the best available efforts to understand the power and problems of using stock as a reward in entrepreneurial firms.

Traditionally, and perhaps stereotypically, labor unions were a villain of choice for small businesses. If entrepreneurial firms are supposed to exist as a contrasting organizational form to conventional small businesses, then there exists the possibility that old animosities might not have an excuse to take hold in these entrepreneurial firms. Batt and Welbourne, in their chapter, "Performance And Growth In Entrepreneurial Firms: Revisiting The Union-Performance Relationship," provide an intriguing explanation why labor unions and entrepreneurial firms could forge a mutually beneficial relationship with a new basis. Building from the common ground of improving worker knowledge and skill, Batt and Welbourne show how a human resource development approach would benefit the workers by improving their skill and claim to higher compensation, support the union tradition of efforts to assure high-quality, high-value labor, and the entrepreneurial firm which prides itself on recruiting, developing and retaining superior talent as a competitive edge in a world where expertise is paramount.

These chapters point up the richness of the relationships that underlie the Human Resource Management process, and the beauty of studying these relationships in entrepreneurial firms is that many of them can be viewed from their inception, and in many cases for the smaller firms, in their entirety. As such, the entrepreneurial firm would seem to offer a tremendous opportunity as a setting in which to conduct HRM research. The chapters in this volume echo this sentiment and build on this belief, helping to describe and project the kinds of research questions that could be usefully addressed in the near term, and offering the in-depth conceptualizations which would need to serve as the foundation for a substantive contribution to the HRM, entrepreneurship and relationship literatures. As you will find on the following pages, the challenge of HRM in entrepreneurial firms is real and significant. It deserves a real and significant involvement on the part of researchers. In that regard, this volume is part of the start.

NOTES

1. Although not represented in this book, we would like to recognize the work being done by a group of professors at Stanford University. Their work on HR practices in emerging companies can be found on the university's web site under the Stanford Project on Emerging Companies.

2. There are two important exceptions to this trend. The first was Mayer and Goldstein (1961), who tracked all of the people trying to start businesses in Rhode Island. The second was McClelland and Winter's (1969) pioneering study of achievement motivation training and its entrepreneurial effects on a sample of volunteers in India.

REFERENCES

Baron, J. N., Burton M. D., & Hannon, M. T. (1996). The road taken: Origins and evolution of employment systems in emerging companies. *Industrial and Corporate Change, 5*(2), 239–275.

Boeker, W. (1989). Strategic change: The effects of founding and history. *Academy of Management Journal, 32*(3), 489–515.

Cyr, L. A., Johnson, D. E., & Welbourne, T. M. (2000). Human resources in initial public offering firms: do venture capitalists make a difference? *Entrepreneurship: Theory & Practice, 25*(1), 77–92.

Eden, D. (1973). Self-employed workers: a comparison group for organizational psychology. *Organizational Behavior and Human Performance, 9*, 186–214.

Eden, D. (1975). Organizational membership *vs.* self-employment: another blow to the American dream. *Organizational Behavior and Human Performance, 13*, 79–94.

Katz, D., & Kahn, R. L. (1978). *The social psychology of organizations* (2nd ed.). New York: Wiley.

Jaques, E. (1976). *A general theory of bureaucracy*. New York: Halsted.

Reynolds, P. (2000). National Panel Study of U.S. Business Startups: Background and Methodology. In: J. A. Katz (Ed.), *Advances in Entrepreneurship, Firm Emergence and Growth* (Vol. 4, pp. 153–228). New York: Elsevier.

Schein, E. H. (1983). The Role of the Founder in Creating Organizational Culture. *Organizational Dynamics, 12,* 13–28.

Weick, K. E. (1969). *The social psychology of organizing*. Reading, MA: Addison Wesley.

Theresa M. Welbourne
Jerome A. Katz
Editors

1. PERFORMANCE IN FAST-GROWTH FIRMS: THE BEHAVIORAL AND ROLE DEMANDS OF THE FOUNDER THROUGHOUT THE FIRM'S DEVELOPMENT

Diane E. Johnson and Karen Bishop

1. INTRODUCTION

> ... the study of organizations should take the social system level as its conceptual starting point, but ... many of the actual measures will be constructed from observations and reports of individual behavior and attitude (Katz & Kahn, 1978, p. 13).

One cannot pick up a newspaper, read a popular journal, listen to the radio, or watch television without finding something on fast-growth firms. Typically, fast-growing firms have been defined as having high growth rates, usually in sales or revenues, that have been sustained over a number of years (e.g. Birch, 1987; Fischer, Reuber, Hababou, Johnson & Lee, 1997). Evidence suggests that these fast-growth firms help fuel the economy (Hambrick & Crozier, 1985) and even Wall Street trading fluctuates based on how these firms perform. Some suggest that firms that grow faster than 20% per year, may account for the majority of job creation in the United States (Birch, 1987). Organizations have rhythms and cycles that are quite independent of their chronological age (Kimberly, 1980b) and these are of particular importance to fast-growth

Managing People in Entrepreneurial Organizations, Volume 5, pages 1–21.

firms facing a rapid pace of change. The literatures discussing organizational transitions have included theoretical bases in the ecological, evolutionary, institutional, resource dependence, and transaction cost approaches (Aldrich, 1999). Thus, from both a theoretical and practical standpoint, it is important that we gain a better understanding of the unique transitional demands of fast-growth firms and how those transitions influence firm performance.

Although organizational theorists recognize that both external and internal factors contribute to fast-growth firm performance, the literature to date has focused predominately on external factors such as the state of the economy, industry issues, and the emergence of new markets. Some have even limited their work to specific industries that have grown abnormally fast (Birch, 1987) or appear to sustain the fastest rate of company growth, such as high technology (e.g. Hanks, Watson, Jansen & Chandler, 1993; Kazanjian & Drazin, 1990). Less attention has been paid to the relationships among internal factors and fast-growth. As Penrose (1952) stated "[W]e have every reason for thinking that the growth of a firm is willed by those who make the decisions of the firm and are themselves part of the firm . . ." (in Kimberly, 1980a, p. 11). Founders of fast-growth firms are called upon to make numerous decisions, but as businesses make these transitions, the level of importance of the factors contributing to firm performance also changes, requiring founder flexibility (Churchill & Lewis, 1983). A unique issue with fast-growth firms is the pace at which they make transitions, demanding rapid changes in founders' behaviors and roles. It is time that entrepreneurial scholars investigate these role and behavioral demands on founders in fast-growth firms, as we have known for quite some time that role behaviors are clearly a crucial aspect of firm success (Katz & Kahn, 1978; Jackson & Shuler, 1995). Thus, the purpose of this chapter is to address behavioral and role demands of founders as they impact decisions that effect fast-growth firm performance. Before achieving this end, we need to first provide the assumptions underlying this chapter as well as the definitions of key concepts.

Assumptions

A primary assumption in this chapter is that fast-growth companies experience a more rapid pace of transition than their slower growing counterparts (Fischer et al., 1997). For most of this chapter, fast-growth is defined as the average three years' sales growth rate of at least 20%. Note, however, that we will argue at several points throughout this chapter that such a definition may be limiting in that what is fast-growth for one industry may be very different in another industry, and yet, both industries may experience similar role and behavioral challenges and demands. We will provide some thoughts on the need for future research on this issue later in the chapter. A second assumption in this chapter is that the term "founder" can include the concept of a group of founders on a top management team as well as subsequent changes in executives, such as a chief executive officer. Other than the need to coordinate multiple members of a top management team, or make transitions to a new CEO, there is nothing in the literature that would lead us to believe that the other behavioral and role demands experienced during fast-growth transitions are different for a single founder or a founding top management team. Thus, founder is defined as the individual or group of individuals whose behaviors and roles shape and often determine the transitional patterns experienced by fast-growth firms. A third assumption is that all firms, regardless of their growth rate, experience transitions. "Organizations are fluid and dynamic; they move in time and in space; they act and react" (Kimberly, 1980a). However, we suggest that fast-growth firms are uniquely different from other, slower-growing firms in that these dynamic movements occur at a very rapid pace and are less likely to occur linearly or even in any kind of order.

The remainder of this chapter is organized into four sections. In the first section, we discuss the literature on the transitional processes that firms experience and highlight issues that may be unique to fast-growth firms. The second section addresses potential role demands of founders, as they specifically apply to their firms' rapid transitions and growth. In the third section, we discuss behavioral demands as illustrated by founders' allocations of time. Finally, we provide some suggestions for potential avenues for future research.

2. ORGANIZATIONAL TRANSITIONS

It is obvious that populations of organizations ebb and flow and that individual organizations are created, grow, sometimes become stagnant, sometimes revitalize, and sometimes pass from the scene (Kimberly, 1980a, p. 6).

The growth of a firm's structure and subsystems and the transitional phases of organizations have been of interest to scholars for quite some time. Historically, the majority of studies of organizational phenomena have focused on mature, rather than new, organizations. However, since Birch's (1987) suggestion that economic vitality rests with job creation in small to medium-sized businesses, interest has increased in the growth patterns and growth rates of these businesses. To assess how prior models of growth apply to fast-growth firms, we first review the literature on models of organizational transitions.

Katz and Kahn (1978) suggested that descriptive studies of growth could take two avenues. The first related to a biography of a single organization or a "synthetic biography" that looked at the development of a single organization (ontogeny). The second was a phylogenetic study of the historical development process of dominant firms. Regardless of the avenue selected, these authors recognized that growth structures could be studied without implying that each step could be easily identified or listed as a specific, historical event. Katz and Kahn's own study of growth stages took a somewhat hybrid view looking at patterns of events as a function of the firm's environment as well as the specific people within the firm.

However, most of the early models of growth were based on the biological metaphor of life cycles and were derived from the more historical or phylogenetic perspective. From about 1967 through 1979, numerous scholars created life cycle models by analyzing the dominant historical sequences experienced by firms as they developed (Adizes, 1979; Downs, 1967; Greiner, 1972; Katz & Kahn, 1978; Kimberly, 1979; Lippitt & Schmidt, 1967; Lyden, 1975; Neal, 1978; Torbert, 1974). Although each of these life cycle studies proposed some differences, they suggested remarkably consistent patterns of progression through time. Notwithstanding, Kimberly (1980a) argued that this previous research was not dynamic enough, suggesting that while chronological age aided our understanding of possible time effects on firm growth and development, the rhythms and cycles experienced by firms were most likely independent of the firm's age. Kimberly's argument was later supported by the research of McCarthy, Krueger and Schoenecker (1990). Nonetheless, while Kimberly believed biological models such as human life cycle stages were imperfect metaphors, he also acknowledged that they provided some logical fashion for studying firm growth.

In 1983, Quinn and Cameron summarized nine of the previously published life cycle typologies describing growth patterns of successfully continuing companies. Although these nine models were based on different factors, Quinn and Cameron were able to determine "dominant criteria of effectiveness" in each of the main life cycle stages for early growth of firms. Using these criteria, Quinn and Cameron developed a four-stage typology of organizational life cycles. They called the earliest stage, entrepreneurial. At this level, flexibility, resource acquisition and growth were preeminent. The second, or collectivity stage, was characterized by the human relations model where informal structures and communication, cooperation among organizational members and morale were the paramount factors. The third stage, which Quinn and Cameron called the formalization stage, was mainly defined by organizational stability, rules and procedures, and planning and goal-setting. Finally, the fourth stage, called elaboration of structure, was primarily defined by decentralization, monitoring of the external environment, and renewal and expansion efforts.

Quinn and Cameron (1983) experienced difficulty in specifying two issues in their analysis. First, only one model in the nine they studied actually addressed decline and death as a life cycle stage. This is not surprising, as Kimberly (1980a) had already suggested that death was not an inevitable feature of firms. Nonetheless, Quinn and Cameron concluded that this stage might be too difficult to predict because in mature firms, "change occurs metamorphically and unpredictably." Second, Quinn and Cameron argued that temporal dimensions were difficult to address since many of the models they assessed did not confront this issue adequately. They found that stage changes could be either rapid or slow and did not closely correspond with any particular age of the firm. Once again, chronological age was recognized by Kimberly (1980a) as a factor likely to be totally different from organizational time. These arguments about temporal dimensions were later supported by the research of McCarthy et al. (1990). Nonetheless, as a result of their findings, Quinn and Cameron (1983) hypothesized neither a decline/death stage nor duration of time for each stage of transition.

Following the taxonomy proposed by Quinn and Cameron (1983), a number of additional models were developed (Adizes, 1989; Churchill & Lewis, 1983; Flamholtz, 1987; Galbraith, 1982; Kazanjian, 1988; Miller & Friesen, 1984; Scott & Bruce, 1987; Smith, Mitchell & Summer, 1985). Once again, these models continued to propose consistent and predictable stages as firms evolved. Then, in 1993, Hanks, et al. argued that although these models seemed theoretically sound, and very little research had actually validated the models empirically. Using a more empirically-based design rather than the previous conceptual approaches, Hanks et al. (1993) collected data from firms in the high technology industry. These authors derived definitions for their life cycle stages from previous models such as Greiner's (1972) as a baseline model, several summary models including Quinn and Cameron's (1983) taxonomy, and five of the recently developed models of the 1980s (see Hanks et al., 1993, for a discussion of these models). Employing exploratory cluster analysis, multivariate analyses, and canonical discriminant analyses, Hanks and his colleagues identified six distinct clusters that they categorized into four life cycle stages. Stage 1 consisted of young, small firms with a mean age of just over four years. Organizations in this cluster were viewed as rapidly growing, simply structured and very informal. As a result, firms in this cluster were titled "start-ups". Firms in Stage 2, called the expansion stage, were somewhat older and larger than start-ups, with a mean age of just over seven years. Expansion stage growth was the highest of all stages, and firms were becoming a bit more formalized at this point with the development of specialized functions and actively marketing their products. Firms in Stage 3, called consolidation, were categorized as late expansion/early maturation firms. Although slightly younger than Stage 2, Stage 3 firms were considerably larger, more than twice the size of expansion firms, and their growth rate, while still rapid, had slowed to some extent from that of stage two firms. Firms at this stage were seen to have more than double the number of specialized functions from Stage 2, with an emphasis on manufacturing. The fourth cluster, Stage 4, entitled diversification, was characterized by the highest level of formalization, more than twice the age of firms in either stages two or three, and clearly the largest of all firms. However, growth had slowed considerably and specialized functions had increased about 150% that of stage three. By far, sales were the largest in this cluster of firms.

As mentioned earlier, Hanks et al. (1993) discerned two additional clusters from their analyses. These latter two groupings of firms did not easily fit into one of the previously described, more traditional stages, and age played a role in distinguishing these groups of firms from the other four stages. The first of these groups represented firms that had the least in employee growth and slower sales growth. While these firms were somewhat similar to those in the start-up stage, they were the oldest group of firms with the highest centralized structure and little formalization. Their products appeared to be well-developed, but the firms seemed to have "disengaged from the growth process." The sixth and final cluster of firms was similar to Stage 2, expansion. However, the firms in this sixth cluster were significantly older, less centralized and slower growing than Stage 2 firms. Hanks, et al. suggested that these firms might have discontinued their development and were in a cycle of "stagnated growth." Although these metaphorically based taxonomies have yet to yield a convergent concept of a general organic pattern of firm development, scholars continue to search for a clearer understanding of how organizations evolve.

More recent models of firm growth and transition shy away from the life cycle metaphor (e.g. Dodge, Fullerton & Robbins, 1994; Van de Ven & Poole, 1995) and some propose an evolutionary-historical framework (Aldrich, 1999). Aldrich argues that an evolutionary approach builds on life cycle models by recognizing that "[o]rganizations emerge in evolving environments that preceded them and will outlive them" (1999, p. 200). Three components that are crucial to this perspective are age (duration of existence), period (external, historical events and forces that have similar effect on all firms regardless of age), and cohort (external, historical events and forces that have different effect on firms of different ages) effects. The evolutionary approach recognizes that firm age is derived not only from duration, but also from the organization's specific life course. Moreover, this perspective acknowledges that ambiguity and uncertainty exist and that firms do not follow fixed patterns of development (Aldrich, 1999).

We have yet to see empirical support for this new perspective. More important is the question of whether or not an evolutionary perspective will provide a needed, and much sought after, foundation for more effectively capturing and/or controlling for the effects of firm evolution in research designs, particularly in studies of fast-growth firms.

In sum, while a great deal of progress has been made and a number of models exist for understanding growth in firms, these taxonomies still present a number of problems for understanding transitions in fast-growth firms. First, while Hanks et al. (1993) have provided an empirical methodology for operationalizing life cycle models of organizational growth, their taxonomy is still phylogenetic in origin and it still proposes a consistent pattern of linear growth. As Hanks et al. (1993) point out, most models assume that "organizations evolve in a consistent and predictable manner." As can be seen from any of the popular press articles on firms in fast-growth industries, little seems predictable! Although the evolutionary approach recognizes that ambiguity and uncertainty exist as firms develop (Aldrich, 1999), this perspective still emphasizes widespread patterns across firms. If such unpredictable patterns exist in a firm's development, how do they apply to fast-growth firms? For example, are their factors or situations that exist to cause fast-growth firms to bypass a particular transformational process? Might some fast-growth firms go through some stages simultaneously due to a rapid pace of change? Is it possible that some fast-growth firms have to repeat some processes because a critical aspect of a transition was not addressed or addressed ineffectively? These questions are not typically addressed by existing life-cycle models or other growth models, making those approaches restrictive in their ability to predict outcomes of fast-growth firms.

Second, if we are to truly understand how firms evolve rapidly, it may be that the conceptual focus should be on the rapid pace of transition and change than on the rapid rate of growth of their financial performance. Most models have been developed from a phylogenetic perspective, outlining a historical development of a variety of firms, often not limited to, and possibly not including, those identified by the traditional definition of fast-growth used in this chapter. Indeed, we propose that the reason chronological age is not equivalent to the stage of an organization's development is *because* of the differing paces of transition among firms. A great deal of what we know about transitions in fast-growth firms has been derived from one dominant industry, namely the high technology industry (Churchill & Lewis, 1983; Fischer et al., 1997; Hanks et al., 1993; Kazanjian, 1988). We have already inferred that fast-growth companies experience a rapid pace of transition due to their fast growth. However, we cannot infer that *only* fast-growth companies experience rapid transitions. Could it be that any firm in any industry might experience the same rapid pace of transition as those we define as fast-growth firms without a recurring 20% sales growth rate? If so, are we seeking to understand only those transitional issues related to rapid sales growth? We think not, in that to do so would be to put the cart before the horse. More importantly the models and discussion to this point have not addressed ontogenetic issues in rapid paces of transition. Are there any unique, firm-specific issues that might better address transitional stages in fast-growth firms? Sandberg and Hofer (1987) suggested that to be successful, each new venture must have a unique strategic approach depending upon its own circumstances. Although some of the existing life cycle models do address transitions from a strategic approach (e.g. Churchill & Lewis, 1983), this view is typically across firms rather than within a particular firm. Such a view has the potential to limit our effectiveness in predicting fast-growth, much less understanding rapid paces of transition in firms.

Third, many of the transitional development models discussed so far do not take into account the role of the founder. Katz and Kahn (1978) argued that "[r]oles, norms, and values ... furnish[ed] three interrelated bases for the integration of organizations." In effect, the roles of individuals within the firm are integrated with the requirements of those roles and the values that underlie those roles. In concert, all contribute to the ongoing life of a firm (Katz & Kahn, 1978). Katz and Kahn (1978) acknowledge that the relative importance of these three factors may vary in different systems. However, the role of the founder should be particularly important in fast-growth firms because changes occur swiftly in these businesses requiring quick, strategic decisions as the environment adapts and adjusts to the presence of a new, fast-growing venture in its markets. Requirements of roles and values behind those roles may not be as crucial because norms and values take time to develop and fast-growth firms may not have that time. Chrisman et al. (1998) support this strategic management approach and outlines specific strategic steps that entrepreneurs must take to be successful. Although the evolutionary approach acknowledges human agency and founder roles and "does not deny that organizations are constructed by people who have strong interests in understanding what they are doing," (Aldrich, 1999, p. 41), this theory also assumes that people are rational and that the roles employed during firm development are borrowed from other firms (Aldrich, 1999). This may or may not be true for fast-growth firms especially in light of Fischer, et al.'s findings that "[r]apid-growth firms often lack directly or even closely comparable competitors against which they might set performance norms." (1997, p. 25). Thus, without specifically studying the impact of founder roles as they evolve through these rapid-paced transitions, we may be missing important components that contribute to growth and changes in fast-growth firms.

Where does all this take us with respect to what we know of developmental transitions in fast-growth firms? We can probably say with certainty that even rapidly growing firms experience some transitional phases or processes of development. Whether or not these transitions are tied similarly with existing traditional models is uncertain without more rigorous study. However, "all the evidence we have indicates that the growth of a firm is connected with attempts of a particular group of human beings to do something; nothing is gained and much is lost if this fact is not explicitly recognized." (Penrose, 1995). Thus, while the environment may precipitate some firm-level transitions (e.g. new markets or technologies), founders' behaviors and role performances are likely to influence how well the firm makes the needed rapid transitions as it grows, which in turn, may impact venture performance and/or sales growth. Regardless of the environmental situation, founders must make decisions on where they are going to apply their own role and behavioral resources (time allocation – discussed in a future section). In fast-growth firms, the pressure to skip or ignore phases may be particularly salient because of the rapid pace of transitions. Moreover, transitions are probably not easy to predict because they are happening so quickly. Thus, regardless of the transitional phase a fast-growth firm is experiencing, the question is not whether or not the firm can grow, but rather what principles govern that growth? (Penrose, 1995.) We suggest that role demands of the founder are critically important conditions that are likely to impact the firm's future growth potential. In the next section, we discuss these role demands and attempt to link them with some of the transitional issues discussed in this section.

3. FOUNDER ROLES

For a firm, enterprising management is the one identifiable condition without which growth is precluded . . . (Penrose, 1995, p. 8).

As we have suggested earlier in this chapter, the roles of founders in fast growth firms may be especially important in light of the rapid pace with which these firms are transitioning. As firms make transitions and grow, those changes require different actions on the part of founders. For fast-growth firms, we suggest that we may gain greater insight into the transitional phases of these rapidly changing firms by investigating founder roles and by identifying the areas of emphasis a founder places on activities that might contribute to firm growth. We do not assume a causal direction for these founder roles in the firm's development. Consistent with prior work in developing the life cycle and other growth models, the firm's apparent transitional stage could be identified, and we could look for identifying roles and behaviors that seem to be occurring at each stage. One would expect that some role demand would be placed on the founder as a result of the firm's entry into its market and its adaptation to environmental changes, such as competitive reactions to the presence of the new firm. Founders may choose to react to these demands or not. However, it may be that the roles enacted by the founders may dictate which transition is being made based upon a strategic decision to emphasize or de-emphasize certain roles. It may even be likely that the roles dictated by founders, in part, guide *how* the firm grows rather than indicate the developmental stages. Thus, role demands made of founders may (or less likely, may not) influence which roles are enacted and emphasized and which may influence how and when the firm grows. To better understand potential role influences in fast-growth firms, a brief review of that literature is warranted.

In general, roles are defined as those behaviors characteristic of one or more persons in context (Biddle, 1979). Katz and Kahn define role behavior as "the recurring actions of an individual, appropriately interrelated with the repetitive activities of others so as to yield a predictable outcome." (1978, p. 189). We contend that although roles are characteristic behaviors or repetitive actions yielding a predictable outcome, individuals enact multiple roles at work, and those actions change as the firm changes. We know that priorities change over the different growth stages (Baird & Meshoulam, 1988; Churchill & Lewis, 1983; Smith, Mitchell & Summer, 1985). Jackson and Schuler (1995) suggest that roles of CEOs and top managers also change significantly across life cycle stages of firms although these latter authors point out that the literature on role changes hasn't been empirically validated. We also know that flexibility (Reuer & Leiblein, 2000; Hitt, 1998) is critical in fast-growth firms because these businesses tend to move through their growth stages rather rapidly. Thus, the question becomes, how can founders of fast-growth firms change their roles and behaviors, simultaneously and quickly enough, to transition effectively into the next stage of their firms' development? Looking at these role changes may be a better way of assessing fast-growth transitions because the roles identify behaviors that specifically lead to changes in firm activities.

A review of any number of the life cycle and other models described in this chapter so far reveal a discussion of different founder and employee behaviors that take place as a firm transitions into each stage. Typically, these behaviors are derived from evaluating size, age, centralization issues, formalized policies, and other contextual, organizational factors. Rarely are founder behaviors determined by specifically identifying what the founder does as his or her firm grows. One of the few studies to address founder changes in fast-growth firms was Churchill and Lewis (1983). These authors specifically analyzed rapidly growing, high technology firms and identified four owner factors that contributed to transitional changes in firms. Although Churchill and Lewis didn't specify roles, they noted that "owner[s'] operational abilities in doing important jobs such as marketing, inventing, producing, and managing distribution" were among some of the activities that changed in importance as the firm grew. While this work offers a glimpse into the more functionally classified founder roles in fast-growth firms, no specific measures or ways to determine which roles are operating and how to assess them are given. If founder roles are to provide clues to fast-growth firms, we must not only be able to identify appropriate roles, but also be able to evaluate those roles. Unfortunately, unlike financial performance which is a fairly objective assessment of a firm, identifying and evaluating role behaviors tends to be subjective, often biased, inaccurate, and difficult to reliably assess.

A promising new diagnostic tool has been developed recently and may provide insight for assessing founder roles in fast-growth firms. Although not completely inclusive of all potential roles, the measure and research that lead to its development, may offer some guidance for evaluating founder roles in fast-growth firms. This tool is the Role-Based Performance Scale (RBPS), developed by Welbourne, Johnson and Erez (1998). Welbourne et al. contend that employees take on different roles, beyond just their specified job duties or tasks, depending on what the firm emphasizes as essential or, as Quinn and Cameron (1983) suggest, based on the "dominant criteria for effectiveness." In this way, through its strategy, the firm dictates desired employee behaviors and promotes these behaviors through its human resource (HR) systems in the hopes of eliciting the necessary and required actions for success in the firm. We suggest that the founder, as a critical member of the fast-growing new venture, experiences role demands and sets role emphases just as do all employees. We also suggest that the effectiveness of the founder in these roles may be more critical than for any other employee. For these reasons, we look more closely to the RBPS as a place to begin considering what these founder roles might entail in a fast-growth firm.

The RBPS has a strong theoretical base and describes five different types of roles at work: job, organization, innovator, career, and team. The job role represents doing tasks specifically required by one's job description. The organization role refers to behaviors above and beyond the call of duty, similar to Organ's (1988) notion of organizational citizenship behaviors. The innovator role recognizes the creativity and innovation one might enact in one's job, and for the firm, as a whole. Career roles are representative of behaviors used to gain necessary skills to progress through the firm. The team role involves working with others toward the success of the firm. The importance of these roles may help shed some light on how both founders and employees influence performance in fast-growth firms.

Again, although the RBPS is unlikely to include all the types of roles a founder may take on, the model under which this measure was developed provides scholars of fast-growth firms a way to investigate the types of founder roles that might be emphasized as these businesses change. Applying the logic of the RBPS to founder roles in fast-growth firms, founders are the individuals who determine the strategic course of a firm. They need to be able to read both external and internal signals that might demand specific role enactment and take on the roles that will best serve their businesses. Moreover, the specifics of a particular role may vary in different circumstances. For example, the founder's job role when a company is forming may involve developing a solid business plan to assist in securing financing as well as hiring and training new employees. This job role might also involve doing whatever it takes to get the firm up and running, even if that means working 12–15 hour days, emptying waste baskets, cleaning offices, answering phone calls, etc. At some later time in the firm's growth, the founder's job role may entail hiring new employees and firing non-productive ones, planning the firm's future direction, and developing more efficient and effective ways of doing things. At this point, while the founder may still work 12–15 hour days, it is likely that emptying waste baskets and cleaning offices will be handled as part of another employee's job role or even outsourced. Even though the specifics of the founder's job role may have changed, more interestingly, the emphasis on the job role is likely to change. The demands on the founder roles may have shifted from specifically doing job-related things to more creative or innovative activities such as getting involved in research and development or possibly improving team cohesion and activities.

Studying founder roles and role shifts may help identify fast-growth transitions better than traditional life cycle models for several reasons. First, life cycle models differentiate broad, dominant patterns of historical events that indicate the stage in a firm's development. As mentioned earlier, due to the rapid pace of evolution in fast-growth firms, these historical events may be too broad, occur simultaneously, or one stage may be skipped all together. How can such models accurately predict successful companies if the stage doesn't exist or occurs at the same time as another stage? In contrast, by investigating founder roles, specific behaviors can be linked to specific changes and/or outcomes that occur in a fast-growth firm. Second, life cycle models assume some linear pattern which may or may not be true for fast-paced firms. Roles make no such linear assumption. Third, life cycle models tend to be based on environmental influences that dictate expected, rational, activities of a firm at each stage of its growth. By investigating role behaviors, we can better account for non-rational decisions influenced by the environment but made by founders that don't fit any specific patterns and contribute nonetheless to the success or failure of a firm. In fact, this may be one of the most important reasons for studying founder roles instead of life cycle stages because the pace at which fast-growth firms transition is likely to be frenetic and many times call for some seemingly irrational or risky behaviors in hopes of achieving success. Thus, without investigating founder role behaviors, we may be missing a critical component of fast-growth firm transitions.

The point is, as the firm goes through its transitions, different role demands will be made on the founder. More importantly, the different roles a founder chooses to enact should have an impact on the transitions his or her firm experiences. Although beyond the scope of this chapter, we would expect that at some point, either before or after the firm "opens its doors" for business, founders' roles begin to differentiate and the RBPS research model might provide a means for examining how founder role enactment influences the pace of transition in fast-growth firms. However, some research suggests that founders of new ventures do shift the amount of time they allocate to certain tasks as the firm grows. This could shed additional light on founder behaviors in fast-growth firms. In the next section we discuss this issue.

4. ALLOCATIONS OF FOUNDER'S TIME

... the speed of strategic decision making in a high-velocity environment [is] challenging because information is poor, mistakes are costly, and recovery from missed opportunities is difficult (Eisenhardt, 1989, p. 570).

One factor that will likely constrain those roles the founder wants to accomplish, to those roles that can realistically be accomplished, is time. Time is a limited resource. This section of the chapter gathers some understanding of the pressures on founders to choose among work demands by looking to research concerning the constraints placed on our cognitive abilities and work behaviors by our limited attentional capacity (i.e. we can only do so much at a time). Just as founders have considerable flexibility in defining their organizational roles as the firm grows, they also have flexibility when making strategic cognitive decisions as to what activities are attended to and which are not (Bishop, 2000; Cooper, Ramachandran & Schoorman, 1997). As time passes on a day-to-day basis for the founder, some things cannot be accomplished: opportunities are not seized; tasks are not finished; calls are not made; employees are not hired; and goals are not reached. Management of this intractable resource (time) requires the founder to adapt to the changing demands of activities as the venture grows and matures (McCarthy et al., 1990). Again, the more rapid the pace of transition within the firm, the more rapidly the founder must flexibly engage in work-related activities to optimize venture performance as much as possible.

Research suggests that entrepreneurs, in all life cycle and firm growth stages, perceive many demands on their time (Bishop, 2000). Choosing among demands that exceed the time available to accomplish them creates stress for the founder. The pressing nature of these demands in confining time frames contributes to a sense of urgency at work (Welbourne, 1997; Welbourne & Cyr, 1999). Exacerbating the need to address the day-to-day pressures of a fast-growing firm, founders in one place of transition also need to develop the readiness and flexibility needed to meet the changes in activities demanding attention as the next transition approaches. As stated before, the founder of a fast-growing venture may experience the pressures to be ready and more flexible even more acutely than would their more slowly-growing counterparts.

There is a great deal of theoretical support for a founder's need to be selective in the activities attended to over the course of the firm's development. An individual founder's capacity to process new information is limited and he or she seeks the minimization of cognitive effort the same as he or she does physical effort (Baron, 1998). In response, mental short-cuts are adopted as time pressures increase or as we experience physical fatigue or stress (Baron, 1998). The difference between intending to do something to actually setting a goal toward its accomplishment is indicated by a deliberate allocation of some level of one's attentional resources (i.e. cognitive effort) toward accomplishing the goal (Kanfer, 1990, 1994). The impact of these many demands on the founder's time influences what he or she decides to do in daily venture activities. In multi-tasking settings, the crux of information processing theory addresses how we allocate our available time to meet the attentional demands of one task versus others and how we perform the selected tasks either simultaneously or in close succession (Proctor & Dutta, 1995). Founders need to know which activities demanding time are more important than others to maintain their motivation toward firm activities. A founder's ability to choose which activities to perform, based on clear relative priorities, influences how satisfied the founder is with the venture's performance, regardless of the levels of performance, and that satisfaction influences their motivation to stay with the venture (Bishop, 2001). McCarthy et al. (1990) found that founder activities do indeed shift over time, supporting the founder's need to multi-task and to juggle the attentional demands encountered as the firm rapidly moves through transitions.

As a firm grows and progresses, a redistribution of the founder's efforts occurs (McCarthy et al., 1990). These redistribution requirements, the need to multi-task, and the cognitive and physical tendencies to create mental short-cuts to minimize effort, all contribute to a founder's conscious choice to judiciously adjust the allocation of his or her valuable time to only the most critical activities. McCarthy et al. (1990) found that shifts in a founder's time allocation are statistically significant between transitional stages.

The first two stages used by McCarthy et al. (1990) are the pre-formation and early start-up (entry into the market) stages. Their third stage is marked by growth in newly hired supervisory personnel or expansion to another location, where the founder moves toward behaviors that are more traditionally viewed as managerial with venture operations more delegated than in the earlier stages. Unfortunately, the McCarthy et al. (1990) study was limited to retail firms with no more than 60 employees, limiting the extent to which growth could be achieved in the labor intensive retail industry. However, the results of their study, for the early stages of venture formation, suggest that founder behaviors and roles undergo significant transition as the firm makes growth transitions and that these transitions are not related to the firm's chronological age. McCarthy and colleagues found that as ventures moved from direct to indirect supervision of employees, significantly more of the founder's time was spent on employees and venture management and less on customer contacts. These variations in activities are based upon founders' changing roles, with no significant relationship to the firm's age. This is significant for fast-growth firms, not because of their age but, because they are making transitions at a very rapid pace and this holds consequences for founder behaviors.

Another interesting point highlighted in McCarthy et al. (1990) is that the average numbers of employees shifts from slightly above three to about nine between their second and third stage. It seems that as the number of employees increases, the complexity of coordinating the venture's operations should also increase. Therefore, the transition toward the second stage would demand that the founder increasingly engage in activities designed to establish informal communication patterns and internal structures. Theoretically supporting this proposition, research on group processes suggests that as group size increases, both interactions and communications begin to break down and cohesiveness decreases. In a venture of nine employees, we already would expect to see any number of existing subgroups self-formed to better perform specific activities because decision quality cannot justify a group larger than five members (Yetton & Bottger, 1983). When groups transition from seven to nine members, not only have sub-groups formed, but coalitions are also possible within and between these sub-groups (Weick, 1969). Therefore, as the number of people involved in a fast-growth venture rapidly increases, the complexity involved in ensuring clear communication and effective interaction among rapidly forming groups and sub-groups increases exponentially.

This should have a significant impact on the relative emphasis of founders' enacted roles as well as the need to make transitions in levels of different founder behaviors. The founder of a fast-growth venture may be quickly facing nine or more employees. The increased demands that come with rapidly growing numbers of employees could mean a very rapid pace of transition in time allocation patterns as well as roles for those founders whose ventures move past 9 employees to 900 in the course of a year. These changes in time allocations could significantly influence short-term and/or long-term venture performance and growth, depending on how effectively a founder can gauge the activity having the highest relative priority and whether doing other activities to a lesser degree will detract from growth and venture performance outcomes. For example, if a firm's sales force increases by 100% and the founder does not have the resources (time and sufficient intermediate supervisory support) to help them become part of the new venture's "team" due to his or her prior customer commitments, sales growth could be affected. Short-term sales may be raised as the new deal is cinched, but future sales may be hampered until the new sales force can be socialized effectively and their learning curves overcome. We would expect that founders of fast-growth companies would have to face these choices. This example could also illustrate the suggestion made earlier in this chapter that the "order" in which fast-growth firms engage in particular life cycle stages may differ from that of their slower growing counterparts based upon founder choices and strategic decisions.

5. CONCLUSIONS AND FUTURE RESEARCH

Exciting times are here for studies of fast-growth firms. With the expansion of many new e-commerce businesses, development of new technologies, and burgeoning entrepreneurial companies, we have numerous opportunities to discover *how* these firms evolve as well as *who* and *what* make a difference in the process. However, those who study organizations have also created numerous opportunities of their own toward these discoveries. Scholars of organizational theory and entrepreneurship are opening the doors to even wider views of how organizations evolve. Organization theorists have "adopted a more contingent and time-based view of organizational change" (Aldrich, 1999, p. 163). Entrepreneurship literature has called for more studies of multi-dimensional cognitive processes observable in entrepreneurs' behaviors toward opportunity discovery, firm creation and firm performance (e.g. Sandberg, 1986; Shaver & Scott, 1991; Venkataraman, 1997). Specifically, these authors indicate that these processes vary among individuals and that these differences matter in entrepreneurial settings. In this chapter, we have responded and have identified several issues that may serve as research ideas for exploiting the opportunities offered.

First, we believe that empirical research on fast-growth firms should embrace a focus on founder roles and behaviors as indicators of transitions rather than the traditional concept of life cycles. Rapid transitions call for flexibility and the ability to take on different roles quickly, or not to take on a role at all, when push comes to shove. Without understanding the roles founders enact, the behaviors required by those roles, and how founders make these rapid transitions as the firm rapidly grows, both scholars and practitioners are missing a vital piece of the puzzle in understanding transitions of fast-growth businesses. Further, we are missing an opportunity to understand what is required to make these transitions effectively. Such missed opportunities affect job creation and economic growth, not to mention personal satisfaction and the rewards attributed to founders of successful firms.

Second, we suggest that all fast-growth firms are not equal and that this inequality makes a difference in research designs and the conclusions we draw from their results. For example, we know that WalMart and Netscape are different in terms of industry characteristics, but their founder roles and behaviors may have taken very different courses. These may be reflected in the evolution of those two companies. The individual differences in behaviors and choices of role emphases of Sam Walton and Jim Barksdale, founders of these two companies, are expected to have made a difference in the rapid growth of their respective companies. Had these two companies been part of a cross-sectional research sample at any point in time, would their firms' transitional challenges have been identified, and if so, could those transitions have explained some of the variance in the rate of firm sales growth beyond industry characteristics or firm age? These are exciting issues that we encourage organizational theorists and entrepreneurship scholars to grapple with as study designs are constructed.

It may be that the organizational development process is not linear. If that is the case, then possibly, the founders of firms are choosing to engage in particular roles and/or related behaviors to some degree based on time demands. If that is also the case, then those transitions previously envisioned as occurring in lock-step order may be postponed or enacted simultaneously out of sheer necessity due to the rapid pace of transition in the firm. Aldrich (1999) suggests that, due to this lack of transitional linearity, clusters rather than individual behaviors might be studied. The work on roles discussed in this chapter would lend support to his suggestion, as well as propose that conceptual linkage is needed between roles and related behaviors during certain transitional role demands, also not yet identified.

Aldrich (1999) also suggests that the issue of historical time may require studying fast-growth firms in cohorts as well as including failed firms from the same time frame. In a rather extreme example, and based upon what we know of the relationship of abilities and behaviors, the study of behaviors in e-commerce start-up companies in 2000 would have entirely different confounding influences than would such a study conducted in 2010. The passage of a decade of historical events since the beginning of the century, not to mention some maturation of the Internet as a technology and as a tool, would find e-commerce founders interacting with an entirely different set of role demands and knowledge constraints. This does not even consider the possibility of new markets, new industries or new technologies entering the world of opportunities between now and then, waiting for an ambitious founder to discover and exploit them.

Although the idea of using cohorts is enticing as an opportunity, we must seek to separate industry effects from the ontogenetic effects in individual companies lead by their founders. As discussed earlier, by only studying rapid paces of transition in companies with annual rates of sales growth exceeding 20%, we may be defining a phenomenon by an outcome rather than by the phenomenon itself. Research has capitalized on the opportunities presented by the fast growing high technology industry and has engaged in research of samples of those companies in an effort to understand both fast growth and control for industry effects on performance. However, by design, such studies have excluded examinations of companies experiencing a rapid pace of change equal to that of the high tech industry, but without the accompanying high rates of sales growth. We need to seriously ask ourselves whether an above-average rate of sales growth adequately defines the concept of "fast-growth" and whether it is time to expand our vision of firm development to the concept of the pace of transition experienced by rapidly growing firms. Is it possible that we might conceive of a definition of fast-growth that is generalizable across industries? Only further exploration of issues discussed in this chapter, and elsewhere, can address that question.

Finally, as we move toward these aims, it behooves us to pursue, not only to describe, and to prescribe those conditions, settings or circumstances where we determine that founder role demands, founder role choices, designated emphasis, and founder behaviors make a difference in the growth and performance of fast-growth firms. To do this, we will have to undertake theory-based, experimental research, pilot studies in settings such as classrooms and laboratories in an effort to control for the effects of treatments designed to make a difference in founder, and therefore, firm performance. Knowledgeable MBA and EMBA students could be subjects with sufficient domain expertise to allow meaningful experiments to evolve. The results of this research must then be moved into entrepreneurial field settings, testing the theories upon which they were based, and shared with our students and practitioners, as well as published, to expand our common body of knowledge. A great deal of the research and theories for this work will need to be integrated from other fields of social science. This endeavor will not only strengthen the field of entrepreneurship in terms of the internal validity of its research, it will also expand the external validity of those theories and measures that are imported into real world entrepreneurial field settings. Accomplishing this is no more daunting than the sights set by the founders we study. We must seek new opportunities, seek new ways to exploit them, make choices in the roles we take on, self-regulate our behaviors, and make decisions as to what transitional leaps we will make. But, when all is said and done, if this is accomplished, we will have the personal satisfaction and the rewards earned by those who follow our path toward the edge of knowledge.

REFERENCES

Adizes, I. (1979). Organizational passages – Diagnosing and treating life cycle problems of organizations. *Organizational Dynamics*, (Summer), 3–25.

Adizes, I. (1989). *Corporate lifecycles: How and why corporations grow and die and what to do about it*. Englewood Cliffs, NJ: Prentice Hall.

Aldrich, H. (1999). *Organizations evolving*. London: Sage Publications.

Baird, L., & Meshoulam, I. (1988). Managing the two fits of strategic human resource management. *Academy of Management Review, 13*, 116–128.

Barron, R. A. (1998). cognitive mechanisms in entrepreneurship: Why and when entrepreneurs think differently than other people. *Journal of Business Venturing, 13*(4), 275–294.

Biddle, B. J. (1979). *Role Theory Expectations, Identities, and Behaviors*. New York: Academic Press, Inc.

Birch, D. L. (1987). *Job creation in America*. New York: The Free Press.

Bishop, K. (2000). Working smart and working hard: The effects of entrepreneurial multi-tasking and intuitive activities on venture performance. Unpublished dissertation. The University of Alabama.

Bishop, K. (2001). The effects of clear priorities in multi-tasking behaviors on entrepreneurs' satisfaction with venture performance. Paper presented at the Babson College-Kauffman Foundation Entrepreneurship Research Conference in Jonkoping, Sweden in June, 2001.

Chrisman, J. J., Bauerschmidt, A., & Hofer, C. W. (1998). The determinants of new venture performance: An extended model. *Entrepreneurship: Theory and Practice, 23*(1), 5–30.

Churchill, N. C., & Lewis, V. L. (1983). The five stages of small business growth. *Harvard Business Review, 61*(3), 30–50.

Cooper, A., Ramachandran, M., & Schoorman, D. (1997). Time allocation patterns of craftsmen and administrative entrepreneurs; Implications for financial performance. *Entrepreneurship: Theory and Practice, 22*(2), 123–136.

Dodge, R. H., Fullerton, S., & Robbins, J. E. (1994). Stage of the organizational life cycle and competition as mediators of problem perception for small businesses. *Strategic Management Journal, 15*(2), 121–134.

Downs, A. (1967). The life cycle of bureaus. In: A. Downs, *Inside Bureaucracy* (pp. 269–309). San Francisco: Little, Brown, and Company.

Eisenhardt, K. M. (1989). Making fast strategic decisions in high velocity environments. *Academy of Management Journal, 32*(3), 543–576.

Fischer, E., Reuber, A. R., Hababou, M., Johnson, W., & Lee, S. (1997). The role of socially constructed temporal perspectives in the emergence of rapid-growth firms. *Entrepreneurship, Theory and Practice, 22*(2), 13–30.

Flamholtz, E. (1987). *How to make the transition from an entrepreneurship to a professionally managed firm.* San Francisco: Jossey-Bass Publishing, Inc.

Galbraith, J. (1982). The stages of growth. *Journal of Business Strategy, 3*(4), 70–79.

Greiner, L. E. (1972). Evolution and revolution as organizations grow. *Harvard Business Review, 50*(4), 37–46.

Hambrick, D. C., & Crozier, L. M. (1985). Stumblers and stars in the management of rapid growth. *Journal of Business Venturing, 1*(1), 31–45.

Hanks, S. H., Watson, C. J., Jansen, E., & Chandler, G. N. (1993). tightening the life-cycle construct: A taxonomic study of growth stage configurations in high-technology organizations. *Entrepreneurship: Theory and Practice, 18*(2), 5–29.

Hitt, M. A. (1998). Presidential address: Twenty-first-century organizations: Business firms, business schools, and the academy. *Academy of Management Review, 23*, 218–224.

Jackson, S., & Schuler, R. S. (1995). Understanding human resource management in the context of organizations and their environments. *Annual Review of Psychology, 46*, 237–264.

Kanfer, R. (1994). Work motivation: New directions in theory and research. In: C. L. Cooper & I. T. Robertson (Eds), *Key Reviews in Managerial Psychology: Concepts and Research for Practice.* New York: John Wiley.

Kanfer, R. (1990). Motivation theory and industrial and organizational psychology. In: M. D. Dunnette & L. M. Hough (Eds), *Handbook of Industrial and Organizational Psychology* (Vol. 1, 2nd ed., pp. 75–170). Palo Alto, CA: Consulting Psychologists Press.

Katz, D., & Kahn, R. R. (1978). *The social psychology of organizations.* New York: John Wiley and Sons, Inc.

Kazanjian, R. K. (1988). Relation of dominant problems to stages of growth in technology-based new ventures. *Academy of Management Journal, 31*(2), 257–279.

Kimberley, J. R. (1979). Issues in the creation of organizations: Initiation, innovation, and institutionalization. *Academy of Management Journal, 22*, 437–457.

Kimberly, J. R. (1980a). The life cycle analogy and the study of organizations: Introduction. In: J. R. Kimberly, R. H. Miles & Associates (Eds), *The Organizational Life Cycle: Issues in the Creation, Transformation, and Decline of Organizations* (pp. 1–17). San Francisco: Jossey-Bass Publishers.

Kimberly, J. R. (1980b). Managerial innovation. In: P. C. Nystrom & W. H. Starbuck (Eds), *Handbook of Organizational Design.* New York: Oxford University Press.

Lippitt, G. L., & Schmidt, W. H. (1967). Crises in a developing organization. *Harvard Business Review, 45*, 102–112.

Lyden, F. J. (1975). Using Parsons' functional analysis in the study of public organizations. *Administrative Science Quarterly, 20*, 59–70.

McCarthy, A. M., Krueger, D. A., & Schoenecker, T. S. (1990). Changes in the time allocation patterns of entrepreneurs. *Entrepreneurship: Theory and Practice, 15*(2), 7–18.

Miller, D., & Friesen, P. H. (1984). *Organizations: A quantum view*. Englewood Cliffs, NJ: Prentice Hall.

Neal, J. A. (1978). *The life cycles of an alternative organization*. Boston, MA: Intercollegiate Case Clearinghouse.

Organ, D. W. (1988). *Organizational Citizenship Behavior: The Good Soldier Syndrome*. Lexington, MA: Lexington Books.

Penrose, E. (1952). *The theory of the growth of the firm*. New York: Oxford University Press.

Penrose, E. (1995). *The theory of the growth of the firm*. New York: Oxford University Press, Inc.

Proctor, R. W., & Dutta, A. (1995). *Skill acquisition and human performance*. Thousand Oaks, CA: Sage.

Quinn, R. E., & Cameron, K. (1983). Organizational life cycles and shifting criteria of effectiveness: Some preliminary evidence. *Management Science, 29*(1), 33–51.

Reuer, J. J., & Leiblein, M. J. (2000). Downside risk implication of multinationality and international joint ventures. *Academy of Management Journal, 43*(2), 203–214.

Sandberg, W. R. (1986). *New venture performance: The role of strategy and industry structure*. Lexington, MA: Lexington Books.

Sandberg, W. R., & Hofer, C. W. (1987). Improving new venture performance: The role of strategy, industry structure, and the entrepreneur. *Journal of Business Venturing, 2*, 5–28.

Scott, B. R., & Bruce, R. (1987). Five stages of growth in small business. *Long Range Planning, 20*(3), 45–52.

Shaver, K. G., & Scott, L. R. (1991). Person, process, choice: the psychology of new venture creation. *Entrepreneurship Theory and Practice, 15*(3), 23–45.

Smith, K. G., Mitchell, T. R., & Summer, C. E. (1985). Top level management priorities in different stages of the organizational life cycle. *Academy of Management Journal, 28*, 799–820.

Torbert, W. R. (1974). Pre-bureaucratic and post-bureaucratic stages of organization development, *International Development, 4*, 1–25.

Van de Ven, A. H., & Poole, M. S. (1995). Explaining development and change in organizations. *Academy of Management Review, 20*(3), 510–540.

Venkataraman, S. (1997). The distinctive domain of entrepreneurship research. *Advances in Entrepreneurship, Firm Emergence, and Growth, 3*, 119–138. JAI Press, Inc.

Weick, K. E. (1969). *The social psychology of organizing*. Reading, MA: Addison-Wesley.

Welbourne, T. M. (1997). Valuing employees: A success strategy for fast-growth firms and fast-paced individuals. *Proceedings of the 17th Annual Babson College Center for Entrepreneurship Studies Research Conference*, 17–31.

Welbourne, T. M., & Cyr, L. A. (1999). Using ownership as an incentive: Does the "too many chiefs" rule apply in entrepreneurial firms? *Group and Organization Management, 24*(4), 438–460.

Welbourne, T. M., Johnson, D. E., & Erez, A. (1998). The role-based performance scale: Validity analysis of a theory-based measure. *Academy of Management Journal, 41*(5), 540–555.

Yetton, P. W., & Bottger, P. C. (1983). The relationships among group size, member ability, social decision schemes, and performance. *Organizational Behavior and Human Decision Processes, 32*(2), 145–159.

2. INDIVIDUAL DIFFERENCES AND THE PURSUIT OF NEW VENTURES: A MODEL OF PERSON-ENTREPRENEURSHIP FIT

Gideon D. Markman and Robert A. Baron

Research on person-organization fit is concerned with the antecedents and consequences of compatibility between persons and the jobs they perform or the organizations in which they work (Kristof, 1996). Such research indicates that individuals are attracted to certain work environments as a result of numerous factors, including their attitudes, values, abilities, personality, as well as various job or organizational dimensions, such as organizational structure and culture (Van Vianen, 2000). For example, Turban and his colleagues (2001) found that while Chinese are more attracted to familiar and foreign- than to unfamiliar and state-owned firms, individual differences seemed to play a moderating role. When participants were more risk averse and had a lower need for pay they were more attracted to state- versus foreign-owned enterprises. While traditional recruiting manuals emphasize matching a person's knowledge, skills, and abilities to the requirements of a particular job, the notion of person-organization fit emphasizes congruence in values, goals, attitudes, and personal preferences. Stated differently, people are attracted to work settings that are consistent with their values and fulfill their needs (Cable & Judge, 1996) and such tendency seems consistent across countries and cultures (Turban et al., 2001).

Managing People in Entrepreneurial Organizations, Volume 5, pages 23–53.
© 2002 Published by Elsevier Science Ltd.
ISBN: 0-7623-0877-X

While much research in personnel selection has focused on important components of fit with respect to existing, well-established organizations, far less attention has been directed to person-organization fit in the context of newly formed organizations. More notably, and despite important progress in research on individual differences in entrepreneurship (see for example the special issue edited by Gartner, Shaver, Gatewood & Katz, 1994), autonomously, neither person-organization fit literature nor entrepreneurship research offers an integrated framework, let alone guidance, regarding factors that make some persons, but not others, pursue new venture formation. The goal of this paper is to fulfill this conceptual gap. To this end, we develop a causally-recursive model (Fig. 1) in which we identify various individual-difference factors that may play an important role in entrepreneurial pursuits.

We couched our arguments to suggest causality, but like social-cognitive theory's triadic reciprocal causation model of self-efficacy (cf. Bandura, 1997), we acknowledge that the relationships illustrated may in fact be successively and reciprocally causal in nature. Our model also suggests some level of equifinality (Gresov & Drazin, 1997). All, or only some, of the elements discussed henceforth, and their dynamic interplay, may lead to tighter person-entrepreneurship fit and subsequently to entrepreneurial pursuits. Finally, the model is not fully inclusive with respect to individual-difference factors. Rather, others factors not discussed here probably also play a role with respect to person-entrepreneurship fit. To be more precise, we recognize that individual differences are multidimensional, and in the context of entrepreneurship, may include diverse aspects or elements that we were (because of limited space and our objective to remain parsimonious) unable to incorporate into our model. Such factors may include motivation (Shane, Locke & Collins, in press; Naffziger, Hornsby & Kuratko, 1994), intentions and propensity to act (Bird, 1988; Krueger & Brazeal, 1994), choice (Shaver & Scott, 1991), personality traits (Ciavarella, Buchholtz, Riordan, Gatewood & Stokes, in press), attitudes (Robinson, Stimpson, Huefner & Hunt, 1991), and cognitions (Baron, 1998, 2000). Nonetheless, we hope that the person-entrepreneurship fit model developed hereinafter will be further developed in the future to more inclusively integrate additional individual difference factors into the field of entrepreneurship.

Our essay is divided into four sections. The first section provides a concise overview of recent person-organization fit research. The second section highlights key differences between mature and start-up companies, and how these variations may be reflected in the role requirements for employees (of mature companies) and entrepreneurs who start new ventures. The most obvious, and

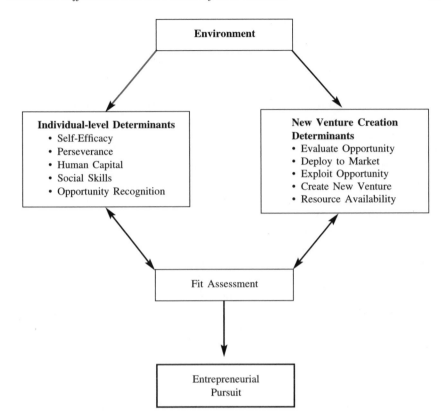

Fig. 1.   Model of Person-Entrepreneurship Fit and Creation of New Ventures.

naturally, the main task that entrepreneurs embark on, either independently or as spin-off from established organization, involves various actions leading to new venture formation. The third section introduces the concept of person-entrepreneurship fit and shows how certain individual-difference variables are crucial for execution of key tasks and functions entrepreneurs fulfill. We conclude this section by outlining our model of person-entrepreneurship fit and entrepreneurial pursuits. The final section suggests new directions for future research on individual differences in entrepreneurship and how such research may further our theoretical understanding of entrepreneurial activities. We conclude this final section with a discussion of practical implications of our framework.

Person-Organization Fit

Research on person-organization fit, or the match between people and the organizations in which they work, is highly diverse. Thus, a comprehensive examination of this topic is beyond the scope of the present paper. As such, we present a succinct overview of key findings in this domain, first and foremost as a means of establishing boundaries of this article (interested readers are referred to several reviews of this topic including but not limited to, Cable & Judge, 1996, 1997; Chatman, 1991; Kristof, 1996; O'Reilly, Chatman & Caldwell, 1991; Schneider, Goldstein & Smith, 1995).

All organizations – established ones and newly founded ones – face intense competitive pressure. Literature on person-organization fit holds that one solution to this problem is to attract, recruit, and retain talented persons who invigorate the organization and mobilize it to achieve its performance goals. For example, Jack Welch used to personally interview all candidates for the top 500 ranking positions at GE. This view that hiring the right people is crucial is not new (cf. Pfeffer, 1998), and it has motivated substantial research on person-organization fit. Cable and Judge (1996) reported that value congruence between job seekers and organizations is more important than whether job applicants and organizational representatives share similar background. Controlling for the attractiveness of job attributes, they also report that high person-organization fit predicts potential employees' job choice and work attitudes. Since socialization may affect turnover, commitment, and the continuity of firms' values and norms (Bauer et al, 1998), it is not surprising that firms use socialization tactics to facilitate person-organization fit (Cable & Parsons, 2001). Building on Kirton's (1976) Adaption-Innovation Theory of problem-solving style at work, Chan (1996) found that although cognitive misfit may not influence engineers' job performance, it does predict their turnover rate for up to three years. Taken together, to the extent that a success depends on committed employees who subscribe to a firm's core values and norms, research on person-organization fit suggests that when newcomers adequately appraise their fit with an organization, it allows them to better manage their future commitment and work attitudes.

Much research questions whether person-organization fit is a function of the person, the situation, or the interaction between the two, as well as the link between such fit and firm performance. Although strong theoretical arguments have been marshaled in support of various positions, an increasing volume of research suggests that both persons and situations – and even more so the interaction between the two – determines individual task performance and organizations' longevity (Bowen, Ledford & Nathan, 1991). The debate over the relative strength of situations and dispositions in organization science is likely to continue. Yet, if it is only institutional environments that shape organizational structures, routines, actions, and outcomes, what is the role of business leaders who make strategic choices (Beckert, 1999)? Building on theories in evolution and organizational ecology, Ghoshal and Lovas (2000) propose that managers and business champions play an important role in shaping their companies' direction and outcomes. In their view, organizations, through managerial foresight and personnel action, have incomplete, yet consequential degrees of freedom to maneuver within their environments. In other words, top management may bring timely interventions that guide and shape the outcomes that firms experience (Balkin, Markman & Gomez-Mejia, 2000).

We propose that because knowledge and intellectual property are becoming more important than physical capital (Rivette & Kline, 2000), individuals may now exert stronger relative control over the fate of their own careers and vocations than was true in the past. Highly skilled or technically trained persons find it easier to change jobs than to change their career. Or as suggested by Neal (1999), technical workers are more likely to change employers within the same industry than to seek alternative lines of work while working for the same employer. The fact that individuals seek opportunities for professional growth, along with increased job mobility, hints that notions of person-organization fit, or better yet, *person-career fit* may have more practical and theoretical implications than researchers had originally thought.

Frequently assessed by the compatibility between organizations and their incumbents on a number of dimensions (Kristof, 1996), person-organization fit is relevant both to employees and their companies. To name a few, adequate fit between incumbents and their organization is commonly associated with job longevity, greater organizational commitment, superior performance, higher job involvement, improved employee attitudes, lower rates of turnover and tardiness, higher levels of socialization and co-workers' likeability, and improved personal health and adaptation, (cf. O'Reilly, Chatman & Caldwell, 1991). Interest in person-organization fit can be traced to Schneider's (1987) attraction-selection-attrition (ASA) model, which suggests that individuals are drawn to organizations as a function of perceived congruence between such characteristics as values and goals (Cable & Judge, 1997; Schneider, Goldstein & Smith, 1995). Schneider's (1987) ASA model holds that people are first *attracted* to organizations when they perceive strong congruence between the institution and their own characteristics (Cable & Judge, 1997; Schneider, Goldstein & Smith, 1995). Then, a positive *selection* occurs when those hired also have the attributes the organization desires. Finally, *attrition* (or separation from the organization) occurs once employees and their firms realize that there is no longer adequate fit. Consistent with the ASA framework, it appears that interviewers use person-organization fit when evaluating and hiring job applicants (Cable & Judge, 1997; Rynes & Gerhart, 1990) and that job applicants self-select into organizations based on compatibility (Cable & Judge, 1996; Schneider, Goldstein & Smith, 1995). On the basis of recent tests of the ASA model, which point out that organizations are relatively homogeneous with respect to incumbents' personal attributes (Schneider, Smith, Taylor & Fleenor, 1998), Van Vianen (2000) has suggested that a match between newcomers' characteristics and those of tenured incumbents also determines a good person-organization fit. Not surprisingly, congruence between persons and their organization is – at least to some extent – a function of resemblance: the extent to which individuals share attitudes and principles, demographics, professional, and social backgrounds, work value, and a host of other factors (e.g. interests, needs, aspirations, etc.).

To recap, research suggests that interactively, persons and their organizations affect attitudes, behaviors, and task performance; that job seekers are attracted to organizations whose mission, values, and culture are congruent with their own; and that incumbents select job candidates who match their values and even background. The same research also shows that incongruence between persons and organizations results in high attrition and turnover rate (e.g. Chatman, 1991).

Differences Between Mature and Start-Up Companies: Implications for the Role Requirements of Employees and Entrepreneurs

According to Shane and Venkataraman (2000) entrepreneurship is a "scholarly examination of how, by whom, and with what effects opportunities to create future goods and services are discovered, evaluated, and exploited" (p. 218). If entrepreneurs are persons who evaluate, discover, and exploit business opportunities, then successful entrepreneurs are those who have the insight to match discoveries with buyers' needs and the stamina, knowledge, skills, and abilities to fruitfully deploy their offerings in the market. The main tasks – though naturally not the only one that entrepreneurs embark upon while creating new companies – range from transforming discoveries into marketable items, working intensely despite uncertainty and limited capital to establish market foothold, and fending off retaliatory actions from rivals in the marketplace. Another role that many entrepreneurs fulfill, particularly when seeking capital, is dealing with external investors. This suggests that similar to definitions of person-organization fit, person-entrepreneurship fit refers to the antecedents and consequences of compatibility between persons – their attitudes and thought processes, knowledge, skills, abilities, and even personality – and the various tasks that they need to fulfill while building and launching a new venture.

Several activities seem to be particularly unique to entrepreneurs, or to persons who build new organizations. Most notably, entrepreneurs must "sell" their business proposition to a small, homogeneous, and normally external group of investors (e.g. business angels, venture capitalists, and bankers). Corporate entrepreneurs must also persuade others to support their ideas, but they normally interact with internal constituencies (e.g. co-workers and supervisors) with whom they normally have stronger historical ties. Nonetheless, it is clear that many of the rolls that entrepreneurs fulfill overlap with duties and tasks that corporate entrepreneurship and even managers of new business units perform. As such, it is worthwhile to note that our analysis of person-entrepreneurship fit may have theoretical and methodological implications for other research (e.g. human resource management, corporate entrepreneurship, etc.), as well as practical applications to executive directors, supervisors, and administrators.

Further appreciation of the diverse roles that entrepreneurs fulfill is apparent when considering key differences between emerging and established organizations. A growing stream of research suggests that although entrepreneurial firms share much in common with established organizations, managerially and operationally, they reflect different stages of organizational lifecycle (Kanzanjian, 1988). Katz and Gartner (1988) suggested that emerging firms might be identified by such properties as intentionality, resources, boundary, and exchange. To name other distinctions, entrepreneurial firms are naturally younger and smaller. They have fewer resources, their product line is limited and largely unknown, they lack name recognition, and thus suffer from the liabilities of smallness, newness, and legitimacy (Aldrich & Fiol, 1994). Entrepreneurs also experience considerably higher internal change and instability than that commonly experienced by managers or incumbents of established firms (Shane & Venkataraman, 2000). In fact, not only do entrepreneurs face volatility and uncertainty, but also their very pursuits of "new combinations" (Schumpeter, 1934) actively instigate further market turbulence and ambiguity. The processes of firm creation – both as an independently formed venture or as a spin-off of new business unit within an established corporation – takes place when teams or individuals successfully convert original discoveries into innovative products and services that benefit society (Arrow, 1962; Kirzner, 1997; Van De Ven, Polley, Garud & Venkataraman, 1999). While many established firms innovate and compete under adverse market conditions, entrepreneurial firms must – simultaneously – build their internal infrastructure, develop routines, and implement their value chain. New ventures and established organizations also vary in terms of access to resources, available capability and assets, and knowledge capital, which again give rise to challenges characteristic of the liabilities of newness and legitimacy. These and other distinct differences explain why young and mature firms often use different operations, strategies, and tactics to achieve their goals (Miller & Friesen, 1982).

Given the distinctions mentioned above, what are the characteristics that distinguish those who choose to build organizations from those who, instead, opt the "secured job" within established organizations? Person-organization fit theory suggests that the inclination and motivation to develop new technology, products, or services and then create organizational infrastructures to sell them vary even among persons enjoying similar levels of knowledge, skills, ability, and motivation. This view coincides with studies suggesting that entrepreneurs and non-entrepreneurs may differ with respect to a number of personal characteristics (cf. Baron, 1998, 2000; Busentiz & Barney, 1997). For example, the annual income of many entrepreneurs is substantially lower than the earnings of comparable employees who have similar knowledge, skills, and ability. Such earning differentials reflect entrepreneurs' readiness to forgo higher pay in exchange for the non-pecuniary benefits such as increased professional autonomy and a sense of personal control (Hamilton, 2000). Additionally, motivational theories, such as goal setting theory, advocate that in almost any context, individual-level performance is a function of personal goals and objectives (Locke & Latham, 1991). Building on the view that more than ability determines variability in achievement and success, Seligman (1991) adds that optimists are more likely to make the effort necessary to achieve their objectives. For example, ability, motivation, and desire to succeed are not always enough without a strong belief that one will eventually succeed. Accordingly, learned helplessness theory states that it is only when individuals believe that they can achieve a desired objective that they will make the effort necessary to attain that goal (Bandura, 1995; Seligman, 1991; Seligman & Schulman, 1986). Other researchers suggest that persons who create new companies and those who work for existing ones may perceive and react to risk differently. Busenitz (1999) and Busenitz and Barney (1997) note that entrepreneurs pursue businesses without fully knowing how the market will react and whether their new products or services will succeed. Since many first-movers and visionary innovators fail to harvest market acceptance only to see second-movers reap these rewards (Tyagi, 2000), persons who create new companies and provide novel services shoulder substantially more risk than persons who run established companies with familiar offerings (Aldrich & Fiol, 1994).

While early empirical studies on individual differences and entrepreneurship were largely inconclusive (cf. Gartner, 1988; Shaver & Scott, 1991), as we discuss below, more recent studies offer support for the view that where entrepreneurship is concerned, individual differences do indeed matter – different people may be better suited to exploit commercial opportunities or create new companies than others. Starting from this premise, Markman, Baron and Balkin (2001) reasoned that because the process of transforming technological discoveries into attractive products or services is inundated with difficulty, snags, setbacks, and disappointment, launching a new venture requires high conviction in one's ability to overcome unavoidable challenges. Indeed, according to their study, patent inventors who start new ventures show significantly higher levels of self-efficacy and perceived capacity to persevere than do inventors who chose to work as employees for established organizations. Interestingly, they also report that regardless of whether one is an entrepreneur or not, patent inventors with higher self-efficacy and strong capacity to persevere (top 20% of the sample) earned some $35,000 more than inventors with lower self-efficacy and weaker capacity to persevere (bottom 20% of the sample).

Cognitive perceptions and biases also seem to shape how individuals cope with risks inherent in their decisions to start ventures (Sarasvathy, Simon & Lave, 1999). Simon, Houghton and Aquino (2000) proposed that entrepreneurs might not realize that certain tasks, important to ventures' longevity, are beyond their control. In their research, such biases as the *illusion of control* and the belief in the *law of small numbers* lowered perceived risk. Earlier evidence also suggests that entrepreneurs and non-entrepreneurs may react to environmental complexity differently and may exhibit variability in their ability to cognitively trim down convolution. Studying organizational complexity and information processing, McGaffey and Christy (1975) predicted that entrepreneurs might differ from non-entrepreneurs in their cognitive processes because the former must actively reduce the unavoidable complexity that is typically associated with new venture formation. Meyer and Dean (1990) suggested that professional managers replace founders once the latter fail to adequately reduce growth-related complexity and thus hinder crucial venture development (a.k.a the "executive limit"). Others found that entrepreneurs, more so than managers, are *less* comprehensive in their decision styles (Fredrickson & Mitchell, 1984). Kaish and Gilad (1991), who studied alertness to opportunity, report that founders of young firms spent significantly more time searching for information and paid attention to different risk cues than did executives of established firms. In contrast, Busenitz and Barney (1997) report that entrepreneurs gather significantly less information, utilize less formal techniques to analyze problems, and follow less rational decision processes than managers of small firms do. Others noted that entrepreneurs recognize patterns in their task environment and make quick decisions (Bird, 1988; Eisenhardt, 1989; Stevenson, Grousbeck, Roberts & Bhidé, 1999). Finally, evidence confirms that shared cognitive scripts may not only explain similarities in venture decision-making among entrepreneurs across cultures but also behavioral differences between entrepreneurs and non-entrepreneurs within countries (Mitchell, Smith, Seawright & Morse, 2000).

To recap, accumulating evidence suggests that entrepreneurs – due to their limited capital, brief presence in the market, questionable legitimacy, and susceptibility to retaliatory actions from resourceful incumbents – encounter substantially different challenges than their counterparts who work for more established firms. Given the evidence that entrepreneurs and corporate entrepreneurs are different, at least along certain roles and dimensions, from non-entrepreneurs, a key question in the field of entrepreneurship is whether, to what extent, and along what personal dimensions, successful entrepreneurs differ from less successful ones. It is to this important question that we now turn.

Individual Differences and Entrepreneurial Pursuits

Person-organization fit theory suggests that environmental forces and situations exert strong influence on entrepreneurial activities, but we agree with Shane and Venkataraman (2000) who point that individuals (and how they react to opportunities) constitute an important hub of the entrepreneurship phenomenon. Like much research on the role of individual differences in business contexts (Chatman, 1989), we distinguish between "strong situations" and "weak situations." Strong situations are particularly powerful contexts whereby individual preferences, motives, and traits cannot strongly influence human behavior or the environment in which they work. However, under weak situations individual differences may have profound impact on behavior – and perhaps on the situation itself. To be more precise, since budding ventures are just being formed as institutions, and generally by a relatively small number of persons, we view entrepreneurial undertakings as "weak situations." Since mature organizations enjoy established aggregations of norms, culture, values, rules, and practices that shape the work and action of many persons, they reflect "strong situations." As young firms are noticeably more open to change than mature firms, it stands to reason that human variation may bear more pronounced weight. Following the person-organization fit rationale presented earlier, it is our view that persons who create new ventures wield stronger and more distinct influences on their environmental ecosystem including their emerging company. Taken together, people continuously shape and are shaped by their workplace ecosystem, but individual differences are particularly noticeable when starting a new business because the process – what we call a weak situation – entails a small group of persons who erect a new organizational infrastructure from the bottom up.

As suggested earlier, initial research seeking to identify individual difference factors that distinguish entrepreneurs from other persons, or successful entrepreneurs from ones who are less successful, met with only modest success. This early, and at time, prolonged failure led some scholars to conclude that individual differences may be somewhat less relevant to entrepreneurship research (Gartner, 1988; Shaver & Scott, 1991). Moreover, some entrepreneurship research relies on population ecology and focused quite unilaterally on environmental characteristics while ignoring individual-difference dimensions (Bygrave, 1993). This is somewhat surprising given recent evidence that studying individual differences furthers management theory, research and practice (Mitchell & Mickel, 1999). Indeed, the view that individual differences matter remained compelling (Pfeffer, 1998), and currently, even economists suggest that firm performance and personal success are determined – to a large extent – by human variability rather than mere exogenous factors such as product differentiation, barriers to entry, or economies of scale (cf. Bhidé, 2000). For instance, recent findings show that young firms' performance and cash flow are more significantly related to their human and organizational resources (e.g. owner's industry experience, commitment, and staff skills) than to their strategy (Brush & Chaganti, 1999). Others have suggested that entrepreneurial success and performance are a function of achievement motivation, risk-taking propensity, preference for innovation (Stewart, Watson, Carland & Carland, 1999), and the capacity to adapt and to tolerate ambiguity (Bhidé, 2000).

Our review of recent entrepreneurship research identified several individual difference variables that seem to distinguish those who successfully start companies from those who don't. While these may include diverse individual characteristics such as locus of control, cognitive ability, attribution, and expectancy, our review centers on ones for which empirical evidence on links to entrepreneurial success seem to be strongest: high *self-efficacy* (Chen, Greene & Crick, 1998; Markman, Balkin & Baron, under review), ability to spot and *recognize opportunities* (Busenitz, 1999; Kirzner, 1997), high personal *perseverance* (Markman, Baron & Balkin, under review; Stoltz, 2000), high *human and social capital* (Honig, 1998), and superior *social skills* (Baron & Markman, 2000).

Self-Efficacy

Self-efficacy refers to one's perceived ability to organize and perform certain tasks (Bandura, 1997; Chen, Greene & Crick, 1998; Gist & Mitchell, 1992). Since self-efficacy positively predicts performance under difficult conditions (Vancouver, Thompson & Williams, 2001), we deduce that entrepreneurs high in self-efficacy will outperform those who are lower on this dimension. Indeed, a rich body of research in applied, social, and cognitive psychology supports this rationale; it shows that superior human functioning is motivated, regulated, and directed by the ongoing exercise of self-efficacy. To give a few examples, empirical research shows that high self-efficacy is fundamental in most domains and activities, including coping styles and dealing with stress (Jex, Blies, Buzzell & Primeau, 2001), efforts at overcoming substance abuse (Bandura, 1999), avoiding homelessness (Epel, Bandura & Zimbardo, 1999), attaining high academic achievement and social influence (Bandura, Pastorelli, Barbaranelli & Caprara, 1999), learning and mastering educational tasks (Bandura, 1993), and – most importantly from the present perspective – performance under task complexity (Bolt, Killough & Koh, 2001) and organizational effectiveness (cf. Bandura, 1997). In short, because one's beliefs in her or his efficacy influence the courses of action as well as how much effort to expend, self-efficacy plays an important role in achievement and performance (Bandura, 1997). Klein (1989) explains that when individuals pursue certain actions, goals, or undertakings, they "process, weigh, and integrate diverse sources of information concerning their capabilities and they regulate their behavioral choices and effort expenditure accordingly" (p. 167). As such, self-efficacy influences beliefs that affect future performance (Bandura, 1997; Gist & Mitchell, 1992).

Since self-efficacy positively affects diverse human activities, it stands to reason that it might have similar consequences in the context of entrepreneurship. For example, Bandura (1997) notes that highly efficacious persons prefer challenging activities and also show higher staying power while pursuing such exigent goals (Bandura, 1997). We reasoned that because the incentive to act is highest when entrepreneurs believe that their actions (e.g. starting a new company) lead to attainable outcomes (e.g. successful venture), high self-efficacy is an important determinant of successful, entrepreneurial behaviors. Initial empirical research on this issue shows that self-efficacy successfully differentiates entrepreneurs from non-entrepreneurs (Chen, Greene & Crick, 1998). Others proposed that because the ability to start a new venture (i.e. obtain capital, recruit key partners, associates, and employees, and ultimately, transform their discoveries into profitable products or services) requires high levels of self-belief, entrepreneurial success would be influenced by one's level of self-efficacy. Indeed, a recent study of patent inventors reports that not only does self-efficacy distinguish between entrepreneurs and non-entrepreneurs (entrepreneurs being significantly higher on this dimension), but also that high self-efficacy is significantly related to inventors' annual earnings (Markman, Balkin & Baron, 2001). Taken together, social cognitive theory and recent empirical studies suggest that success in entrepreneurial pursuits may be influenced by individual differences in self-efficacy. As such, our model indicates that entrepreneurs who are relatively high in self-efficacy will outperform entrepreneurs who are lower on this dimension.

Opportunity Recognition

In their early work on market processes, Hayek (1948) suggested that entrepreneurial activity involves market participants who acquire better information than fellow economic agents, whereas Mises (1949) maintained that entrepreneurial activity is driven by daring, imaginative, and speculative reactions to market opportunities. Clearly, both knowledge and audacity contribute to entrepreneurship, and as we argue below, have their origin (at least in part) in the way individuals react to information. Yet, most traditional economic models overlook the role of information and continue to assume that competitive acts bring the market closer to equilibrium. As economic agents must outdo one another by offering goods and services that are characterized by higher quality or lower cost, the essence of competition – which is underplayed by neoclassical equilibrium models – is dynamic rivalry (Kirzner, 1997).

Rejecting microeconomics' view that markets are in a state of equilibrium, entrepreneurial discovery theory (cf. Kirzner, 1997) distinguishes between levels of knowledge and information. Focusing on "unthought-of" knowledge, the theory seems to appreciate human role in discovering market opportunities. To be more specific, according to efficient markets theory, all known information is priced into equities and other derivatives, so when investments yield above normal returns, they also bear correspondingly greater risks (Kirzner, 1997). However, since certain opportunities may yield exceptional returns *without* exceptional risk, entrepreneurial discovery theory suggests that information leading to such opportunities will continue to frustrate market equilibrium. The challenge for entrepreneurs then is to discover new information that will enable them to distinguish excellent opportunities from strategies that simply yield high returns by reason of correspondingly higher underlying risks. Or, as stated by others, entrepreneurial or Schumpeterian rents are achieved by entrepreneurial discoveries (Cooper, Folta & Woo, 1995; Kirzner, 1997; Rumelt, 1987).

A recent longitudinal study of 12 radical innovation projects in 10 large U.S. firms suggests that opportunity recognition is highly dependent on individual initiative and capacity, rather than routine practices and procedures instituted by firms (Leifer et al., 2000). Keeping this in mind, we note that individuals differ greatly in their abilities to spot, recognize, and capitalize on abstract, implicit, and changing information (Miller, 1996). This suggests – in contrast to traditional economic theory that assumes a uniform risk-return ratio across opportunities (e.g. the better the return; the higher the risk) – that one's ability to identify favorable opportunities (e.g. those with high versus low market potential) may provide an important edge to those who strive to launch new ventures. Since markets' downfall risk and upside potential create a powerful incentive for entrepreneurs to obtain full and accurate information, it stands to reason that those who are more alert and better as monitors would stand a better chance than those who are less adept on these dimensions. We propose that although most individuals scan their environment, successful entrepreneurs may be better at discovering opportunities, as well as otherwise unforeseeable obstacles, embedded in their environment. To echo Kirzner (1997, p. 72), alertness, or "lookout for hitherto unnoticed features of the environment", allows successful entrepreneurs to spot high-potential opportunities and thus use them to overcome commercial newness. Since starting a new venture is an inherently uncertain process, lacking information may exacerbate uncertainties and heighten chances of failure. Indeed prescriptions for new-venture failure, such as misunderstanding customers, designing cost-ineffective products, and disregarding intermediate and end-users' needs (Dougherty, 1992), suggest that alertness may have broader implications than previously assumed. Moreover, it appears that an initial recognition of opportunity may trigger subsequent acts of opportunity recognition, which over time, lead to new venture launch (Leifer et al., 2000).

Research on entrepreneurial alertness and opportunity recognition may focus on diverse attributes including behaviors, background, and cognitions. For example, entrepreneurs and non-entrepreneurs who work in the same industry seem to react differently to opportunities in their task environment (McCline et al., 2000). Kaish and Gilad (1991) assessed the number of reading materials or amount of time entrepreneurs and managers spend thinking about their business. They concluded that the two groups scan and search for information differently. Entrepreneurs spend more time on nonverbal scanning and pay special attention to risk cues, whereas managers tend to focus on the economics of the opportunity. Interestingly, a replication study failed to support the entrepreneurial alertness hypothesis (Busenitz, 1996). While some findings suggest that novice entrepreneurs tend to search for information *less* extensively than more seasoned entrepreneurs (Cooper, Folta & Woo, 1995), it is unclear what the specific stimulus configuration of such opportunities is, and the cognitive processes through which successful entrepreneurs identify them. It remains to be seen whether successful entrepreneurs are indeed more adept than less successful ones at recognizing viable opportunities.

In another pertinent study (Shane, 2000), individuals from very different technological backgrounds assessed an invention (i.e. 3DP™). Results indicated that they recognized and then developed divergent business opportunities with respect to this invention. Shane's study suggests that different personal and vocational backgrounds may influence the type of opportunity identified. Additional support for the view that different backgrounds may play an important role is provided by Sarasvathy, Simon and Lave (1998), who used think-aloud verbal protocols to show that entrepreneurs and bankers think and process information differently. Sarasvathy and her colleagues report that while entrepreneurs accept risk as inevitable and take greater personal responsibility for its outcomes, bankers try to control risk by avoiding situations that involve higher levels of exposure to risk.

One additional line of research – that dealing with *regulatory focus theory* (e.g. Higgins, 1998) also points to the conclusion that individual difference factors may play a key role in the ability to recognize opportunities. As noted recently by Baron (in press), this framework suggests that in regulating their own behavior in order to achieve desired end-states, individuals adopt one of two contrasting perspectives (e.g. Higgins, 1998). In the first, known as a *promotion* focus, individuals focus on the goal of accomplishment – attaining positive outcomes. When they adopt this regulatory focus, persons seek to generate many hypotheses and to explore all possible means to reaching the goals they desire. In a *prevention* focus, in contrast, the ultimate goal sought is safety – avoiding negative outcomes. Individuals adopting this regulatory focus tend to generate fewer, but "safe" hypotheses, and center their attention on avoiding mistakes – actions or decisions that will produce negative outcomes. Many studies (e.g. Higgins & Silberman, 1998) indicate that individuals differ in their preferences for a promotion or prevention focus. In addition, individuals can be induced to adopt one or the other of these two foci by situational factors (e.g. instructions to focus either on achieving gains or avoiding losses, Liberman et al., 2001).

Regulatory focus theory suggests that when individuals adopt a promotion focus (an emphasis on accomplishment), they concentrate on what *signal detection theory* terms hit, on recognizing a stimulus when it is present and avoiding misses or failing to recognize a stimulus that is in fact present. In contrast, regulatory focus theory suggests that when individuals adopt a prevention focus (an emphasis on avoiding negative outcomes), they tend to concentrate on avoiding errors. Prevention-focused persons are especially vigilant to achieve correct rejections (correctly concluding that the stimulus is not present when it is indeed absent) and to avoid false alarms (concluding that a stimulus is present when it is not).

These predictions have clear implications for the process of opportunity identification by potential entrepreneurs. Specifically, persons who adopt a promotion focus are more likely to be vigilant for the existence of opportunities and to generate many hypotheses concerning potential opportunities. Further, they tend to set lower criteria for concluding that an opportunity exists. While this may result in many false alarms (assuming an opportunity exists when it really does not), it also increases the odds that opportunities that do exist will be recognized. So overall, the greater individuals' disposition to adopt a promotion focus, the more likely they are to identify opportunities. In contrast, persons who adopt a prevention focus are more likely to be vigilant for false alarms and for correct rejections; they tend to set higher criteria for concluding that an opportunity exists.

When these two theories, are combined, they cast potentially valuable light on the question of why some entrepreneurs are more successful than others – especially in terms of identifying viable opportunities. Regulatory focus theory suggests that both successful and unsuccessful entrepreneurs may show a tendency to adopt a promotion focus. Both groups are primarily oriented toward accomplishment so both seek to generate many hypotheses they can test in their efforts to obtain positive outcomes. But a key difference between successful and unsuccessful entrepreneurs may lie in the fact that while those who are successful temper this promotion focus with some aspects of a prevention focus (e.g. concern over avoiding false alarms), unsuccessful entrepreneurs adopt what might be termed a *pure promotion focus*. They show much less concern over avoiding negative results. In more specific terms, both successful and unsuccessful entrepreneurs show high motivation to maximize hits – to correctly notice opportunities that are present. But while successful ones are concerned with correctly avoiding false alarms and are also concerned with misses (failing to notice opportunities that are present), unsuccessful entrepreneurs show low concern with avoiding false alarms or to avoid misses. These and related predictions are summarized in Table 1.

In sum, a recent development in cognitive science (e.g. regulatory focus theory) and long a mainstay of research on perception (e.g. signal detection theory) combine to provide a new perspective on the process of opportunity recognition. The field of organizational behavior, with its focus on human cognition and its long-standing interest in several aspects of perception, provides a natural bridge between these basic lines of research and the field of entrepreneurship. And since individuals vary in their adoption of a promotion or

Table 1. Predicted Regulatory Focus (Promotion Prevention) of Successful and Unsuccessful Entrepreneurs.

Successful Entrepreneurs (Mixed Promotion and Prevention Focus)		Unsuccessful Entrepreneurs (Pure Promotion Focus)	
High on	Hits	High on	Hits
	False Alarms		Misses
Moderate	Correct Rejections	Low on	False Alarms
Low on	Misses		Correct Rejections

prevention focus, or some combination of the two, this framework, too, suggests that individual differences may play an important role in key aspects of the entrepreneurship process.

Perseverance

As they try to create and sell "new combinations," entrepreneurs encounter substantial obstacles including considerable uncertainty about market accept-ability and consumers' demand. In fact, the more radical the innovation, the higher the barriers that entrepreneurs must shatter or circumvent, and the more likely they are to bring upon themselves additional costs stemming from efforts to educate skeptical investors and persuade disinclined customers. Entrepreneurs also endure many personal detriments; they bear the opportunity cost of other alternatives, a liquidity premium for time and capital, risk stemming from uncertainty, financial and social perils, and other hazards due to rapidly changing trends and markets. Launching an independent company – even in the context of corporate entrepreneurship – entails a reality of limited resources, unfamiliar brand name, partial product offerings, and uncertain access to markets. Naturally, inherent in such undertaking is vulnerability to economic failure, sometimes precipitated by prolonged and painful struggle to keep the budding organization running. Even when success appears reachable, entrepreneurs still bear numerous disincentives due to market unpredictability and retaliatory rivals. The nature of entrepreneurial work then is inseparable from ambiguous conditions; contexts that may bring financial breakdown, legal liability, and total failure. This suggests that entrepreneurs incur, sometimes personally, substantial amount of financial and social adversity.

Steadfastness and persistence may be seen as escalation of commitment in the face of failure or strategic persistence in the wake of success, but research remains adamant that under challenging circumstances, perseverant individuals perform more adeptly than yielding individuals (cf. Bandura, 1997). As we noted above, successful entrepreneurs must maintain conviction and rise above numerous obstacles despite outcome uncertainty; they must establish market foothold with frail resources and capital, fend off competitors' strikes, and overcome liabilities of newness, smallness, and legitimacy. Entrepreneurs may also endure personal difficulties, such as financial or legal liabilities and periods of social or economic isolation (cf. Baron & Markman, 2000). Since entrepreneurs encounter repeated resistance, rejection, hostility, setbacks, snags, obstacles, and dis-appointment (to name a few), the ability to withstand, quarantine, and quickly overcome adversity would be an important personal advantage.

Learned industriousness theory states that depending on their history of persistent and effortful performance, different individuals display different levels of perseverance (Quinn, Brandon & Copeland, 1996). Also, depending on their *explanatory styles* – the customary ways in which individuals explain setbacks and failures – some tend to give up while others persist. Stoltz (2000), who conducted studies with over 100,000 persons from diverse organizations, points that individuals react to and sustain adversity differently. Applying Stoltz's construct, *Adversity Quotient* (AQ) to patent inventors, Markman, Baron, and Balkin (2001) report two interesting findings. First, successful inventors had significantly higher AQ scores than less successful inventors. Second, inventors who used the patents granted to them to start new companies had significantly higher levels of perceived control over adversity they faced and higher accountability for the outcome of the adversity than those who did not use their patents for that purpose.

While more research is certainly necessary, taken together, such studies hint that perseverance in the face of business difficulties may be as important for ultimate success as the idea or the opportunity itself. If this is so, then perhaps venture capitalists and corporate leaders could rely on measures of AQ to screen and identify technical people who will then be successful as champions of new business units. To recap, since perseverance reliably predicts personal effectiveness and performance under difficult circumstances across many professional domains, and since creating a new company is an ongoing challenge that demands lasting personal persistence, we propose that perseverant entrepreneurs will outperform those who are less persistent.

Human and Social Capital and Social Skills

While traditional means of production constituted a major share of a firm's tangible assets, today's capital is human talent and ingenuity; persons carry within them knowledge, expertise and other factors vital to their firm's success. Incumbents' knowledge, skills, ability, and experience are the driving force of firms' capacity to compete, and able labor force and its intellectual capital are now becoming even more central to their business enterprises (Rivette & Kline, 2000). Persons who have access to vital information become powerful agents in business creation processes (Shane & Venkataraman, 2000). Human capital consists of both abilities, which are influenced in part by innate factors (e.g. intelligence, health, personality dispositions, appearance) as well as acquired skills such as education, training, experience, and interpersonal relationships (Shanahan & Tuma, 1994). Evidence suggests that human capital is related to firm survival and growth (cf. Pennings, Lee & Van Witteloostuijn, 1998). First, even among firms of equal economic strength, longevity is related to variability in human capital (Gimeno et al., 1997) and research shows that human capital affects firm performance (Boone, De Brabander & Van Witteloostuijn, 1996). Similarly, persons with high human capital deliver higher performance, and firms championed by such persons are better able to attract and retain clients and strategic allies (Honig, 2001). Finally, and mainly in the absence of financial track record, investors assess entrepreneurs' human capital (e.g. professional credentials and accolades) as screening devices. To echo Arrow (1973), successful persons seem to have better access to their professional circles than less successful persons. This suggests that formal degrees, practical experience, and industry ties function as screening and filtering techniques to weed high-potential from low-potential individuals.

Like Dess and Shaw (2001) we consider social capital a tacit resource that encompasses relations within and across organizations. While social capital is frequently studied at organizational rather than individual level, because it is a tacit resource and cannot be fully protected against loss, incursion, or unauthorized transfer, many scholars agree that social capital is also an individual-level phenomenon (Miller & Shamsie, 1996). For example, social capital may capture opportunities enabled by social structure (Maman, 2000) when resources are made available through organizational ties, affiliation with elite institutions, social networks and contacts, and relationships with others. As such, human capital and social capital are complementary (Dess & Shaw, 2001). High levels of social capital facilitate knowledge attainment, access to resources, and may contribute to one's success (Nahapiet & Ghoshal, 1998). In entrepreneurship, high social capital provides access to information and thus, increased cooperation and trust from others. To be more precise, research among 1,700 new business ventures in Germany shows positive relationships between social capital and venture success (Bruderl & Preisendorfer, 1998). Moreover, entrepreneurs who have high social capital (e.g. extensive social networks, status, industry ties, and reputation) are more likely to attract venture capitalists' funds than entrepreneurs who are lower on this dimension (Cable & Shane, 1997). High social capital and high human capital – controlling for other factors – are related to business profitability (Honig, 1998). Similarly, variability in human capital results in significant differences in the viability and longevity of new ventures (Boden & Nucci, 2000).

Recent research found that social skills – competencies that enable individuals to interact effectively with others – play a key role entrepreneurs' success (Baron & Markman, 2000; in press). This finding is not surprising given that social skills can positively influence the outcomes of various situations, including job interviews (Riggio & Throckmorton, 1988), performance reviews (Robbins & DeNisi, 1994), and even legal proceedings (McKelvie & Coley, 1993). For instance, a study involving more than 1400 employees in a diverse set of jobs found that social skills were the single best predictor of job performance and promotion ratings (Wayne, Liden, Gran & Ferris, 1997). Similarly, social skills influence negotiation outcomes (Lewicki, McAllister & Bies, 1998), the frequency of conflict and aggression (Baron & Richardson, 1994), and personal happiness (Thomas, Fletcher & Lange, 1997).

In the context of new venture formation, social skills are important because entrepreneurship is embedded in social contexts (Steier, 2000); many of the tasks entrepreneurs must accomplish in order to succeed require some socialization and interpersonal interaction. Raising capital, generating enthusiasm and commitment in employees from a wide range of backgrounds, communicating effectively with advisors and potential investors, attracting effective partners, developing networks and strategic alliances, establishing market trust and legitimacy, and negotiating with buyers, suppliers, and rivals over diverse issues, require good social skills. Thus, since new venture creation requires entrepreneurs to work with many constituencies in numerous contexts and under varying degrees of stress and ambiguity, proficiency in dealing with others may be a key ingredient in entrepreneurs' success.

Baron and Markman (2000; in press), who conducted a study with entrepreneurs from two very different industries (cosmetics and high-tech), reported that higher social skills were associated with greater financial success. To be more precise, for both groups of entrepreneurs, social perception (the ability to perceive other persons accurately) was significantly related to financial success and for entrepreneurs in the cosmetics industry, social adaptability (the ability to adapt to a wide range of social situations and to interact with individuals from many different backgrounds) was a significant predictor of financial success. The inference Baron and Markman drew is that while human and social capital may be particularly crucial for accessing resources, social skills might be particularly important once such access is attained – that is, during the building stages of a new venture. Indeed, Ensley and his colleagues (in press) suggest that the success of new ventures hinges, at least in part, on entrepreneurs' ability to work together to commercialize their discoveries. Moreover, social skills may assist entrepreneurs in forming strategic alliances with other companies (e.g. Gulati & Westphal, 1999), in securing orders from new buyers, hiring talented employees, and so on. Given the positive impact social skills have on diverse human functioning, it is surprising that entrepreneurship research has, at least until recently, been somewhat reluctant to recognize it as an important factors in the context of new business formation.

Taken together, the above sections provide a foundation for our model of person-entrepreneurship fit and entrepreneurial pursuits depicted in Fig. 1. As briefly mentioned at the beginning of this article, our model suggests that becoming an entrepreneur places people in situations where certain individual difference factors might be instrumental to their decision to pursue a new venture formation and to their success. Stated differently, the weaker the situation, the greater the person-entrepreneurship fit, the higher the likelihood of (successful) entrepreneurial pursuits. As drawn, the model presents a "snapshot" of the process at a single point in time. However, it is meant to incorporate both iterative and recursive interactions. That is, the model captures the nonlinear interplay among several individual difference factors (e.g. self-efficacy, ability to recognize opportunities, personal perseverance, human and social capital, and superior social skills) in the context of tasks that entrepreneurs undertake (e.g. evaluate, recognize, seek resources, deploy to market, and exploit opportunities to create new firms). We suggest directionality, causality, and some level of equifinality (Gresov & Drazin, 1997), and we acknowledge that the relationships illustrated are successively and reciprocally causal in nature; some or even all of the five elements discussed and their dynamic interplay may correlate with person-entrepreneurship fit and entrepreneurial pursuits. For instance, as articulated during this discussion, highly efficacious persons or individuals with high human capital may be more inclined to pursue entrepreneurial opportunity at the same time that entrepreneurial pursuits foster stronger self-efficacy and raises one's human capital.

Finally, the role of individual differences in entrepreneurship is obviously multidimensional; individual differences may include diverse factors or elements that we were unable to incorporate into the model. Nonetheless, we believe that our person-entrepreneurship fit model could accommodate other individual-level factors that, though not discussed here, seem to play a role with respect to entrepreneurship (cf., special issue by Gartner, Shaver, Gatewood & Katz, 1994).

DISCUSSION

Shaver and Scott (1991) suggested that research on new venture creation should also attempt to show how entrepreneurs' thought processes might be translated into action. A few years later, a special issue of Entrepreneurship Theory and Practice (Gartner, Shaver, Gatewood & Katz, 1994) introduced several "paradigm-expanding" (p. 5) papers and encouraged entrepreneurship researchers to assess individual-level as well as social and psychological processes involved in entrepreneurial activity. Recently, Shane and Venkataraman (2000, p. 218) stated that entrepreneurship research should study "how, *by whom*, and with what effects opportunities to create future goods and services are discovered, evaluated, and exploited" (italic added). Clearly, the overarching thread is to encourage further scholarly dialogue on the importance of the persons – the entrepreneurs – to the phenomenon of new business formation. This chapter should be seen in this context.

An individual-difference perspective in assessing person-entrepreneurship fit may have important implications for corporate entrepreneurship. We noted that to the extent that corporate entrepreneurs score high on a number of *measurable* individual-difference dimensions (e.g. self-efficacy, opportunities recognition, perseverance, human and social capitals, and social skills), the closer the anticipated person-entrepreneurship fit. This view is based on observations that given comparable conditions, individuals – even if equipped with similar knowledge, skills, and abilities – are unlikely to equally recognize opportunities and even less so to harvest these opportunities by launching new ventures. Our earlier debate about weak and strong situations suggested that new ventures, even within matured firms, are conspicuously more acquiescent to human variation. As such, identifying, assessing, and monitoring these individual differences, while anticipating their likely effect, are important.

We examined potential relationships between research on person-organization fit and entrepreneurship, but more empirical and conceptual work is needed in order to confirm and extend our preliminary framework. For example, what does the future hold for research and theory development once other human factors – such as motivation (Naffziger, Hornsby & Kuratko, 1994), intentions and propensity to act (Bird, 1988; Krueger & Brazeal, 1994), choice (Shaver & Scott, 1991), the big five personality traits (Ciavarella, Buchholtz, Riordan, Gatewood & Stokes, in press), attitudes (Robinson, Stimpson, Huefner & Hunt, 1991), and cognitions (Baron, 1998, 2000) are incorporated into our model of person-entrepreneurship fit? Because, at its core, corporate entrepreneurship requires multitasking and diverse skills, we encourage executives and managers to go beyond merely matching employees' knowledge, skills, and abilities with clearly articulated job descriptions (Bowen, Ledford & Nathan, 1991). While "body parts" approach (e.g. searching for mere helping hands, muscles, or brute physical force) may sometimes fuel, at least for a short while, established and resource-rich organizations, emerging, resource-starved firms require intrinsic commitment and personal ownership. These issues were not addressed here, and they remain open and should be carefully examined in future research.

Because new business creation is multidimensional with diverse jobs, multi-tasks, and transient duties, our perspective complements other selection models that call for person-career or person-organization fit rather than theories of person-job fit (O'Reilly, Chatman & Caldwell, 1991; Schneider, Goldstein & Smith, 1995; Van Vianen, 2000). While several personal and organizational characteristics were assessed, future studies should empirically assess concerns regarding the utility of selection models in these contexts. Human variability would probably also be of interest to scholars who focus on motivation, team-work, and organizational design. As such, person-entrepreneurship fit should, at the very least, be taken into account in broader human resource functions such as selection, recruitment, placement, and retention programs (Mitchell & Mickel, 1999).

Since many selection procedures are exploitable, subject to legal challenge, and are only indirectly related to superior performance, practitioners are reluctant to rely on person-organization fit measures (Van Vianen, 2000). Nonetheless, job candidates continue to join organizations once there is a perceived fit between existing incumbents and new comers (Van Vianen, 2000). Research shows that interviewers can assess with high levels of accuracy applicant-organization value congruence, and that subjective fit assessments influence hiring decisions (Cable & Judge, 1997). In entrepreneurship, which we dubbed as a "weak situation," founding team members do much of the recruiting and retention (e.g. through their reputation, personal attributes, and industry ties). This suggests that entrepreneurs have, at least initially, much influence on, and discretion, regarding both social and cultural infrastructure, as well as strategic and technological orientation of their budding organization. Further, since new hires cannot fully assess the culture or climate of a new venture until later in the socialization process, perceptions of founding teams – their personalities, attitudes, behaviors, reputations, and professional and social affiliations – carry heavy weight in evaluating expected fit. Interestingly, although most entrepreneurs are probably unaware of person-organization theory, they seem to rely on its principles; they use ethnicity, race, and other identity cues as low-cost screening devices before they hire new employees, contract suppliers, and invite new partners (Silverman, 1999).

Finally, and in contrast to stable or unchanging human traits, the individual-difference factors our model used are readily open to modification. Indeed, techniques for enhancing self-efficacy and perseverance, or improving human and social capital as well as social skills have been developed and used with considerable success in many business contexts (e.g. Bandura, 1997; Stoltz, 2000; Waldroop & Butler, 2000). Seligman (1991) notes that cognitive styles like pessimism and helplessness can be changed through training techniques whereby individuals are taught to overcome self-defeating beliefs and thoughts. This suggests that identifying and providing entrepreneurs with appropriate training in such skills and attributes might assist them in their efforts to exploit opportunities and build new organizations. Since entrepreneurs' success and failure have significant ramifications not only for them personally, but to their societies as well (Venkataraman, 1997), efforts to provide them with skills serving to tip the balance in favor of success is well justified.

CONCLUSION

Although research on person-organization fit is multidisciplinary (cf. Judge & Ferris, 1992; Kristof, 1996; Schneider, Goldstein & Smith, 1995), to date, little effort has been made to integrate its various conceptualizations, operational-izations, or measurement strategies with the field of entrepreneurship. We explore the potential contributions of a person-organization fit framework to address the basic question: "Why some persons, but not others, are so much more successful as entrepreneurs?" Our person-entrepreneurship fit framework may provide an initial answer; possession of some or all of the characteristics identified above may be part of the reason why some persons, but not others, choose and excel at new business creation. To the extent this view is confirmed by future research, it would also appear that techniques could be developed for assessing the extent to which individuals are suited for diverse entrepreneurial roles, just as standard techniques of personnel selection (cf. Smith, 1994) are used to determine whether job applicants should be hired and students be admitted to graduate programs. To the best of our knowledge, this is a new and potentially fruitful perspective for research in entrepreneurship.

In closing, it is important to note that despite our focus and research on person-entrepreneurship fit, we in no sense imply that the effects of individual-difference factors are stronger or more important than other variables in determining entrepreneurial pursuits. We fully share the perspective, reflected in strategic management and other organization science research, that many factors – including market forces, industry trends, new technological discoveries, and so on – interact in complex ways to ultimately shape the nature and success of entrepreneurial pursuits (cf. Venkatarman, 1997; Shane & Venkatarman, 2000; Van De Ven, Polley, Garud & Venkataraman, 1999). We merely wish to emphasize here that one important unknown is the extent to which potential entrepreneurs possess "what it takes" – the skills, abilities, and characteristics required for creating a new venture, and have speculated that when person-entrepreneurship fit is high, "people don't choose their careers; they are engulfed by them" (Dos Passos, 1959).

REFERENCES

Aldrich, H. E., & Fiol, C. M. (1994). Fools rush in? The institutional context of industry creation. *Academy of Management Review, 19*(4), 645–670.

Arrow, K. (1962). Economic welfare and the allocation of resources for invention. In: R. Nelson (Ed.), *The Rate and Direction of Inventive Activity: Economic and Social Factors*: 609–626. Princeton, NJ: Princeton University Press.

Balkin, D. B., Markman, G. D., & Gomez-Mejia, L. R. (2000). Is CEO pay in high-technology firms related to innovation? *Academy of Management Journal, 43*(6), 1118–1129.

Bandura, A. (1993). Perceived self-efficacy in cognitive development and functioning. *Educational Psychologist, 28*(2), 117–148.

Bandura, A. (1997). *Self-efficacy: The exercise of control*. New York: W. H. Freeman & Company.

Bandura, A. (1999). A sociocognitive analysis of substance abuse: An agentic perspective. *Psychological Science, 10*(3), 214–217.

Bandura, A, Pastorelli, C., Barbaranelli, C., & Caprara, G. V. (1999). Self-efficacy pathways to childhood depression. *Journal of Personality & Social Psychology, 76*(2), 258–269.

Baron, R. A. (1998). Cognitive mechanisms in entrepreneurship: Why and when entrepreneurs think differently than other people. *Journal of Business Venturing, 13*, 275–294.

Baron, R. A. (2000). Counterfactual thinking and venture formation: The potential effects of thinking about "what might have been." *Journal of Business Venturing, 15*, 79–91.

Baron, R. A. (in press). Organizational behavior and entrepreneurship: Why both may benefit from closer links. In: B. M. Staw & R. Kramer (Eds), *Research in Organizational Behavior*. Greenwich, CT: JAI Press.

Baron, R. A., & Richardson, D. R. (1994). *Human Aggression* (2nd ed.). New York, NY: Plenum Press.

Baron, R. A., & Markman, G. D. (2000). Beyond social capital: The role of social competence in entrepreneurs' success. *Academy of Management Executive, 14*(1), 106–116.

Baron, R. A., & Markman, G. D. (in press). Social skills and entrepreneurial success: Why the ability to get along well with others may really matter. *Journal of Business Venturing*.

Bauer, T. N., Morrison, E. W., & Callister, R. R. (1998). Organizational socialization: A review and directions for future research. *Research in Personnel and Human Resource Management, 16*, 149–214.

Beckert, J. (1999). Agency, entrepreneurs, and institutional change. The role of strategic choice and institutionalized practices in organizations. *Organization Studies, 20*(5), 777–799.

Bhidé, A. V. (2000). *The Origin and Evolution of New Business*. NY: Oxford University Press.

Bird, B. (1988). Implementing entrepreneurial ideas: The case for intention. *Academy of Management Review, 13*(3), 442–453.

Boden, R. J. Jr., & Nucci, A. R. (2000). On the survival prospects of men's and women's new business ventures. *Journal of Business Venturing, 15*(4), 347–362.

Bolt, M. A., Killough, L. N., & Koh, H. C. (2001). Testing the interaction effects of task complexity in computer training using the social cognitive model. *Decision Sciences, 32*(1), 1–20.

Boone, C., de Brabander, B., & Van Witteloostuijn, A. (1996). CEO locus of control and small firm performance: An integrative framework and empirical test. *Journal of Management Studies, 33*(5), 667–699.

Bowen, D. E., Ledford, G. E. Jr., & Nathan, B. R. (1991). Hiring for the Organization, Not the Job. *Academy of Management Executive, 5*(4), 35–51.

Bruderl, J., & Preisendorfer, P. (1998). Network support and the success of newly founded businesses. *Small Business Economics, 10*(3), 213–225.

Brush, C. G., & Chaganti, R. (1999). Businesses without glamour? An analysis of resources on performance by size and age in small service and retail firms. *Journal of Business Venturing, 14*(3), 233–257.

Busenitz, L. W. (1996). Research on entrepreneurial alertness. *Journal of Small Business Management, 34*(4), 35–44.

Busenitz, L. W. (1999). Entrepreneurial risk and strategic decision making: It's a matter of perspective. *Journal of Applied Behavioral Science, 35*(3), 325–340.

Busenitz, L. W., & Barney, J. B. (1997). Differences between entrepreneurs and managers in large organizations: Biases and heuristics in strategic decision-making. *Journal of Business Venturing, 12*(1), 9–30.

Bygrave, W. D. (1993). Theory building in the entrepreneurship paradigm. *Journal of Business Venturing, 8*(3), 255–280.

Cable, D. M., & Judge, T. A. (1996). Person-organization fit, job choice decisions, and organizational entry. *Organizational Behavior and Human Decision Processes, 67*(3), 294–311.

Cable, D. M., & Judge, T. A. (1997). Interviewers' perceptions of person-organization fit and organizational selection decisions. *Journal of Applied Psychology, 82*, 546–561.

Cable, D. M., & Parsons, C. K. (2001). Socialization tactics and person-organization fit. *Personnel Psychology, 54*(1), 1–23.

Cable & Shane (1997). A prisoner's dilemma approach to entrepreneur-venture capitalist relationships. *Academy of Management Review, 22*(1), 142–176.

Chan, D. (1996). Cognitive misfit of problem-solving style at work: A facet of person-organization fit. *Organizational Behavior and Human Decision Processes, 68*(3), 194–207.

Chatman, J. (1989). Improving interactional organizational research. *Academy of Management Review, 14*(3), 333–349.

Chatman, J. (1991). Matching people and organizations: Selection and socialization in public accounting firms. *Administrative Science Quarterly, 36*, 459–484.

Chen, C. C., Greene, P. G., & Crick, A. (1998). Does entrepreneurial self-efficacy distinguish entrepreneurs from managers? *Journal of Business Venturing, 13*, 295–316.

Ciavarella, M. A., Buchholtz, A. K., Riordan, C. M., Gatewood, R. D., & Stokes, G. S. (in press). The big five and venture success: Is there a linkage? *Journal of Business Venturing*.

Cooper, A. C., Folta, T. B., & Woo, C. Y. (1995). Entrepreneurial information search. *Journal of Business Venturing, 10*(2), 107–120.

Dess, G. G., & Shaw, J. D. (2001). Voluntary turnover, social capital, and organizational performance. *Academy of Management Review, 26*(3), 446–456.

Dos Passos, J. (1959). *New York Times*, October 25th.

Dougherty, D. (1992). A Practice-Centered Model of Organizational Renewal Through Product Innovation. *Strategic Management Journal, 13*, 77–92.

Eisenhardt, K. M. (1989). Making fast strategic decisions in high-velocity environments. *Academy of Management Journal, 32*, 543–576.

Ensley, M. D., Peterson, A. W., & Amason, A. C. (in press). Understanding the dynamics of new venture top management teams: Cohesion, conflict, and new venture performance. *Journal of Business Venturing.*

Epel, E. S., Bandura, A., & Zimbardo, P. G. (1999). Escaping homelessness: The influences of self-efficacy and time perspective on coping with homelessness. *Journal of Applied Social Psychology, 29*(3), 575–596.

Fredrickson, J. W., & Mitchell, T. (1984). Strategic decision processes: Comprehensiveness and performance in an industry with an unstable environment. *Academy of Management Journal, 27*, 399–423.

Gartner, W. B. (1988). Who is the entrepreneur? is the wrong question. *American Journal of Small Business, 12*, 11–32.

Gartner, W. B., Shaver, K. G., Gatewood, E., & Katz, J. (1994). Finding the entrepreneur in entrepreneurship research. *Entrepreneurship Theory and Practice, 18*(3), 5–10.

Ghoshal, S., & Lovas, B. (2000). Strategy as guided evolution. *Strategic Management Journal, 21*, 875–896.

Gimeno, J., Folta, T. B., Cooper, A. C., & Woo, C. Y. (1997). Survival of the fittest? Entrepreneurial human capital and the persistence of underperforming firms. *Administrative Science Quarterly, 42*(4), 750–783.

Gist, M. E., & Mitchell, T. R. (1992). Self-efficacy: A theoretical analysis of its determinants and malleability. *Academy of Management Review, 17*, 183–211.

Gresov, C., & Drazin, R. (1997). Equifinality: Functional equivalence in organization design. *Academy of Management Review, 22*(2), 403–428.

Gulati, R., & Westphal, J. D. (1999). Cooperative or controlling? The effects of CEO-board relations and the content of interlocks on the formation of joint ventures. *Administrative Science, 44*(3), 473–506.

Hamilton, B. H. (2000). Does entrepreneurship pay? An empirical analysis of the returns to self-employment. *The Journal of Political Economy, 108*(3), 604–631.

Hayek, F. A. (1948). *Individualism and economic order.* Chicago: University of Chicago Press.

Higgins, E. T. (1998). Promotion and prevention: Regulatory focus as a motivational principle. In: M. P. Zanna (Ed.), *Advances in Experimental Social Psychology* (Vol. 30, pp. 1–46). New York: Acadmie Press.

Higgins, E. T., & Silberman, I. (1998). Development of regulatory focus: Promotion and prevention as ways of living. In: J. Heckhausen & C. S. Dweck (Eds), *Motivation and Self-Regulation Across the Life Span* (pp. 798–113). New York: Cambridge University Press.

Honig, B. (1998). What determines success? Examining the human, financial, and social capital of Jamaican microentrepreneurs. *Journal of Business Venturing, 13*, 371–394.

Honig, B. (2001). Human capital and structural upheaval: A study of manufacturing firms in the West Bank. *Journal of Business Venturing, 16*(6), 575–594.

Jex, S. M., Bliese, P. D., Buzzell, S., & Primeau, J. (2001). The impact of self-efficacy on stress-or-strain relations: Coping style as an explanatory mechanism. *Journal of Applied Psychology, 86*(3), 401–409.

Judge, T. A., & Ferris, G. R. (1992). The elusive criterion of fit in human resource staffing decisions. *Human Resource Planning, 15*(4), 47–67.

Kaish, S., & Gilad, B. (1991). Characteristics of opportunities search of entrepreneurs versus executives: Sources, interest, general alertness. *Journal of Business Venturing, 6*, 45–61.

Kanzanjian, R. K. (1988). Relation of dominant problems to stages of growth in technology-based new ventures. *Academy of Management Journal, 31*, 257–279.

Katz, J., & Gartner, W. B. (1988). Properties of Emerging Organizations. *Academy of Management Review, 13*, 429–441.

Kirton, M. (1976). Adaptors and innovators – A description and measure. *Journal of Applied Psychology, 61*(5), 622–635.

Kirzner, I. (1997). Entrepreneurial discovery and the competitive market process: An Austrian approach. *Journal of Economic Literature, 35*, 60–85.

Klein, H. J. (1989). An integrated control theory model of work motivation. *Academy of Management Review, 14*, 150–172.

Kristof, A. L. (1996). Person-organization fit: An integrative review of its conceptualizations, measurement, and implications. *Personnel Psychology, 49*(1), 1–49.

Krueger, N. F. Jr., & Brazeal, D. V. (1994). Entrepreneurial potential and potential entrepreneurs. *Entrepreneurship Theory and Practice, 18*(3), 91–104

Leifer, R., McDermott, C. M., O'Connor, G. C., Peters, L. S., Rice, M., & Veryzer, R. W. (2000). *Radical Innovation: How Mature Companies Can Outsmart Upstarts.* Boston, MA: Harvard Business School Press.

Lewicki, R. J., McAllister, D. J, & Bies, R. J. (1998). Trust and distrust: New relationships and realities. *Academy of Management Review, 23*(3), 438–458.

Liberman, N., Moldon, D. C., Idson, L. C., & Higgins, E. T. (2001). Promotion and prevention focus on alternative hypotheses: Implications for attributional functions. *Journal of Personality and Social Psychology, 80*, 5–18.

Locke, E. A., & Latham, G. P. (1991). *A Theory of Goal Setting & Task Performance.* Prentice Hall, Englewood Cliffs, NJ.

Maman, D. (2000). Who accumulates directorships of big business firms in Israel?: Organizational structure, social capital and human capital. *Human Relations, 53*(5), 603–630.

Markman, G. D., Balkin, D. B., & Baron R. A. (2001). Inventors' cognitive mechanisms as predictors of new venture formation. Working Paper, Rensselaer Polytechnic Institute.

Markman, G. D., Baron, R. A., & Balkin, D. B. (2001). Adversity quotient: Perceive perseverance and new business formation. Paper presented at Academy of Management Meeting. Washington, D.C.

McCline, R. L., Bhat, S., & Baj, P. (2000). Opportunity recognition: An exploratory investigation of a component of the entrepreneurial process in the context of the health care industry. *Entrepreneurship Theory and Practice, 25*(2), 81.

McGaffey, T. N., & Christy, R. (1975). Information processing capability as a predictor of entrepreneurial effectiveness. *Academy of Management Journal, 18*(4), 857–863.

McKelvie, S. J., & Coley, J. (1993). Effects of crime seriousness and offender facial attractiveness on recommended treatment. *Social Behavior & Personality, 21*(4), 265–277.

Meyer, G. D., & Dean, T. J. (1990). An upper echelons perspective on transformational leadership problems in high technology firm. *Journal of High Technology Management Research, 1*, 223–242.

Miller, D., & Friesen, P. H. (1982). Innovation in conservative and entrepreneurial firms: Two models of strategic momentum. *Strategic Management Journal, 3*, 1–25.

Miller, D., & Shamsie, J. (1996). The resource-based view of the firm in two environments: The Hollywood film studios from 1936–1965. *Academy of Management Journal, 39*, 519–536.

Miller, S. M. (1996). Monitoring and blunting of threatening information: Cognitive interference and facilitation in the coping process. In: I. G. Sarason, G. R. Pierce & B. R. Sarason (Eds), *Cognitive Interference; Theory, Methods, and Findings*. Mahwah, NJ: Lawrence Erlbaum Associate Publishers.

Mises, L. (1949). *Human action: A treatise on economics*. New Haven, CT: Yale University Press.

Mitchell, R. K., Smith, B., Seawright, K. W., & Morse, E. A. (2000). Cross-cultural cognitions and venture creation decision. *Academy of Management Journal, 43*(5), 974–993.

Mitchell, T. R., & Mickel, A. E. (1999). The meaning of money: An individual-difference perspective. *Academy of Management Review, 24*(3), 568–578.

Nahapiet, J., & Ghoshal, S. (1998). Social capital, intellectual capital, and the organizational advantage. *Academy of Management Review, 23*(2), 242–266.

Naffziger, D. W., Hornsby, J. S., & Kuratko, D. F. (1994). A proposed research model of entrepreneurial motivation. *Entrepreneurship Theory and Practice, 18*(3), 29–42.

Neal, D. (1999). The complexity of job mobility among young men. *Journal of Labor Economics, 17*(2), 237–261.

O'Reilly, C. A, Chatman, J., & Caldwell, D. F. (1991). People and organizational culture: A profile comparison approach to assessing person-organization fit. *Academy of Management Journal, 34*, 487–516.

Pennings, J. M., Lee, K., & Van Witteloostuijn, A. (1998). Human capital, social capital, and firm dissolution. *Academy of Management Journal, 41*(4), 425–440.

Pfeffer, J. (1998). *The Human Equation: Building Profits by Putting People First*. Boston, MA: Harvard Business School Press.

Quinn, E. P., Brandon, T. H., & Copeland, A. L. (1996). Is task persistence related to smoking and substance abuse? The application of learned industriousness theory to addictive behaviors. *Experimental & Clinical Psychopharmacology, 4*(2), 186–190.

Riggio, R. E., & Throckmorton, B. (1988). The relative effects of verbal and nonverbal behavior, appearance, and social skills on evaluations made in hiring interviews. *Journal of Applied Social Psychology, 18*(4), 331–348.

Rivette, K. G., & Kline, D. (2000). *Rembrandts in the Attic*. Boston, MA: Harvard Business School Press.

Robbins, T. L., & DeNisi, A. S. (1994). A closer look at interpersonal affect as a distinct influence on cognitive processing in performance evaluations. *Journal of Applied Psychology, 79*(3), 341–353.

Robinson, P. B., Stimpson, D. V., Huefner, J. C., & Hunt, H. K. (1991). An attitude approach to the prediction of entrepreneurship. *Entrepreneurship Theory and Practice, 15*(4), 1332.

Rumelt, R. P. (1987). Theory, strategy and entrepreneurship. In: D. J. Teece (Ed.), *The Competitive Challenge: Strategies for Industrial Innovation and Renewal* (pp. 137–158). New York: Harper & Row.

Rynes S. L., & Gerhart, B. (1990). Interviewer assessments of applicant "fit:" An exploratory investigation. *Personnel Psychology, 43*, 13–35.

Sarasvathy, D. K., Simon, H. A., & Lave, L. (1999). Perceiving and managing business risks: Differences between entrepreneurs and bankers. *Journal of Economic Behavior and Organization, 33*, 207–225.

Schneider, B., Goldstein, H. W., & Smith, D. B. (1995). The ASA framework: An update. *Personnel Psychology, 48*, 747–773.

Schneider, B., Smith, D. B., Taylor, S., & Fleenor, J. (1998). Personality and organizations: A test of the homogeneity of personality hypothesis. *Journal of Applied Psychology, 83*, 462–470.

Schumpeter, J. (1934). *Capitalism, socialism, and democracy*. New York: Harper & Row.

Seligman, M. E. P. (1991). *Learned Optimism*. New York: Knopf.

Seligman, M. E. P., & Schulman, P. (1986). Explanatory style as a predictor of productivity and quitting among life insurance sales agents. *Journal of Personality and Social Psychology, 50*, 832–838.

Shanahan, S. E., & Tuma, N. B. (1994). The sociology of distribution and redistribution. In: N. J Smelser & R. Swedberg (Eds), *The Handbook of Economic Sociology* (pp. 733–765). Princeton, NJ: Princeton University Press.

Shane, S. (2000). Prior knowledge and the discovery of entrepreneurial opportunities. *Organization Science, 11*, 448–469.

Shane, S., Locke, E. A., & Collins, C. J. (in press). Entrepreneurial motivation. *Human Resource Management Review*.

Shane, S., & Venkataraman, S. (2000). The promise of entrepreneurship as a field of research. *The Academy of Management Review, 25*, 217–226.

Shaver, K. G., & Scott, L. R. (1991). Person, process, and choice: The psychology of new venture creation. *Entrepreneurship Theory and Practice*, (Winter), 23–42.

Silverman, R. M. (1999). Ethnic solidarity and black business: The case of ethnic beauty aids distributors in Chicago. *The American Journal of Economics and Sociology, 58*, 829–841.

Simon, M., Houghton, S. M., & Aquino, K. (2000). Cognitive biases, risk perception, and venture formation: How individuals decide to start companies. *Journal of Business Venturing, 15*(2), 113–134.

Smith, M. (1994). A theory of the validity of predictors in selection. *Journal of Occupational and Organizational Psychology, 67*, 13–31.

Steier, L. (2000). Entrepreneurship and the evolution of angel financial networks. *Organization Studies, 21*(1), 163–192.

Stevenson, H. H., Grousbeck, H. I., Roberts, M. J., & Bhidé, A. (1999). *New Business Venture and The Entrepreneur* (5th ed.). Boston, MA: Irwin McGraw-Hill.

Stewart, W. H. Jr, Watson, W. E., Carland, J. C., & Carland, J. W. (1999). A proclivity for entrepreneurship: A comparison of entrepreneurs, small business owners, and corporate managers. *Journal of Business Venturing, 14*, 189–214.

Stoltz, P. G. (2000). *Adversity Quotient at Work*. New York, NY: HarperCollins Publishers.

Thomas, G., Fletcher, G. J. O., & Lange, C. (1997). On-line empathic accuracy in marital interaction. *Journal of Personality & Social Psychology, 72*(4), 839–850.

Turban, D. B., Lau, C. M., Ngo, H. Y., Chow, I. H. S., & Si, S. X. (2001). Organizational attractiveness of firms in the People's Republic of China: A person-organization fit perspective. *Journal of Applied Psychology, 86*(2), 194–206.

Tyagi, R. K. (2000). Sequential product positioning under differential costs. *Management Science, 46*(7), 928–940.

Van De Ven, A. H., Polley, D. E., Garud, R., & Venkataraman, S. (1999). *The Innovation Journey*. Oxford, NY: Oxford University Press.

Van Vianen, A. E. M. (2000). Person-organization fit: The match between newcomers' and recruiters' preferences for organizational cultures. *Personnel Psychology, 53*, 113–149.

Vancouver, J. B, Thompson, C. M., & Williams, A. A. (2001). The changing signs in the relationships among self-efficacy, personal goals, and performance. *Journal of Applied Psychology, 86*(4), 605–620.

Venkataraman, S. (1997). The distinctive domain of entrepreneurship research: An editor's perspective. In: J. Katz & R. Brockhous (Eds), *Advances in Entrepreneurship, Firm Emergence, and Growth* (Vol. 3, pp. 119–138). Greenwich, CT: JAI Press.

Waldroop, J., & Butler, T. (2000). *Maximum Success: Changing the 12 Behavior Patterns That Keep You from Getting Ahead*. Doubleday.

Wayne, S. J., Liden, R. C., Graf, I. K., & Ferris, G. R. (1997). The role of upward influence tactics in human resource decisions. *Personnel Psychology, 50*, 979–1006.

3. HUMAN RESOURCE MANAGEMENT MODELS FOR ENTREPRENEURIAL OPPORTUNITY: EXISTING KNOWLEDGE AND NEW DIRECTIONS

Robert L. Heneman and Judith W. Tansky

It has long been recognized that managing human resources is a critical variable in the growth of emerging firms (Penrose, 1959). Although this fact is well known, there is precious little theory and research to guide the study of managing human resources in the entrepreneurial organization. A recent review of the literature found not only a paucity of theory and research in this area, but that the existing theory and research is disjointed (Heneman, Tansky & Camp, 2000). A similar observation was made about entrepreneurial research in general (Shane & Venkataraman, 2000). As a result, models and frameworks are needed to organize and direct theory development in entrepreneurship (Shane & Venkataraman, 2000).

When there is a lack of well-developed models and frameworks, two issues may arise concerning the creation of new knowledge. First, scholars may be reluctant to do research on managing human resources in entrepreneurial firms. It is very difficult to conduct meaningful research for publication when there are no existing models or frameworks to use as a basis for one's ideas. Second,

Managing People in Entrepreneurial Organizations, Volume 5, pages 55–81.
© 2002 Published by Elsevier Science Ltd.
ISBN: 0-7623-0877-X

it is difficult to know whether one's ideas are adding value to the knowledge base since previous theoretical efforts and research are disjointed and difficult to follow. Given these two issues, it is not surprising that many articles conclude that we need more and better research concerning the management of human resources in entrepreneurial firms. Our objective in this chapter is to add structure and direction to the study of managing human resources in entrepreneurial firms in order to promote the development of more and better research.

In order to meet our objective, we undertake four steps. First, we make the case for why human resource management theories should be studied in emerging firms. Second, we review existing human resource management models to see what relevance, if any, they have to the management of human resources in entrepreneurial firms. Most of these models have been developed primarily for the study of human resource departments in large, bureaucratic companies. Thus, we do not expect to find a large amount of direction from use of these models. Nevertheless, for due diligence reasons and, more importantly, because there are some parallels between managing human resources in large and small firms, we will not omit these models from the chapter. Third, we pose some new frameworks and models that have direct relevance to entrepreneurship. Based on our review, we will point out to scholars the direction for theory and research indicated by each model and framework. Our hope is that our effort might: (1) attract scholars to this area of study and (2) provide a context in which to assess the value of contributions to this field. Lastly, we provide our own framework to integrate these various models. Also, we offer the start to a new model based on theory from physics.

THE IMPORTANCE OF HRM THEORY FOR EMERGING FIRMS

Human resource management (HRM) can be defined as an organizational, decision-making system concerned with aligning the interests of employees with company goals in order to maximize firm performance. In order for the interests of employees to be aligned with the goals of the organization, companies must select and/or train people to have the needed knowledge, skills, and abilities as well as reward employees for goal accomplishment. In order for firm performance to be maximized, employees must be successful at meeting the goals of the organization and be loyal to the company by remaining with the company as a productive employee.

The importance of HRM to entrepreneurial firms has been clearly identified in two ways. First, focus group data gathered by the Kauffman Foundation on over 173 CEO/founders of emerging firms clearly indicated in a content analysis of responses that human resource management issues are one of the most critical issues that they face (Heneman, Tansky & Camp, 2000). Second, research clearly pointed out that HRM practices have an impact on the economic performance of the firm (Heneman et al., in press). Consequently, entrepreneurship researchers and practitioners need to pay attention to developments in human resource management. Human resource management may be as much, or more, of a source of sustained competitive advantage for emerging firms as technology or capital (Barney & Wright, 1999). While technology is quickly initiated by competitors and capital is plentiful for emerging companies, sound HR systems are difficult to find and/or imitate.

HRM researchers and practitioners need to be more sensitive to the needs of emerging companies. Most HRM practices are based on theories relevant to large and bureaucratic firms. While these types of firms are vital to the success of our economy, it is the smaller, entrepreneurial firms that are the engines for economic growth in the United States. In the United States in 1995, 99.7% of the companies had fewer that 500 employees and 78.8% has fewer than 10 employees (USSBA, 1997). HR researchers and practitioners that ignore the need to develop theory and practices for emerging companies run the risk of becoming obsolete.

ORGANIZING FRAMEWORK AND MODELS

Frameworks and models to be examined in this chapter are shown in Exhibit 1. They are categorized by three major types of frameworks and models. The category labels for each set of frameworks and models comes from Delery and Doty (1996). The "universal perspectives" suggest that there are "best" or universalistic practices in managing human resources that are applicable to all organizations, including entrepreneurial firms. The "contingency perspectives" suggest that human resource management practices must be carefully matched to characteristics of the firm, such as its business strategy and organizational structure. The "configurational perspectives" look at how patterns or interactions of human resource variables relate to firm performance. There may be certain patterns of human resource variables that are more likely to be related to firm performance in entrepreneurial firms than in non-entrepreneurial firms. In a study of 1,050 financial institutions of all sizes, Delery and Doty (1996) found that all three of these different types of categories of human resource practices are related to firm performance. Unlike Delery and Doty (1996), who only studied one model or framework within each category, we take a more expansive view of each category label. In our review, we cover multiple frameworks and models within each category. Some of these frameworks and models are old,

Exhibit 1.   Organizing Framework for Human Resource Management
           Frameworks and Models of Entrepreneurship.

Universal Perspectives

- Functional
- Legal
- High Performance Work Systems

Contingency Perspectives

- Strategic Human Resource Management
- Market System
- Growth Stage

Configurational Perspectives

- Resource Based View of the Firm
- Role Based Theory
- Visionary Model

some are new. For the new frameworks and models that we are proposing,
we will provide both qualitative and quantitative data to verify our claims
whenever possible.

UNIVERSAL PERSPECTIVES

Universal frameworks and models are grounded in the concept that certain
human resource practices add value to the performance of all firms. Each framework and model is differentiated from the other on the basis of the type of
practice to be followed. Although these frameworks and models are independent
of one another, they are not mutually exclusive.

Functional Human Resource Management

Arguably, the most often used framework for human resource management is
the functional model whereby human resource activities are grouped by content
area. Typical content areas include staffing, training and development, compensation, and employee relations. This approach is used by most large companies
to organize their human resource management function, and it is also used in
most human resource textbooks to describe the human resource practices of
large firms. Upon occasion, it has also been used to describe the practices that
small and medium-sized firms should use (e.g. Arthur, 1995).

Functional human resource management is a very efficient method of organizing human resource activities based on economies of scale. For example, an organization with two large business units can have one compensation department rather than two to eliminate duplication of activities across business units. The functional approach also provides a schema for human resource professionals to group similar human resource activities.

This approach has been criticized first by academics (H. Heneman Jr., 1969) and later by practitioners (Ulrich, 1997) because of the focus of managers on activities rather than outcomes. That is, staffing, compensation, and training are means to a business end rather than ends in and of themselves. End states toward which these activities are directed include, but are not limited to, performance, attendance, and retention. Line managers in both entrepreneurial and non-entrepreneurial firms tend to cognitively process human resource activities in terms of desired business outcomes rather than human resource practices.

Models and frameworks of entrepreneurial organizations might also be developed around outcomes rather than activities. Human resource activities can be tied into important intermediate (e.g. productivity) and ultimate (e.g. financial performance of the business) business goals. An example of this approach is with Economic Value Added (EVA) models that (Ehrbar, 1998) are path diagrams showing how resources, including human ones, are linked to the economic goals of the organization.

Legal Human Resource Management

A myriad of laws and regulations govern the human resource activities of the firm. Many of the laws and regulations apply to employers with fifteen or more employees. As a result, as firms grow, they must eventually become aware of, and take responsibility for, these laws and regulations or subject themselves to potential lawsuits and financial penalties if found guilty.

In large firms, these concerns are often handled by legal departments and/or separate departments (e.g. Equal Employment Opportunity and Affirmative Action). In smaller firms, these issues may be handled by general legal counsel or, as is often the case, they are ignored until some issue arises. For example, diversity and discrimination are non-issues until inconsistent rules for bonuses are applied to a male and a female. The female then seeks legal counsel and files discrimination charges. The owner of the smaller firm usually does not have the funds, time or knowledge to effectively deal with this type of issue. Legal fees and losing the lawsuit may even bankrupt the company.

In both entrepreneurial and non-entrepreneurial firms, there may be utility in reframing the schema used to view human resource management laws and regulations. Two perspectives appear useful. One is a diversity perspective where activities undertaken to provide equal opportunity and affirmative action may help the organization identify otherwise unrecognized talent or business opportunities in the market. The firm is encouraged to act upon these various opportunities. Second, is a risk management perspective whereby human resource laws and regulations are made part of the portfolio of laws and regulations needed to be assessed and monitored over time to prevent the firm from subjecting themselves to devastating consequences under various scenarios. By taking a diversity perspective and a risk management perspective, the management of laws and regulations regarding people becomes aligned with the goals of the business rather than by a separate functional human resource activity.

Care must be taken with the legal model because it focuses on only one aspect of managing human resources that may add value to the firm. If entrepreneurial firms treat human resources only as a cost, then avoidance of lawsuits becomes the goal. If entrepreneurial firms treat human resources as an investment, then legal human resource management can further goals of the organization through diversity and risk management. Moreover, other human resource functional areas can help generate revenues as well as minimize costs as demonstrated in the research literature. For example, a meta-analysis indicted that management by objectives (MBO), as a method of performance appraisal, is associated with a 42% increase in productivity (Rodgers & Hunter, 1991). Principles of performance appraisal that have been found to be successful as a defense in discrimination cases (Field & Holley, 1982) are consistent with performance appraisal practices followed in MBO.

High Performance Work Systems

Research has shown that some human resource management practices add more value to the firm than do others (Wright et al., 1999). Pfeffer (1998) defines a high performance work system as one where high performance management practices can be utilized because within the organization, people are viewed as a critical, strategic asset. When people are viewed as intelligent, motivated and trustworthy, a culture develops that allows performance management practices to be implemented that, in turn, lead to performance results and sustained profits. A high performance work systems approach indicates that these practices with above average returns should always be followed. For example, ServiceMaster which provides low technology cleaning services, achieved a return to stockholders of 25% compounded annually for a twenty-five year period. The company values people and has been very willing to invest in leadership training and courses to help people develop communication skills. Developing management talent and instilling the organization's key values has been critical to the success of ServiceMaster (Pfeffer, 1998, p. 297). Although there is great debate as to which practices are most valuable to the firm, Pfeffer (1998, pp. 64–65) provides a current list of human resource management practices that appear on most lists as adding value to the firm are shown in Exhibit 2.

Pfeffer (1998), and others, review the evidence that these practices do indeed work across a large number of organizations. Hence, there is some utility for entrepreneurial firms to review this list as a means of being successful managing human resources. Also, a line of research to be pursued is the extent to which these practices are indeed effective in entrepreneurial firms. One would expect, for example, that employment security is unlikely in entrepreneurial firms given the volatility of the environment in which most entrepreneurial firms operate. Also, for those organizations that differentiate themselves on the basis of innovation, as is the case with many entrepreneurial firms, a constant flow of employees into and out of the firm may be very desirable. This constant flow of employees may be necessary in order to generate new ideas on an ongoing basis and also to have the appropriate human capital available at the right time(s) in the growth of the firm.

Future developments in this area should focus on whether there are universalistic practices associated with entrepreneurial firms that are unique to entrepreneurial firms. For example, profit and stock sharing plans may be more effective in entrepreneurial firms than nonentrepreneurial firms. In entrepreneurial firms, it is likely that employees have more influence over the

Exhibit 2.   High Performance Work Systems Characteristics.

---

(1) Employment security.

(2) Selective hiring of new personnel.

(3) Self-managed teams and decentralization of decision making as the basic principles of organizational design.

(4) Comparatively high compensation contingent on organizational performance.

(5) Extensive training.

(6) Reduced status distinctions and barriers, including dress, language, office arrangements, and wage differences across levels.

(7) Extensive sharing of financial and performance information throughout the organization.

Source: Pfeffer, J. (1998). *The human equation: Building profits by putting people first*. Boston, MA: Harvard Business School Press.

outcomes needed to be attained in order for the company to generate profits and distribute stocks. In nonentrepreneurial firms, the amount of influence over organizational outcomes may be less, and as a result, profit and stock sharing maybe less motivational to nonentrepreneurial employees.

CONTINGENCY PERSPECTIVES

Contingency perspectives offer frameworks to show under what circumstances various human resource practices are likely to be advantageous to the firm. Contingencies vary somewhat depending upon the model and framework. General support for this perspective is reviewed by Gomez-Mejia and Balkin (1992).

Strategic Human Resource Management

Strategic human resource management models rely on the concept of "fit" between the strategic goals of the organization and human resource practices. Under this umbrella concept of fit is the concept of alignment and integration, both of which must be present for fit to exist. Alignment refers to the development of human resources practices for *each* functional area of human resources that are consistent with the business strategy of the organization. Hence, researchers speak of staffing strategies, compensation strategies, and training strategies. Integration refers to the development of human resource practices that are consistent with one another (R. Heneman, in press). The belief behind integration is that synergies are possible between human resource strategies. When synergy occurs, the practices used together in concert with one another add more value to the firm than each practice used alone. In statistical terms, the interaction effect between human resource practices are likely to explain variance in firm performance above and beyond the main effects of each practice.

The empirical research to date does not provide strong support for either the alignment or integration concepts associated with fit. Main effect models (i.e. universalistic) are likely to receive more empirical support than interaction effect models in the limited amount of research conducted to date (Gerhart, Trevor & Graham, 1996). One reason for this lack of support for strategic human resource management models may be the lack of sound theoretical models to guide predictions regarding integration and alignment.

It is very unlikely that the simple extension of existing strategic human resource management research to entrepreneurial firms will yield meaningful results. This approach has not worked well in extending human resource practices from large to small firms (Barber, Wesson, Roberson, & Taylor, 1999) and is unlikely to work well with the extension of findings from nonentrepreneurial firms to entrepreneurial firms. A better strategy will be to develop theory specific to the entrepreneurial firm as to strategic practices. For example, Rothchild Gourmet Foods installed a goal-sharing incentive plan that provided financial rewards for the accomplishment of business objectives, including controllable costs, sales and quality. This compensation plan, in the eyes of the employees, became the strategic plan as it organized employee goals relative to company goals.

Market System

Another contingency approach is to match patterns of human resources practices with characteristics of the firm. One pattern that has been investigated has been labeled a "market" pattern as compared with an "internal" pattern (Delary & Doty, 1996). Internal human resource systems are considered to be consistent with a defender business strategy where the firm is focused on defending their current portfolio of products and services (Miles & Snow, 1978). Market patterns are considered to be consistent with prospective business strategies where the firm is seeking to expand their portfolio of products and services (Miles & Snow, 1978). Internal human resource practices are shown in Exhibit 3. Market based human resource management practices are shown in Exhibit 4. In a study of financial institutions, there was some limited support for these hypothesized matches between business strategy and human resource practice with firm performance (Delery & Doty, 1996).

Exhibit 3. Internal Based Human Resource Practices.

(1) Internal career opportunities

(2) Formal training systems

(3) Behavior based appraisal

(4) Hierarchy-based compensation (i.e. little profit sharing)

(5) Employment security

(6) Employee voice

(7) Tightly defined jobs

Source: Delery, J. E., & Doty, D. H. (1996). Modes of theorizing in strategic human resource management: Tests of universalistic contingency, and configurational performance patterns. *Academy of Management Journal, 39*, 802–825.

Exhibit 4. Market Based Human Resource Practices.

---

(1) Few internal career opportunities

(2) Lack of formal training systems

(3) Output based appraisals

(4) Profit sharing systems

(5) Little employment security

(6) Little employee voice

(7) Broadly defined jobs

Source: Delery, J. E., & Doty, D. H. (1996). Modes of theorizing in strategic human resource management: Tests of universalistic contingency, and configurational performance patterns. *Academy of Management Journal, 39,* 802–825.

One implication of this finding is that multiple characteristics of the firm need to be focused on simultaneously rather than one characteristic of the firm or business strategy being considered by itself as was done in this study. Lawler (1996) makes forceful arguments that human resource practices should be considered in the context of strategy, organizational structure, and business process.

Another implication is that the dichotomous pattern of human resource practices may be overly simplistic. There may be variations along each dimension of human resource practice that must be considered in empirical investigations. Qualitative case study research might be conducted in entrepreneurial firms to establish the various patterns that exist and under what circumstances they are used.

Growth Stage

Growth is a critical goal of entrepreneurial organizations (Heneman & Tansky, 1999). Aldrich (1999) argues that as an organization is socially constructed and evolves, one of the issues becomes developing organizational boundaries. People, in the form of the management team that has evolved, and employees that are added become a crucial piece in developing and maintaining organizational boundaries. Thus, as organizations evolve, the area of human resources evolves to help develop and maintain the organization. The demands placed upon the specific human resource activities that are conducted, and who conducts these activities, varies (Greer, Youngblood & Gray, 1999; Klaas, McClendon & Gainey, 1999). Human resource practices to be emphasized and who will perform these activities are shown in Exhibit 5.

Exhibit 5.   Growth Stage Model of Human Resource Management.

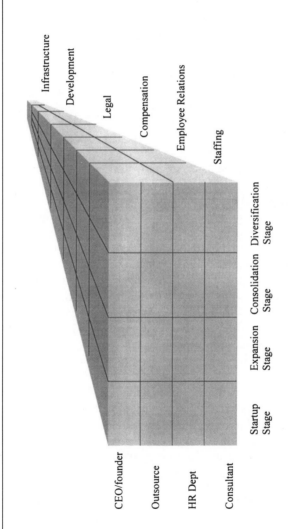

Exhibit 5. (continued).

Activity Order	Cell in Model
1	CEO/founder, Startup Stage, Staffing
1	CEO/founder, Startup Stage, Employee Relations
2	Outsource, Expansion Stage, Compensation
2	Outsource, Expansion Stage, Legal
3	HR Department, Consolidation Stage, Development
4	Consultants, Diversification Stage, Infrastructure

Aldrich (1999) argues that we know little about human resources in evolving firms until they reach the older stages of growth and have become medium-sized or large because that is where research has focused. Thus, although this framework is newly proposed and very coarse, it suggests several propositions for entrepreneurial, evolving firms. Initial stages of growth are likely to be associated with the CEO/founder performing various human resource practices. As the organization grows, the owner's time becomes compromised by human resource practices, and the CEO/founder must outsource the function. As the firm continues to grow, a human resource department may be added for efficiency sake as well as for support of the unique capabilities of the organization that have been developed. Eventually, the organization may need to outsource specialized services (e.g. incentive plan design).

In the initial stages, employee relations and staffing are likely to be the focus of the CEO/founder. With growth comes issues of compensation (e.g. payroll) and legal concerns. As the firm continues to grow, development of human resources becomes an issue to prevent skill obsolescence so a full time human resource staff is hired to do firm specific training. Eventually, human resource practices are again outsourced to develop a human resource infrastructure for the firm (e.g. human resource information system) and to perform specialized services (e.g. incentive plan design).

CONFIGURATIONAL PERSPECTIVES

The configurational perspective looks at interactions of human resource variables likely to be related to firm performance. In addition, these patterns of human resource practices must not only be consistent internally but must match up with patterns of business strategy. Under a configurational approach, business strategy is viewed as a multidimensional construct. Lastly, these patterns of human resource practices are ideal types (Delary & Doty, 1996).

Resource Based View of the Firm

According to a resource based view of the firm, in order for organizations to exploit market opportunities and to sustain competitive advantage once attained, organizations must develop distinct capabilities (Barney, 1997). One capability that can be used toward these ends is the human resource (Barney & Wright, 1998). For example, Nordstrom's Department Stores has taken what is considered to be a relatively homogeneous labor pool and exploited the rare characteristics of its employees to gain a competitive advantage by maintaining the highest sales per square foot of any retailer in the nation (Barney & Wright, 1998, p. 34). Nordstrom's provides a highly incentive-based compensation system that allows salespersons to make as much as twice the industry average. At the same time, the culture encourages sales clerks to make heroic efforts to meet customers' needs. In order to be successful in achieving these ends with human resources, human resource practices must meet the criteria shown in Exhibit Six.

To the extent that these criteria are met with human resource practices, other organizations will have a difficult time copying these practices. Critical capabilities vary by organization. Critical human resource capabilities are developed by human resource practices. In essence, organizations form an ideal type of critical capability for their organization. For example, one large retailer with small shops around the world established fashion taste and sense as a critical competency. In turn, all of the human resource practices (e.g. staffing, compensation, development) were developed to support this critical capability as well as others (R. Heneman & Thomas, 1997).

The resource-based view of the firm has great applicability to managing human resources in entrepreneurial firms. Rather than developing human

Exhibit 6.   Characteristics of Critical Human Resource Competencies.

- Valuable
- Rare
- Inimitable
- Nonsubstitutable

Source: Barney, J. (1997). *Gaining and sustaining competitive advantage*. Reading, MA: Addison-Wesley.

resource activities for the sake of efficiency and administrative ease as with functional human resources, human resource activities are organized around the goal of providing human resource practices that add value to the organization by supporting core capabilities of the firm. Interestingly, the human resource practices themselves may become critical capabilities in the firm. For example, in organizations that are facing very tight labor markets, as is currently the case, organizations that have human resource practices that successfully attract and retain talent are more likely to be successful.

Role Based Theory

There has been a recent resurgence in interest in role theory in human resource management research (Ilgen & Hollenbeck, 1991). Roles are defined as expected patterns of behavior for people (Naylor, Pritchard & Ilgen, 1980). In general, roles are of current interest in human resource management research because of the increasingly organic nature of organizations and the need to move from jobs to roles to accommodate the flexibility required of employees in organic organizations (R. Heneman, Ledford & Gresham, in press).

A universal model of roles has been developed by Welbourne, Johnson, and Erez (1998). They develop theory and use empirical data to support the notion that across a wide spectrum of different organizations, there are critical roles that employees must perform. These roles include job, innovation, career, team, and organization. These roles are defined in Exhibit 7. The data they collected

Exhibit 7.   Roles in Organizations.

Role	Definition
Innovator	Role requires creativity on behalf of the organization, not the individual, which contributes to the effectiveness and adaptability of the organization.
Job	Role represents the traditionally held view of employee performance.
Career	Role focuses on career accomplishment, participating in training and acquiring new skills, and emphasizes joint career responsibility of employer and employee in new employment contract.
Team	Role recognizes the importance of being a team member in today's organization because of increasing reliance on teams and cooperation among team members.
Organization	Role parallels behaviors associated with organizational citizenship behaviors (Organ, 1988).

Source: Welbourne, T. M., Johnson, D. E., & Erez, A. (1998). A role-based performance scale: Validity analysis of a theory-based measure. *Academy of Management Journal, 41*, 540–555.

show construct and predictive validity support for these ideal type roles in entrepreneurial and nonentrepreneurial firms.

Jobs and careers may not be clearly articulated in entrepreneurial firms. Hence, there may be other roles that employees are expected to perform. These roles can be formulated on the basis of leader-member exchange theory (LMX; Graen, Novak & Sommerkamp, 1982). That is, LMX provides the theoretical rationale to develop roles appropriate to entrepreneurial firms that can supplement the list developed by Welbourne et al. (1998). As applied to an entrepreneurial environment, LMX theory suggests the following. CEO/founders of entrepreneurial firms form perceptions of in-groups and out-groups of employees. In-group members receive a high degree of trust, interaction, support, and rewards from the CEO/founder while out-group members receive a low degree of trust, interaction, support, and rewards, (R. Heneman, Greenberger & Ananyuo, 1989). Out-group employees are marginal employees that can be replaced. In-group members drive the success of the business. Within the in-group, the CEO/founders will look to employees to fulfill special roles. These roles can be thought of in terms of intellectual capital (Youndt, Subramanian & Snell, 1999) needed by the CEO/founder. Intellectual capital is divided into three dimensions by Youndt et al. (1999): human capital (knowledge, skill, and abilities), social capital (knowledge available through social relationships), and organizational capital (institutionalization of knowledge).

The CEO/founder goes to certain people with technical skills to perform functions of the business that the CEO/founder does not have expertise in (e.g. finances). Hence, human resource practices must be arranged such that the correct human capital is available to the CEO/founder. The CEO/founder also needs to have trusted employees that he can confide in when discussing various issues of change in the business. Hence, human resource practices must be arranged to support the social capital needed by CEO/founder in the in-group (Leana & Van Buren, 1999). Productive family relationships within family businesses would be another example of social capital. Lastly, the CEO/founder needs for knowledge to be institutionalized in the organization so that it can be recalled when needed. Although this knowledge may be stored electronically, much of the tacit knowledge in entrepreneurial firms resides within employees (e.g. the "old hand"). Hence, human resource practices must be developed to support organizational capital that resides in people in the business.

As an example of this framework, compensation practices might be used to support these different roles in different ways. Skill-based pay may need to be used to bolster human capital while recognition rewards may sustain social capital. Retention bonuses may be necessary to retain employees in possession of organizational capital. As another example of this framework, it is likely that social capital is needed before human capital in emerging firms during the start-up phase in order to attract the necessary capital, physical and human resources.

Visionary Model

Traditionally, human resources was viewed as a reactionary function in the organization-designed to process transactions (e.g. payroll) and to comply with government laws and regulations. Contemporary depictions of human resources are more likely to depict human resources as proactive. From a proactive perspective, steps are taken in the organization to add value. Human resource practices are designed to fit the strategy and culture of the organization (R. Heneman & Gresham, 1998). So, for example, selection processes are undertaken to not only match the person to the job, but to match the person the goals of the larger organization as well (H. Heneman, Judge & R. Heneman, 2000).

To test this difference in models, we conducted a factor analysis with an existing database. The database resulted from the *1998 Survey of Innovative Practices* mailed in the fall of 1998 to 6,000 Entrepreneur of the Year Institute (EOYI) members. EOYI members are CEOs (primarily founders) from arguably the most innovative and admired firms in the world. The survey was commissioned to explore key non-financial items that were believed to impact a firm's ability to achieve and sustain a high rate of growth. Six hundred and seventy-two usable responses were received. The 672 firms averaged 5.9% net profit, 18 years in business, and employed an average of 269 employees in 1995. Although retail trade was somewhat under-represented, and manufacturing was over-represented, the distribution across industrial sectors was fairly representative.

Using the items in this database, we formulated a "maintenance" model that depicts the reactive approach to human resource management. We also constructed a "visionary" model with items that capture a proactive approach. The results of the factor analysis are shown in Exhibit 8. As can be seen in this exhibit, the results confirmed our model. The results were also confirmed in a qualitative study where we categorized focus group comments by CEO/founders (R. Heneman & Tansky, 1999).

Given that there are two models, the next step will be to see to what extent these models correlate with operational (e.g. productivity), behavioral (e.g. turnover), financial (e.g. returns), and growth objectives of entrepreneurial firms. Our belief is that both models will add value to the entrepreneurial firm relative to a null model. As pointed out in the description of the chapter on legal and functional human resource models, both these models have historically been grounded in well-conceived practices. On the other hand, it is also our belief

Exhibit 8. Visionary vs. Maintenance Human Resource Practice Factor
Analysis Results.

	Factor Loadings	
Item	Maintenance	Visionary
Training and development	0.125	0.561
Complying with employment regulations	0.796	0.111
Maintaining employment records	0.757	0.268
Setting competitive compensation levels	0.205	0.631
Managing workers' compensation	0.707	0.165
Maintaining productivity	−0.041	0.721
Maintaining morale	−0.096	0.800
Dealing with labor/union issues	0.549	−0.079
Eigen Value	2.387	2.687
% Variance Explained	23.9%	26.9%

that the visionary model will add value above and beyond the maintenance
model for reasons spelled out in other models in this chapter (e.g. role theory,
high performance work systems).

EVALUATION OF FRAMEWORKS AND MODELS

Current perspectives on entrepreneurship include the identification and explanation of market opportunities along with the growth of the firm (Shane &
Venkataraman, 2000). Moreover, entrepreneurial firms may be located in large
or small companies. It appears, based upon our review of the various HR
perspectives, that some frameworks and models lend themselves better to some
aspects of entrepreneurship and company size than do others. Our views are
summarized in Exhibit 9 and Exhibit 10 and described below.

Functional Human Resource Management

Functional HR appears to have a low level of relevance to the identification
and exploitation of market opportunities. Fewer individuals are usually involved
in this process, and human resource practices are usually very organized with
little need to compartmentalize human resource practices. As the firm grows in

Exhibit 9.   Relevance of HR Frameworks and Models for the Study of
Entrepreneurship Facet.

| | Entrepreneurship Facet | | |
Frameworks and Models	Identification	Market Exploitation	Growth
Functional	Low	Low	Moderate
Legal	Low	Moderate	High
High Performance	Low	Low	Moderate
Strategic	Moderate	Moderate	Moderate
Market	High	Moderate	Low
Growth	Low	Moderate	High
Resource Based	High	High	High
Role Based	High	High	High
Visionary	High	High	High

size, however, traditionally, it has been viewed that there is an increasing need
to compartmentalize HR practices for the sake of efficiency. This assumption
is being challenged, however, with many firms, both large and small,
outsourcing the functional activities (Klaas, McClendon & Gainey, 1999).

Legal Human Resource Management

Legal HR has the greatest relevance as firms grow in size because as previously
noted, most laws and regulations apply to firm with fifteen or more employees.

Exhibit 10.   Relevance of HR Frameworks and Models for the Study of
Large and Small Entrepreneurial Firms.

| | Firm Size | |
Frameworks and Models	Small	Large
Functional	Low	Moderate
Legal	High	High
High Performance	Low	High
Strategic	Moderate	Moderate
Market	High	Low
Growth	High	High
Resource Based	High	High
Role Based	High	Moderate
Visionary	High	High

However, the diversity concept embodied in legal human resource management has value as previously pointed out in finding new ways to identify and exploit market opportunities. Both small and large entrepreneurial firms face these issues.

High Performance Human Resource Management

High performance HR has a low level of relevance for the identification and exploitation of human resources. The limited availability of capital makes many of the universal best practices impractical (e.g. employment security, extensive training, profit sharing). On the other hand, as the firm grows and capital accumulates, there may be some opportunity to initiate some of these best practices. Small entrepreneurial companies are particularly likely to lack the funds for high performance work practices.

Strategic Human Resource Management

Strategic human resource management seems to have a moderate level of value to the study of entrepreneurship. The alignment of human resource practices with the business plan of the organization would seem vital to all entrepreneurial activities in both small and large entrepreneurial firms. On the other hand, the integration of human resource practices with one another may have less value to the entrepreneurial firm.

Depending upon which facet of entrepreneurship one is addressing, there may be different combinations of human resource practices that are advantageous to the firm. For example, in terms of integration, job analysis may be ignored in developing selection plans to have the human capital needed to identify opportunities in the market and to figure out ways to exploit these opportunities. On the other hand, when the process of firm creation and growth is considered, attention may indeed need to be given to job analysis when selecting employees to ensure that support roles necessary for effective functioning of the firm are present.

As an example related to the concept of alignment, human resource systems may not need to be in alignment for the firm to be successful at identifying and exploiting market opportunities. On the other hand, when the market exploitation strategy has been formulated, and firm creation is of the essence, then it is essential to have human resource practices consistent with the chosen strategy of the firm. Otherwise, employees may be pursuing strategies inconsistent with the intended direction of the firm.

Market System

The market system approach lends itself very well to the identification and exploitation of market opportunities. The recommended market practices (e.g. broadly defined jobs) pose few constraints upon the initial formulation of ideas. As the firm grows in size, however, more high performance based practices, may be more effective and possible with expanding capital pools.

Growth Stage

The growth stage model of human resources plays a more important role in the exploitation of market opportunities and firm growth than in the initial identification of market opportunities phase. As the CEO/founder must develop exploitation, and eventually, growth opportunities, there is a need to bring in more specialized help to guide human resource strategy development.

Resource Based View

The resource-based view of the firm adds value to all phases of entrepreneurship. It provides insight as to the goal of human resources in organizations. Human Resources need to add unique value to the organization at any phase relative to other resources that may be substitutable for human resources (e.g. technology).

Role Based Theory

Roles are critical to all aspects of entrepreneurism. If we were forced to select a theory that has the most relevance to entrepreneurship, especially in smaller companies, role theory would be the one. The study of roles, unlike functional human resource management, for example, allows for the ongoing creation of roles for people in entrepreneurial firms. Role negotiation formation appears to be a very vital and ongoing part of entrepreneurship that happens more frequently than in nonentrepreneurial firms.

Visionary View

The visionary view appears to be critical to all aspects of entrepreneurism in both large and small entrepreneurial firms. The vision of the CEO/founder permeates everything that is done in the entrepreneurial firm including the management of human resources. As such, it provides the impetus for selection of human resource practices to be used or not used by the organization. What appear to be idiosyncratic practices at dot.com companies may be very consistent with the view of the CEO/founder being at odds with traditional HR practices. For example, solving puzzles was instituted as a selection device by Gates in the early days of Microsoft, and the practice continues today (Gimein, 2001).

TOWARDS INTEGRATION

Our view of human resource management models leads us to conclude that traditional models of human resource management in and of themselves have limited relevance to entrepreneurial firms. They need to be supplemented with new models and frameworks. Toward this end, we offer an integration of parts of these frameworks and models in Exhibit 11.

Human resources are grouped by functional human resource areas for purposes of efficiency as with functional human resource models. Synergies may exist between human resource practices as indicated by strategic human resource models and as shown by arrows within the human resource practices box. Legal issues and high performance work system features can be slotted into each functional area as well.

Human resource practices are goal-directed toward the vision of the CEO/founder per strategic human resource management models and toward role formulation per role theory. Roles formed are also depicted as a function of the CEO/founder vision. In turn, vision and roles are directed toward establishing critical capabilities for the organization and in turn ultimately influence performance of the firm. Human resource practices themselves may upon occasion directly influence critical capabilities of the firm, but usually it is only an indirect effect at best. Human resource practices have been shown to influence performance of the firm (Wright, Dyer, Boudreau, & Milkovich, 1999), but the magnitude of these impacts is usually small and suggests an indirect, rather than direct, effect. Firm performance directly influences HR practices, owner vision and role formulation. As firms grow in size, for example, human resource practices become more institutionalized as suggested by growth theories.

LIMITATIONS AND NEW BEGINNINGS

The approach that we have taken in this chapter is to build upon the existing human resource literature by reviewing it and integrating it into an integrative model. Such an approach is consistent with our positivist academic training that emphasized incremental empirical research to advance knowledge in a particular

Exhibit 11. An Integration of HR Frameworks.

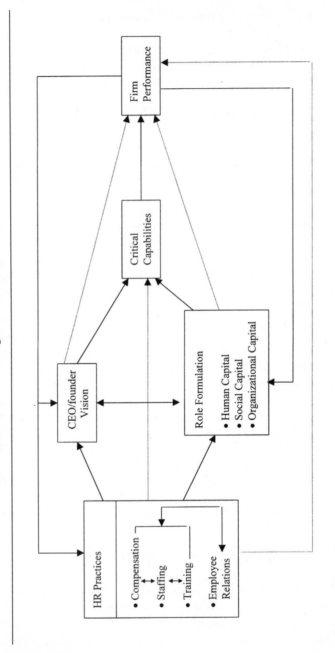

Note: ——— direct effect
.... indirect effect

area. While the reader benefits from a cumulative knowledge base using this approach, the reader also suffers from significant advances that are made by stepping out of the existing paradigm and developing a new body of theory. Unique perspectives may help us to come to an even better understanding of HRM in entrepreneurial firms because they are not constrained by previous assumptions.

It is our belief that both approaches are needed to better understand HRM in entrepreneurial organizations. In spirit of new beginnings, we offer the following explanation of the emergence of HRM in entrepreneurial organizations as an example of a somewhat more new approach than offered by our integrative model. Our model draws upon physics. We may need to draw theory outside management and to begin to form ideas.

In physics, great attention is being paid to theory development to explain the emergence of the universe and the ultimate end state of the universe (i.e. infinite expansion versus ultimate collapse). Similarly, attention needs to be paid to the emergence of HRM in emerging companies. Perhaps big-bang theory from physics applies to HRM as shown in Exhibit 12.

Energy may build up in the form of creative ideas about how to best manage human, social, and organizational capital in order to provide a needed product or service to the market in the most effective manner. Eventually, this energy may result in an explosion that leads to a HRM unit in the organization. Initially, that unit may be an internal person or external person (e.g. consultant, call center). Over time, as employees are added, the HRM unit may become a codified set of policies, a department, or some combination. An HRM unit is needed in order to channel the explosion of energy into the correct path. The energy released in the explosion may result in outcomes negative to the organization (e.g. law-suits), positive to the organization (e.g. productivity enhancement), or both. Borrowing again from physics, the HRM unit may operate on the basis of "string theory" to channel energy at multiple dimensions of reality including observable (e.g. behaviors) and unobservable (e.g. morale) systems. Using this approach, the explanation of HRM effectiveness in organizations may have more to do with the channeling of energy in appropriate directions, than with policies and procedures.

CONCLUSION

Although there has not been a great deal of research regarding the management of human resources in emerging companies, there is a resurgence in interest (R. Heneman, Tansky & Camp, 2000). We are pleased to see that several of the latest articles are empirical in nature and well designed (e.g. H. Heneman

Exhibit 12. A "Big-Bang" Model of HRM.

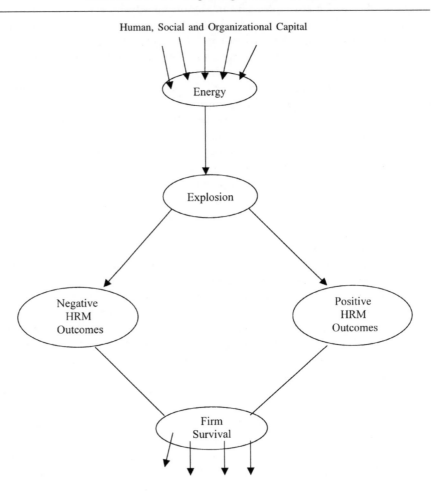

III & Berkeley, 1999; Barber et al., 1999). We would also like to see concurrent theory development take place with this resurgence. In order to guide future theory development in this area we believe that configurational models, especially role theory, along with our synthesized model offer the most promise. The traditional functional view of HR has little to offer entrepreneurial firms in search of sustained, competitive advantage through the unique configuration of people in the organization.

ACKNOWLEDGMENTS

The authors would like to thank the Kauffman Center for Entrepreneurial Leadership for funding the research for this paper. We would also like to acknowledge that the views presented here are those of the authors and may not necessarily represent the views of the Kauffman Center. The authors would also like to thank Theresa Welbourne and Jerry Katz for their helpful comments on previous drafts of this manuscript.

REFERENCES

Aldrich, H. (1999). *Organizations Evolving.* London: Sage Publications, Ltd.

Arthur, D. (1995). *Managing human resources in small and mid-sized companies.* New York: American Management Association.

Barber, A. E., Wesson, M. J., Roberson, Q. M., & Taylor, M. S. (1999). A tale of two job markets: Organizational size and its effects on hiring practices and job search behavior. *Personnel Psychology, 52,* 841–868.

Barney, J. (1997). *Gaining and sustaining competitive advantage.* Reading, MA: Addison-Wesley.

Barney, J. B., & Wright, P. M. (1998). On becoming a strategic partner: The role of human resources in gaining competitive advantage. *Human Resource Management, 37*(1), 31–46.

Delery, J. E., & Doty, D. H. (1996). Modes of theorizing in strategic human resource management: Tests of universalistic contingency, and configurational performance patterns. *Academy of Management Journal, 39,* 802–825.

Ehrbar, A. (1998). *Stern Stewart's economic value added (EVA): The real key to creating wealth.* New York: John Wiley & Sons, Inc.

Field, H. S., & Holley, W. H. (1982). The relationship of performance appraisal system characteristics to selected employment discrimination cases. *Academy of Management Journal, 25,* 392–406.

Gimein, M. (2001). Smart is not enough. *Fortune,* (January 22), 124–134.

Gerhart, B., Trevor, C. O., & Graham, M. E. (1996). New directions in compensation research: Synergies, risk, and survival, *Research in Personnel and Human Resources Management, 14,* 143–203.

Gomez-Mejia, L. R., & Balkin, D. B. (1992). *Compensation, Organizational Strategy, and Firm Performance.* Cincinnati: South-Western Publishing Co.

Graen, G., Novak, M., & Sommerkamp, P. (1982). The effects of leader-member exchange and job design on productivity and job satisfaction: Testing a dual attachment model. *Organizational Behavior and Human Performance, 30,* 109–131.

Greer, C. R., Youngblood, S. A., & Gray, D. A. (1999). Human resource management outsourcing: The make or buy decision. *The Academy of Management Executive, 13,* 85–96.

Heneman, H. G. Jr. (1969). Toward a general conceptual system of industrial relations: How do we get there? In: G. Somers (Ed.), *Essays in Industrial Relations Theory.* Ames, Iowa: The Iowa State University Press.

Heneman, H. G. III. (1999). Applicant attraction practices and outcomes among small businesses. *Journal of Small Business Management, 37*(1), 53–74.

Heneman, H. G. III, Judge, T., & Heneman, R. L. (2000). Staffing Organizations (3rd ed.). New York: McGraw-Hill (722 pages).

Heneman, R. L. (in press). *Integrating Compensation Policies and Corporate Business Strategies.* New York: AMACOM.

Heneman, R. L., Greenberger, D., & Ananyuo, C. (1989). Attributions and exchanges: The effects of interpersonal factors on the diagnosis of employee performance. *Academy of Management Journal, 32,* 466–476.

Heneman, R. L., Ledford, G. E., & Gresham, M. (in press). Compensation and the changing nature of work. In: S. Rynes & B. Gerhart (Eds), *Compensation in Organizations: Progress & Prospects* (Society for Industrial and Organizational Psychology Frontiers of Industrial and Organizational Psychology Series). San Francisco: New Lexington Press.

Heneman, R. L., Tansky, J. W., & Camp, S. M. (2000). Human resource management practices in small and medium size enterprises: Unanswered questions and future research perspectives. *Entrepreneurship: Theory and Practice, 25*(1), 11–26.

Heneman, R. L., & Tansky, J. W. (1999). *Human resource strategies for the high growth entrepreneurial firm.* Columbus, OH: Fisher College of Business, The Ohio State University.

Heneman, R. L., & Gresham, M. (1998). Performance-Based Pay Plans. In: J. W. Smither (Ed.), *Performance Appraisal: State-of-the Art Methods for Performance Management* (Society for Industrial and Organizational Psychology Professional Practice Series) (pp. 496–536). San Francisco: Jossey Bass.

Heneman, R. L., & Thomas, A. L. (1997). The Limited Inc.: Using strategic performance management to drive brand leadership. *Compensation and Benefits Review, 27*(6), 33–40.

Ilgen, D. R., & Hollenbeck, J. R. (1991). The structure of work: Job design and roles. In: M. Dunnette & L. Hough (Eds), *Handbook of Industrial & Organizational Psychology* (2nd ed., Vol. 2, pp. 165–208). Palo Alto, CA: Consulting Psychologists Press.

Klaas, B. S., McClendon, J., & Gainey, J. W. (1999). HR outsourcing and its impact: The role of transaction costs. *Personnel Psychology, 52,* 113–136.

Lawler, E. E. III. (1996). *From the ground up: Six principles for building the new logic corporation.* San Francisco: Jossey Bass.

Leana, C. R., & Van Buren, III. (1999). Organizational social capital and employment practices. *Academy of Management Review, 24,* 538–555.

Miles, R. E., & Snow, C. C. (1978). *Organizational strategy, structure, and process.* New York: McGraw-Hill.

Naylor, J. C., Pritchard, R. D., & Ilgen, D. R. (1980). *A theory of behavior in organizations.* New York: Academic Press.

Organ, D. W. (1988). A restatement of the satisfaction-performance hypothesis. *Journal of Management, 14,* 547–557.

Penrose, E. T. (1959). *The theory of the growth of the firm.* Oxford: Basil Blackwell.

Pfeffer, J. (1998). *The human equation: Building profits by putting people first.* Boston, MA: Harvard Business School Press.

Rodgers, R., & Hunter, J. E. (1991). Impact of management by objectives on organizational productivity. *Journal of Applied Psychology, 76,* 322–336.

Shane, S., & Venkataraman, S. (2000). The promise of entrepreneurship as a field of study. *Academy of Management Review, 25,* 217–226.

Ulrich, D. (1997). *Human resource champions: The next agenda for adding value and delivering results.* Cambridge, MA: Harvard Business School Press.

United States Small Business Administration Office of Advocacy (1997). *Characteristics of small business employers and owners.* www.sba.gov.

Welbourne, T. M., Johnson, D. E., & Erez, A. (1998). A role-based performance scale: Validity analysis of a theory-based measure. *Academy of Management Journal, 41,* 540–555.

Wright, P. M., Dyer, L. D., Boudreau, J. W., & Milkovich, G. T. (1999). *Research in personnel and human resource management*. Supplement 4: Strategic human resources management in the twenty-first century. Stamford, CT: JAI Press.

Youndt, M. A., Subramaniam, M., Snell, S. A., & Golden, T. (1999). *Intellectual capital profiles: An examination of investments and returns*. University Park, PA: Institute for the Study of Effective Organizations, Smeal College of Business Administration, Pennsylvania State University.

4. SMALLER BUT NOT NECESSARILY WEAKER: HOW SMALL BUSINESSES CAN OVERCOME BARRIERS TO RECRUITMENT

Ian O. Williamson, Daniel M. Cable and
Howard E. Aldrich

INTRODUCTION

For small firms, one of their most difficult but important goals is locating and
hiring new qualified employees that enable them to offer products and services.
In fact, despite the currently slowing economy, a recent Conference Board
survey of leaders of small and mid-size firms identified scarcity of qualified
employees as the most often cited threat to business growth, identified by almost
50% of those surveyed. By contrast, less than 25% of the sample saw the
slowing growth in the economy as a threat to firm growth, and only 10% were
worried about a collapse in stock prices (Muson, 2001). Consistent with these
findings, in a recent National Federation of Independent Business (NFIB) survey
of small businesses, 35% reported having difficult-to-fill job openings, a record

Managing People in Entrepreneurial Organizations, Volume 5, pages 83–106.
Copyright © 2002 by Elsevier Science Ltd.
All rights of reproduction in any form reserved.
ISBN: 0-7623-0877-X

high since the NFIB began conducting the survey in 1973 (Small Business Economic Trends, 2001).

Small businesses dominate the landscape of the United States, representing over 99% of all employers, creating two out of every three new jobs, and producing 39% of the gross national product (SBA, 1999a), but very little research has examined the issues they face when recruiting employees. Past small business research on recruitment has largely focused on simply describing what recruitment practices are utilized, without developing a theory about why these practices may be successful (e.g. Bartram, Lindley, Marshall & Foster, 1995; Windolf, 1986). Within the human resource management (HRM) literature, research on recruitment has almost exclusively focused on large firms (Barber, 1998; Williamson, 2000). This focus on large firms is problematic because there are theoretical reasons to suggest that small firms may face different barriers in the recruitment process than larger firms. Specifically, relative to large businesses, small firms face at least two unique challenges: lower levels of external awareness of their existence and image, and greater pressures to conform to institutional norms.

For example, past recruitment research indicates that organizational awareness is an important predictor of job seekers' early job search decisions (e.g. Cable & Graham, 2000; Gatewood, Gowan & Lautenschlager, 1993; Schwab, Rynes & Aldag, 1987). However, unlike larger, well-known firms, small businesses often cannot rely on their name, their reputation in the industry, or their market share to attract new employees (Aldrich, 1999; Aldrich & Von Glinow, 1991). In addition, when evaluating the attractiveness of prospective employers, job seekers' preferences are likely to be influenced by the system of specific norms, values, and beliefs within a particular industry (Salancik & Pfeffer, 1978). Such industry norms are largely shaped by the actions of large organizations, to the disadvantage of smaller firms (Hannan & Freeman, 1984). As a result, newly formed or small organizations may be constrained in their recruitment activities when competing with large organizations (Aldrich & Auster, 1986; Stinchcombe, 1965). Unfortunately, past small business and HRM research has neglected to examine differences between large and small organizations, and has not considered how these differences may influence recruitment success (Barber, 1998).

This chapter attempts to address these limitations of past research by drawing on marketing and sociological principles to discuss small business recruitment issues. We argue that small businesses face various unique barriers that may limit their ability to compete successfully with large organizations for talented employees. Based on this assumption, we suggest that research and writing in both the recruitment and small business literatures would benefit from a multidisciplinary investigation of small business recruitment.

For the purposes of this discussion, we define small businesses as all firms employing 500 or fewer employees, which is consistent with the standard used by the Small Business Administration in most industries (SBA, 1999b). This definition encompasses small firms without regard to their growth orientation, as well as young and old small firms, because effective recruitment is important to the performance and survival of all small businesses. In addition, our discussion specifically focuses on the efforts of small businesses to recruit job seekers who are skilled professionals (e.g. MBAs, CPAs, and IT workers). We focus on this segment of the labor force because skilled professionals tend to be in high demand, increasing the likelihood that small organizations will be in competition with large firms for their services. Additionally, norms and standards tend to be more established in this segment of the labor pool due to central organizations such as universities, professional associations, or trade associations that both create and disseminate information about industry employment norms (DiMaggio & Powell, 1983). Thus, institutional pressures are likely to constrain organizational efforts to recruit skilled professionals (Williamson, 2000).

Finally, in this chapter we are mainly concerned with those recruitment strategies small firms use to recruit "strangers." Strangers are defined as job seekers with whom founders and managers of small businesses do not share existing personal relationships (Baker & Aldrich, 1994). Because organizational growth and performance are closely linked with the ability of organizations to recruit non-family members or friends, a better understanding of how small organizations can successfully compete with large firms to recruit strangers has implications for organizational survival.

The first section of the chapter discusses disadvantages small firms face in the recruitment process relative to large organizations, focusing specifically on two issues: job seekers' organizational knowledge and organizational legitimacy. *Organizational knowledge* refers to what job seekers know about a prospective employer. *Organizational legitimacy* refers to job seekers' perceptions or assumptions that an organization is a desirable, proper, and appropriate employer, given the system of norms, values, and beliefs within an industry (Suchman, 1995). We argue that small firms tend to have lower levels of organizational knowledge and legitimacy, relative to large organizations. As a result, small businesses may be disadvantaged when competing for recruits with large organizations. The second section of the paper considers strategies small businesses can use to overcome these barriers. First, we suggest that small businesses may be able to improve job seekers' organizational knowledge by utilizing brand-marketing strategies. Second, drawing on institutional theory, we suggest that small businesses may enhance their legitimacy through the strategic imitation of established and culturally accepted human resource (HR) practices and the development of interorganizational linkages. Finally, we discuss the interactive and potentially conflicting effects that brand-marketing and institutional theory strategies may have on small business recruitment efforts and how the concept of strategic balance point can be utilized to manage this tension.

SMALL BUSINESS RECRUITMENT BARRIERS

Job Seekers' Organizational Knowledge

Job seekers must rely on their beliefs about an employer when deciding whether or not to apply for a job, to sign up for an interview, or to accept a position with a prospective employer. Thus, fundamentally, what job seekers know about employers, or their *organizational knowledge*, determines whether employers will be successful in recruiting. In this section of the chapter, we review two different types of knowledge that job seekers have about employers: the *familiarity* of an organization to job seekers, and job seekers' beliefs about an employer's *image*. We then use these two types of knowledge to consider how small businesses are often handicapped during the recruitment process.

Organizational Familiarity
Job seekers cannot be attracted to an organization, or apply for one of its jobs, unless it is salient to them. *Organizational familiarity* is defined as the likelihood that an employer comes to a job seeker's mind, and the ease with which it does so (Keller, 1993). Two ways to operationalize familiarity are through recognition and recall. Recognition refers to a job seeker's ability to confirm prior exposure to an employer when primed with the organization's name (e.g. "yes, I'm familiar with a company called InterLan"). Measuring recognition captures the ease with which an organization's name can be retrieved from a job seeker's memory. Recall, on the other hand, refers to a job seeker's ability to produce an employer's name when cued with some attribute of the organization (e.g. an employer in the Internet hosting industry). Thus, recall gives insight into an employer's position in job seekers' beliefs, relative to competing employers.

For an organization to remain competitive in recruiting, organizational familiarity must be high among a targeted market of job seekers. Otherwise, an organization will not enter job seekers' consideration sets (Roberts & Lattin, 1997). A *consideration set* refers to the subset of the total group of options that meets a decision maker's most basic evaluation criteria. Job choice research suggests that an organization must enter a job seeker's consideration set before it is considered as an employment option (e.g. Power & Aldag, 1985). In fact, organizational familiarity may be the most important predictor of *early* job search decisions, when job seekers otherwise have little information about recruiting organizations (e.g. Schwab et al., 1987). Thus, when they lack adequate information to discriminate meaningfully between organizations on other criteria, job seekers make early decisions, such as whether to apply for a job, based largely on organizational familiarity.

Perceived Organizational Image
Awareness that an organization exists is eventually accompanied by *content* information about the organization (e.g. what type of organization is it?). Thus, after an organization is known and recognized as a potential employer, it develops an image as being a certain type of employer with a certain image (Gatewood et al., 1993). *Organizational image* refers to job seeker's beliefs about an employer's characteristics, such as its culture, industry, history, the type of people that work there, geographic location, and HR policies. Job seekers' beliefs about organizational image are important because they allow job seekers to differentiate between employers. Moreover, beliefs about organizational image also allow job seekers to judge the fit between different employers and their own personal attributes, such as their values, personality, and needs (Cable & Judge, 1996; Turban & Keon, 1994). Thus, job seekers' beliefs about organizational image affect their willingness to consider becoming an employee and also their assessment of whether they would fit in (Kristof, 1996; Rynes, 1991).

Small firms face obstacles that limit their recruitment success relative to large firms, given that job seekers' reactions to employers are governed by their familiarity with the firms and knowledge about their images. First, smaller firms are generally less familiar to job seekers because they make far fewer investments in recruitment marketing than larger firms because of financial constraints (Rynes & Boudreau, 1986). Small firms also are less likely than large firms to be part of job seekers' everyday experiences, because they attract less media coverage, have fewer customers, and have smaller product and service distribution networks than large firms (Aldrich & Auster, 1986). Given that employers must be known before they are even considered as employment options, lack of awareness or familiarity can doom small firms to recruitment failure.

Small firms also may lag behind larger firms in recruitment because it is more difficult for job seekers to acquire credible information about small firms. Research suggests that job seekers place more trust in information from informal word-of-mouth sources (such as friends and family), rather than in formal recruitment sources (such as brochures, advertisements, and recruiters). Sorenson, Rhode and Lawler (1973) found that the most credible sources of information about accounting jobs were professors and other accounting students, rather than organizational representatives. Likewise, Fisher, Ilgen and Hoyer (1979) suggested that sources outside a company might be the most trusted by job seekers because they are seen as sources of information rather than persuasion.

Thus, job seekers appear to rely heavily on company information that they obtain from informal sources, which are generally more available from larger than smaller firms. About 60% of the U.S. workforce is employed in firms employing 100 or more people (Aldrich, 1999), making large organizations more salient than smaller ones to most people. Likewise, because they hire fewer people and have fewer open positions, smaller firms generally have difficulty establishing recruitment networks with high-volume sources of employees, such as colleges and job placement agencies. For example, at the University of Maryland, College Park, no small businesses recruited through the MBA program placement office in 1999 or 2000. Thus, representatives from small firms are less likely to have formed ongoing relationships with professors, career office advisors, and alumni. Correspondingly, there are fewer informal sources to help job seekers learn about the organizational images of small firms, compared to large ones.

Organizational Legitimacy

Successful organizational recruitment requires not only that job seekers be aware of a small business and its image, but also that they view the firm as a desirable or attractive employer. Thus, it is understandable that most of the research on organizational attractiveness in the HRM literature has adopted a congruence perspective and has focused on how job seekers' individual attributes or preferences, such as personality, values, and demographic characteristics, influence organizational attractiveness perceptions (Brass, 1995). From this perspective, job seekers will be more attracted to organizations with images that are congruent with their individual preferences (see Barber, 1998; Kristoff, 1996 for reviews).

Job seeking does not take place in a social vacuum, however. Small business recruitment efforts take place within a social environment where established norms of behavior guide external constituents' evaluations of organizations

(Scott, 1998). Small business recruitment success is therefore based not only on the preferences of individual actors, but also on industry norms (Deephouse, 1996). Institutional theory provides an alternative to congruence models for understanding why and how societal norms may influence small business recruitment. Specifically, institutional theory suggests that *organizational legitimacy* strongly influences the ability of small businesses to acquire sustained support from external constituents (Meyer & Rowan, 1977).

In a broad sense, organizational legitimacy represents an overall evaluation of a firm, based on its activities or characteristics (Suchman, 1995). Constituents evaluate organizations by comparing their practices to established and culturally sanctioned practices within an organization's industry, rather than solely to their own individual preferences (Suchman, 1995). Thus, those firms displaying practices that have a strong similarity to industry norms are perceived as more legitimate than organizations using non-institutionalized practices (Meyer & Scott, 1983).

Acquiring legitimacy influences the level of support organizations receive from external actors (Parsons, 1960; Pfeffer & Salancik, 1978). Organizational legitimacy enhances efforts to garner resources because it bolsters an organization's perceived credibility and strengthens expectations that it can carry out constituents' objectives (Rao, 1994; Suchman, 1995). For example, in their examination of mental health centers, D'Aunno, Sutton and Price (1991) found that health centers utilizing institutionalized mental health practices garnered greater legitimacy from parent organizations, resulting in greater resource support for operating and payroll expenses, staffing, supplies, and office space. They suggested that parent organizations were more likely to support health centers adopting standard industry practices because they perceived that such health centers would meet their expectations for how mental health care should be provided. Another benefit of legitimacy is that external constituents may be motivated to develop more favorable exchange relationships, in terms of financial rewards, with legitimate firms. Developing a tie with an organization that has a high level of legitimacy may enhance the legitimacy of an external constituent, thus increasing its credibility (Deephouse, 1999; Pfeffer & Salancik, 1978).

Organizational legitimacy may influence organizational recruitment success to the extent that job seekers view firms with higher levels of legitimacy as more predictable, meaningful, and trustworthy employers than firms with lower levels of legitimacy (Suchman, 1995). Job seekers face a great deal of uncertainty in discerning whether prospective employers will be able to meet their employment goals, such as salary, advancement, work/life balance, and job security. High levels of organizational legitimacy can be a signal to job seekers that an organization treats its employees well, thus dampening their fears concerning employment prospects at the firm. In addition, job seekers may be motivated to seek employment at an organization with high levels of legitimacy because of their belief that membership in that organization will provide greater opportunities later in their careers should they leave. This may have the dual effect of making a firm more attractive in the eyes of job seekers, as well inducing job seekers to forgo higher salaries from other firms with lower levels of legitimacy.

Smaller firms, however, face a potential legitimacy deficit, relative to larger firms, that may hamper their recruiting efforts. In particular, small firms face two liabilities that affect their legitimacy: they have limited influence on industry norms, and they have weak ties to organizations that educate and place the most skilled members of the workforce. We consider each liability, in turn.

First, industry norms are primarily shaped by the largest and most visible organizations in the population, rather than small firms (Haveman, 1993). This is especially true in mature industries (Aldrich, 1999). Thus, large organizations, because of their prominence, are able to shape their environments and turn industry norms to their advantage by influencing the criteria external constituents use when evaluating organizations (Freeman, 1982; Meyer & Rowan, 1977).

For example, past research suggests that HR practices, such as recruitment procedures, compensation policies, and work-family practices, symbolize an organization's working conditions to job seekers (Barber & Roehling, 1993; Honeycutt & Rosen, 1997; Rynes, Bretz & Gerhart, 1991; Williams & Dreher, 1992). Thus, HR practices serve as an important basis by which job seekers compare organizations within an industry. Large organizations tend to have formal HR departments staffed with HR professionals, resulting in well developed internal labor markets, formal career development systems, and integrated HR practices (Aldrich & Auster, 1986; Guthrie & Olian, 1991). Conversely, most small firms do not have personnel departments, or even a person in a specialized role that handles human resource issues (Bartram et al., 1995). Indeed, in their examination of 360 small to medium size firms making their initial public offering, Welbourne and Cyr (1999) found that only 26 (7%) had a senior HR management executive. Thus, small firms tend to adopt a "muddle-through" HR approach, adopting idiosyncratic practices as needed and lacking a clear overarching strategy (Windolf, 1986). Given that large firms have a significant influence on industry norms and that firms whose practices conform to current norms enjoy greater legitimacy than non-conforming firms, this "muddle through" approach to HR may reduce small firms' legitimacy, relative to the large organizations. As a result, job applicants are likely to view large firms more favorably than small firms.

Second, large organizations often develop strong exchange relationships with central institutions that educate a large fraction of the highly skilled workforce, such as colleges and trade associations, while small organizations often lack such interorganizational relationships (Aldrich & Zimmer, 1986; Stinchcombe, 1965). For highly educated workers, colleges and professional associations provide the framework within which the recruitment process operates, thus establishing norms of behavior that shape job seekers' behaviors. For example, in their examination of the recruitment efforts of small and large organizations, Barber, Wesson, Roberson and Taylor (1999) found that large organizations were more likely to utilize college campus placement services than small firms. As a result, job seekers who utilized campus placement services were more likely to pursue work with large organizations than small ones. As large organizations develop interorganizational relationships with colleges and associations, they shape expectations in ways that lead to small firms being viewed as peripheral rather than core employers (Thomas, 1989).

Thus marketing and sociological perspectives on recruitment suggest that small businesses face organizational knowledge and legitimacy barriers that limit their ability to successfully recruit job seekers, relative to large organizations. It is important to point out that these barriers are predicted to affect small business recruitment success independent of the level of financial compensation a small firm can offer to pay a job seeker. Past research has found that, on average, small firms pay less than large firms, which may negatively affect small business recruitment efforts (Brown, Hamilton & Medoff, 1990; Evans & Leighton, 1989). However, from an organizational knowledge perspective, even if a small business were able to equal or exceed the financial compensation provided by a large business, it might still face recruitment barriers because job seekers are less aware of its existence and lack information on its image.

Thus, job seekers will be less likely to include the small business in their consideration set of potential employers, compared to a large firm, reducing the small firm's recruitment success. Conversely, organizational legitimacy theory suggests that *even if* job seekers are knowledgeable about a particular small business, that firm may still have lower recruitment success than large organizations. Because small firms are less likely to conform to culturally established industry norms than large firms, they are perceived as less credible and less attractive employers. These distinctions between the organizational knowledge and organizational legitimacy approaches are important because they suggest two fundamentally different strategic recruiting solutions for small firms. In the next section, we consider several strategic options for overcoming the recruitment limitations we have identified.

STRATEGIC IMPLICATIONS

Brand-Marketing Approach

We have argued that small business recruitment effectiveness is tied to job seekers' organizational knowledge, comprising organizational familiarity and information about organizational image. To enhance its recruitment success, a small business must manage the organizational information that job seekers hold about the company. Unfortunately, we know surprisingly little from the recruitment research literature about how firms can manage the information flow to job seekers. As Rynes (1991) noted, decisions about how to present recruitment information to applicants, and the order of information presentation, have been largely unexplored.

Rather than relying on the recruitment literature, we turned to the marketing literature for suggestions on how small organizations might improve job seekers' organizational knowledge. We chose the marketing literature because when firms seek to manage the flow of knowledge to a targeted group of job seekers, they are essentially marketing the organization as a "brand," just as they would try to convey information to consumers. Thus, in both their marketing and recruitment functions, organizations compete through communication and persuasion to attract a limited, targeted market of individuals.

A basic finding of the marketing and persuasion literatures is that individuals process information differently, depending on their motivation to pay attention to and learn from an information source. Thus, the effectiveness of communication methods in increasing individuals' knowledge about an organization depends upon an audience's motivation. For example, the elaboration likelihood model (Petty & Cacioppo, 1986), which describes the process through which individuals' opinions and attitudes can be changed, suggests that *peripheral* modes of communication should be used when audiences have low levels of motivation to search out or closely scrutinize information. Peripheral modes of communication include the sending of simple informational cues to people, such as ads, brochures, and leaflets. Conversely, when the audience's motivation to scrutinize information is relatively high, a *central* mode of communication is the most effective means of communicating information accurately (MacInnis, Moorman & Jaworski, 1991; Petty & Cacioppu, 1986). Central communication methods are exemplified by detail-oriented communications, such as information sessions.

Research supporting the elaboration likelihood model suggests several strategic implications for how small businesses should convey information to job seekers. Small businesses must capture job seekers' awareness and motivation before they can effectively communicate information about organizational image. To develop a higher level of organizational familiarity, the elaboration likelihood model suggests that small businesses focus on peripheral routes of communication. Such routes could include developing relationships with professors and career office directors, establishing and advertising their presence at places where their targeted job seekers congregate (e.g. career fairs), and offering free company gifts to catch job seekers' attention.

Such efforts should increase the recognition and recall that job seekers have about an organization, thus raising its familiarity to them. After small firms have established a higher level of familiarity, targeted job seekers should be more motivated to scrutinize the information the firms make available. Small firms can then begin to engage in central routes of communication, such as holding information sessions and interviews. These central modes of communication should increase job seekers' knowledge about small businesses' images.

An important implication of the above discussion is that small businesses must measure and understand job seekers' existing level of knowledge about their company before they can decide what types of recruitment interventions and investments will return the greatest value. In other words, when it comes to delivering information to job seekers and improving organizational knowledge, no single set of "best recruitment practices" exists for all small firms. Instead, employers must discover their familiarity in the minds of their target market before developing and implementing their recruitment strategy and interventions. Indeed, from a financial perspective, the consideration of job seekers' impressions is especially important in the case of small businesses, to prevent the wasting of limited resources and increase the likelihood of attaining a desired level of return on recruitment investments. A small business might accomplish this by surveying or conducting focus groups with targeted job seekers to ascertain their perceptions of the organization's image. For example, a North Carolina technology firm in the Research Triangle Park recently assessed organizational image by administering surveys to job seekers at eleven different universities to learn how they were perceived among a targeted group of potential applicants.

Institutional Theory Approach

A brand-marketing approach provides direction on how small businesses can improve job seekers' organizational knowledge, but it does not address the legitimacy barriers they face. No single strategy, other than growth, would allow a small firm to gain enough influence in its social environment to completely overcome the liabilities of smallness. However, institutional theory does suggest certain strategies that may allow small businesses to convince job applicants that they can meet the standards of employment within a particular industry. For the purposes of this chapter, we focus on two strategies: strategic isomorphism and the development of interorganizational linkages.

Strategic Isomorphism

Institutional theorists suggest that one way for firms to gain legitimacy and external support is by imitating practices used by other legitimate organizations within their industry (e.g. DiMaggio & Powell, 1983; Haveman, 1993; Oliver, 1991). This practice of imitation has been defined as *strategic isomorphism*. The underlining logic of strategic isomorphism is that legitimized practices carry with them positive culturally embedded information that is attributed to the firms using them (DiMaggio & Powell, 1983). Thus, by manipulating their practices and policies so that they conform to industry norms, organizations may improve their credibility and increase the likelihood that external constituents will view them as legitimate (Suchman, 1995).

Research on large organizations has found a strong link between strategic isomorphism, organizational legitimacy, and organizational support (e.g. Arnold, Handelman & Tigert, 1996; D'Anno, Sutton & Price, 1991; Deephouse, 1996; Westphal, Gulati & Shortell, 1997). Given the sensitivity of job seekers to organizations' HR practices (Barber, 1998), the strategic imitation of normative HR practices may also be a viable means for small firms to gain legitimacy and improve their recruitment success. While financial capital constraints may limit the ability of small firms to imitate precisely the practices of large firms, small businesses could pattern their recruitment practices so that they incorporate the core features of the practices utilized by large firms. For example, in situations of evaluative uncertainty, external constituents are apt to view the way in which information is exchanged as a symbolic proxy for the credibility of an organization (Aldrich, 1999). Thus, imitating standard forms of job advertisements and recruitment brochures may increase the amount of legitimacy attributed to small firms by job seekers (Aldrich & Fiol, 1994). Consistent with this logic, Baker and Aldrich (1994) found that small firms attempting to recruit strangers into their organizations for the first time were most successful when they relied on more institutionally acceptable recruitment practices, such as newspaper advertisements, college recruiting offices, and well-defined job positions.

Similarly, small firms may also enhance their legitimacy through the effective use of Internet technologies. The use of Internet technology in the recruitment process has increased tremendously in recent years (Mosley, 1998). As a result, in some industries (e.g. information technology) Internet recruitment has developed a "taken for granted" status. Thus, the utilization of Internet recruitment technologies may allow small businesses to reduce job seekers' concerns about their legitimacy, particularly in those industries where the use of this practice is widespread. However, a recent Arthur Anderson and National Small Business United (2000) survey estimated that only 9% of small businesses used some form of Internet technology to recruit employees. Small businesses thus have a great deal of catching up to do.

Interorganizational Linkages

In addition to strategic isomorphism, small businesses may also be able to enhance their legitimacy by developing interorganizational relationships with legitimate organizations within their industry. When external constituents are uncertain about the quality and capabilities of an organization, they are inclined to evaluate a firm based on the attributes of its network partners, due to a presumption that network partner characteristics are highly correlated with a focal firm's qualities (Podolny, 1994; Podolny & Stuart, 1995). Thus, interorganizational ties to legitimate actors may offer small organizations a way to overcome the liabilities of smallness. For example, in their examination of childcare service organizations, Baum and Oliver (1991) found that interorganizational linkages to central organizations (e.g. service agreements with government agencies) diminished liabilities of smallness, enhanced service organizations' legitimacy, and as a result, reduced organizational mortality. Similarly, Stuart, Hoang and Hybels (1999) found that the attributes of biotechnology start-up firms' network partners (e.g. commercial and technical prominence) were positively related to the rate at which these firms went public and also to their market evaluation by investors. Furthermore, the greater the level of uncertainty investors faced when evaluating biotechnology firms, the greater the impact network partner attributes had on investors' evaluations.

Therefore, the development of interorganizational linkages to central providers of labor and other legitimate organizations may convey a message to job seekers that a small firm is a legitimate employer, increasing the probability that they will view it as reliable and credible. These interorganizational linkages could take a variety of forms. For example, small businesses could advertise any certifications or accreditations they receive from prestigious organizations (e.g. ISO 9000). Small businesses could also enhance their legitimacy by developing ties with colleges and universities through the sponsorship of work-study or internship programs that produce students with company relevant skills or encouraging employees to serve as representatives on university advisory committees (Engler, 1999). Similarly, small business owners could become involved in industry professional associations through committee work or by serving as speakers and panelists at conferences.

Another way in which small businesses could use interorganizational linkages to enhance legitimacy is by using recruitment literature to highlight supplier relationships or strategic partnerships with large legitimate organizations within their industry. In addition to conveying to job seekers that a small business is stable and reliable, the publicizing of these ties may also cause job seekers to view employment opportunities in the small business as a means of acquiring industry connections that can enhance their career mobility. A popular press example of a company effectively utilizing this approach is AllBusiness.com (dot.com), a 120 employee business-to-business Internet-firm specializing in providing office supplies, and services to other small businesses. NBC Internet Inc, a subsidiary of General Electric Co, is a major investor in AllBusiness.com. Thus, when recruiting potential employees, the firm highlights the fact that employees in the organization have the opportunity to work with a business-to-business Web site that is backed by NBC Internet, the seventh highest trafficked company on the Internet (Internetweek, 2000).

Interaction Between Brand-Marketing and Institutional Theory Strategies

Institutional theory suggests that imitating legitimated industry practices and developing strategic interorganizational linkages will enhance the legitimacy of small businesses, which in turn will have a positive influence on their recruitment success. It is conceivable that these two strategies may also provide small firms with communication advantages that enhance organizational knowledge. For example, the imitation of Internet recruitment techniques may provide small businesses with cost savings and increase exposure to job seekers (Abraham & Newcorn, 2000). Similarly, interorganizational linkages may serve as a means for firms to disseminate job information to job seekers, thus increasing the firm's familiarity.

However, the institutional perspective does not address the possibility that small firms may derive certain recruitment benefits by adopting practices that promote distinctiveness instead of conformity. Indeed, the elaboration likelihood model suggests that the initiation of communication that draws attention to an organization will enhance its familiarity and increase its recruitment success. For example, the popular press is full of examples where small businesses have been able to successfully recruit employees by purposely adopting practices that are a radical departure from industry norms, such as vague or non-existent job descriptions or the use of stock-based compensation (Alexander, 1999; Carton, 1995). Thus, an inherent tension exists between institutional theory and the brand-marketing view.

One approach to potentially resolving this tension is to recognize that small businesses may need to adopt a dual strategy of distinctiveness and imitation in order to maximize their ability to recruit job seekers (Williamson, 2000). Specifically, strategic balance theory proposes that small firms seeking to maximize recruitment success should attempt to be as different as legitimately possible (Deephouse, 1999). Within an industry there exists variance in the preferences of job seekers and the norms on what constitutes a proper employment environment (Glynn, Barr & Dacin, 2000). As such, small firms can maintain some degree of distinctiveness from their competitors and still be viewed as legitimate. Thus, small businesses should adopt recruitment strategies that allow them to be within a "range of acceptability" (Deephouse, 1999). Small firms outside this range risk job seekers questioning their legitimacy as an employer and thus viewing them as unattractive employers.

However, small firms that are able to strategically maintain moderate levels of similarity to industry norms reduce the likelihood of their legitimacy as an employer being challenged by job seekers. These firms gain the flexibility of promoting their unique features in order to distinguish themselves from other competitors and realize higher levels of recruitment success. Thus, recruitment success may be maximized at the level of strategic isomorphism where the competitive advantage provided by firm distinctiveness, through greater levels of familiarity and awareness, equals the cost associated with diminished employer legitimacy. This point of maximization can be described as the strategic balance point (Deephouse, 1999).

A clear illustration of how strategically balancing distinctiveness and isomorphism can improve organizational efforts to acquire resources from external constituents is found in Elsbach and Sutton's (1992) study of radical social movement groups. Elsbach and Sutton found that by adopting illegitimate practices, social movement groups were able to gain recognition and support from a narrow segment of society that endorsed their controversial actions. However, focused innovativeness did *not* damage groups' legitimacy in the larger society. Indeed, by strategically conforming to specific societal norms, the social movement groups were still able to acquire organizational legitimacy from broader segments of society, resulting in the acquisition of important organizational resources (e.g. pubic endorsements by credible organizations, financial support, and increased organizational membership).

Extrapolating these findings to the recruitment context of small businesses, small firms might purposively highlight their attributes that are *not* consistent with industry norms. They can therefore attract job applicants who have preferences for these deviant characteristics. For example, younger job applicants have been shown to have a strong "contempt for bureaucracy," and many wish to try new ideas with employers who value results more than rules (Cable, Mulvey, Aiman-Smith & Edwards, 2000). Thus, small firms may develop a competitive recruitment advantage over large firms when recruiting job seekers in this segment of the work force by purposively highlighting that they are less bureaucratic and hierarchical than large firms (e.g. stressing the "family environment" of the organization in recruitment literature). By coupling these practices with the necessary level of socially accepted recruitment and HR policies, small businesses may still garner legitimacy.

Establishing legitimacy is important to small firm recruitment success because past research suggests that while some individuals have a strong preference for working in small organizations, such individuals represent a small portion of the total labor pool. For example, in their study of 585 senior business and engineer majors Barber and colleagues (1999) found that only 15% preferred to work for small firms, whereas 39% held no preference towards employer size, and 46% preferred large organizations. Thus, by strategically balancing distinctiveness with isomorphism, small businesses may be able to increase the size of the applicant pool they attract, improving their recruitment outcomes. For example, small firms might gain legitimacy by participating in major career fairs but distinguish themselves from larger competitors by sending top-level executives to interact with job seekers. This unique practice will stand out in comparison to the actions of large firms. As a result, job seekers may be more likely to recall and remember the firm, thus increasing its organizational awareness (Keller, 1993). Moreover, the use of legitimized venues will allow a small firm to be seen as a viable employment option by a broader segment of job seekers.

The balance point of distinctiveness vs. isomorphism that will place small firms within "the range of acceptability" will likely vary, depending on a variety of firm and industry-level factors. Three such factors, intended to be illustrative rather than all-inclusive, are the type of position a small business is attempting to fill, the industry in which it is recruiting, and the life stage of its industry. In terms of position type, small businesses attempting to fill idiosyncratic positions may derive more benefit from isomorphic recruitment practices than firms attempting to fill positions that are standardized within an industry. Firms filling idiosyncratic jobs may benefit because job seekers may place greater importance on the reliability and credibility of the firm making the idiosyncratic hire if they perceive that the job's skills and experiences may not easily transfer to other organizational settings, reducing their potential marketability. Conversely, if a small firm is attempting to fill a position that is standardized across their industry, they may need to work harder to distinguish their firm from larger organizations.

Industry differences in employment norms may also influence the extent to which small businesses may need to adopt an isomorphic vs. distinctiveness strategy, as well as determine what types of practices small firms may need to imitate. For example, past research suggests that work-family HR policies (e.g. flexible career paths, on-site child care, and adoption subsidies) have become institutionalized norms in the health care and financial service industries. However, such practices are not widely utilized in manufacturing sectors (Goodstein, 1994; Milliken, Martins & Morgan, 1998). Thus, small businesses attempting to recruit in the health care and financial service industries may face greater pressure to adopt elements of these policies and promote their use in order to retain legitimacy in the eyes of job seekers. Conversely, firms recruiting in the manufacturing sector may not face pressure to adopt these types of policies. Indeed, the adoption of work-family policies in the manufacturing sector industry could represent a strategy of distinctiveness and benefit small businesses by providing greater visibility.

Finally, the life stage of a small business's industry may also influence what constitutes the optimal balance point for recruitment activities, such that in developing industries a small business may benefit from emphasizing distinctiveness while in mature industries a small firm may experience more recruitment success by emphasizing isomorphism. The institutionalization of industry norms often varies as a function of an industry's development (Westphal, Gulati & Shortell, 1997). In newly forming industries, institutional norms are typically undeveloped and are largely shaped by the actions of innovative small firms (Aldrich & Fiol, 1994). In this setting, small firms are not likely to face strong institutional norms and may experience more recruitment success by adopting distinctive practices. For example during the early stages of the development of the computer software and personal computer (PC) industries, small firms were successful in attracting employees by using what at that time were radical HR practices, such as stock options for all employees, allowing casual attire, and telecommuting. However, as industries mature, successful novel practices are adopted by more organizations within the industry and become institutionalized norms (Aldrich & Fiol, 1994). Thus, in mature industries, the strategic balance point for small firms may entail placing a greater emphasis on imitating institutionalized recruitment practices in order to garner legitimacy, as opposed to adopting distinctive practices. Consistent with this logic, as the PC and software industries have matured the use of stock options has widely increased and is now widely used by most organizations. Thus, small firms recruiting in these industries are forced to consider the use of stock options if they wish to garner legitimacy from job seekers.

SUMMARY AND RESEARCH IMPLICATIONS

Summary

The overwhelming majority of organizations in the U.S. have fewer than 500 employees (SBA, 1999a). Nonetheless, few researchers have examined how small businesses recruit employees to meet the labor demands of organizational growth and routine attrition. We have addressed this issue by utilizing marketing and sociological principles to examine the potential barriers facing small businesses. In addition, we illustrated how the initiation of brand-marketing, strategic isomorphism, and interorganizational networking strategies may allow small firms to overcome recruitment barriers. Table 1 provides a summary of the hypothesized recruitment barriers faced by small firms and potential strategic solutions to these barriers.

Several implications for small business owners as well as academics can be drawn from our analysis. Perhaps the most important practical implication of this paper is that small businesses need to consider both job seekers' organizational knowledge and perceptions of organizational legitimacy when deciding what types of recruitment practices to adopt. Thus, the use of benchmarking or "best practice" strategies, whereby organizations adopt recruitment practices solely on the basis that they have provided instrumental efficiency for other organizations, may not be beneficial for all small firms. Conversely, we suggest that small firms attempting to compete with large, well-known organizations should first assess job seekers' knowledge about their organizations. Based on this assessment, small firms should make immediate investments on developing awareness or perceptions of organizational image through the use of peripheral (e.g. distributing gifts with company logo, advertising at career fairs) or central (e.g. holding information sessions, interviews) modes of recruitment communications. However, when selecting recruitment practices to increase job seekers' organizational knowledge, decision makers must also give considerable consideration to how these practices fit within the established recruitment norms of their industry. As a result, small businesses may be constrained to selecting from a subset of practices that are either endorsed or adopted by legitimate institutional leaders (Aldrich & Fiol, 1994).

From an academic perspective, an important implication of this paper is that marketing and sociological theories should be integrated into research on small business recruitment in particular, and employee recruitment in general. Most recruitment research has focused on understanding how job seekers' individual preferences influence their evaluations of prospective employers' attractiveness (Barber, 1998). Few studies, however, have developed theoretical models to

Table 1. Recruitment Barriers Faced by Small Businesses and Strategic Solutions.

Barriers Faced by Small Firms in the Recruitment Process	Causes of Barriers	Strategic Initiatives to Alleviate Barriers
Job Seekers' Have Low Organizational Knowledge	Low Organizational Familiarity	Use of Peripheral Forms of Communication in Recruitment Practices • Free company gifts • Presence at career fairs
	Job Seekers Lack Information About Organizational image	Use of Central Forms of Communication in Recruitment Practices • Information sessions • Interviews
Low Perceptions of Organizational Legitimacy in the Eyes of Job Seekers	Low Influence on Industry Norms	Strategic Isomorphism • Imitation of established recruitment practices • Imitation of established human resource policies
	Lack of ties to Central Organizations	Interorganizational Linkages • Develop ties with Colleges and Universities • Develop ties with professional associations
	Poorly Developed Human Resource Systems	• Advertise Supplier Relationships and Partnerships with Prominent Organizations • Advertise Accreditations

understand how recruitment activities influence job seekers' perceptions of an organization or how social norms and institutional contingencies influence how job seekers evaluate the attractiveness of prospective employers (Colarelli, 1996; Ryans, 1991). Taking job seekers' organizational knowledge into account may assist researchers by providing a theoretical basis for understanding the contingencies affecting when certain recruitment practices will be effective. In addition, integrating institutional theory into recruitment research may provide a theoretical basis for understanding how environmental factors constrain or enhance the recruitment efforts of firms.

A second theoretical contribution of this chapter is the formal recognition that small businesses may need to adopt a dual strategy of distinctiveness and isomorphism to optimize their recruitment outcomes. Institutional perspectives have often been criticized for failing to account for the occurrence of non-conforming behavior: "institutional theorists, by virtue of their focus, have tended to limit their attention to the effects of the institutional environment on structural conformity and isomorphism and have tended to overlook the role of active agency and resistance in organization-environment relations" (Oliver, 1991, p. 151). Our application of strategic balance theory provides an understanding of how strategies of distinctiveness and imitation may be coupled to improve the recruitment success of small firms.

Areas of Future Research

To date no study has empirically tested how job seekers' organizational knowledge and perceptions of organizational legitimacy affect small businesses' recruitment efforts. Future studies might use qualitative methods such as verbal protocol analysis (a process-tracing method requiring subjects to "think aloud" while making decisions or judgments) to determine the level of organizational knowledge job seekers have about small firms. They may also examine the factors job seekers utilize to evaluate organizational legitimacy, such as HR policies or recruitment practices (Barber & Roehling, 1993; Martin & Klimoski, 1990). These results could be used to develop surveys assessing job seekers' organizational knowledge and legitimacy evaluations. The surveys could then be used to test the empirical relationship between these constructs and specific recruitment out-comes, such as applicants per vacancy and average days-to-fill. In addition, future research should also examine the relationship between strategic isomorphism, interorganizational linkages, and job seekers' perceptions of small firms' organizational legitimacy. Finally, we have proposed that small firms may benefit from the simultaneous adoption of distinct and isomorphic practices. However, future research is needed to determine what an optimal combination of these two strategies should be for small businesses recruiting employees and how this balance point may vary by organizational or industry contingencies.

REFERENCES

Abraham, K., & Newcorn, C. (2000). Online recruiting – A powerful tool for small businesses. *The National Public Accountant*, *45*, 32–35.

Aldrich, H. E. (1999). *Organizations Evolving*. London: Sage Publications.

Aldrich, H. E., & Auster, E. R. (1986). Even dwarfs started small: Liabilities of age and size and their strategic implications. In: B. Staw & L. Cummings (Eds), *Research in Organizational Behavior* (Vol. 8, pp. 65–198). Greenwich. CT: JAI Press.

Aldrich, H. E., & Fiol, C. M. (1994). Fools rush in? The institutional context of industry creation. *Academy of Management Review*, *19*, 645–670.

Aldrich, H. E., & Von Glinow, M. A. (1991). Business Start-ups: The HRM imperative. In: S. Birley, I. Macmillan & S. Subramony (Eds), *International Perspectives on Entrepreneurship Research* (Vol. 18, pp. 233–253). New York: Elsevier Science Publishers B.V.

Aldrich, H. E., & Zimmer, C. (1986). Entrepreneurship Through Social Networks. In: D. Sexton & R. Smilor (Eds), *The Art and Science of Entrepreneurship* (pp. 3–23). New York: Ballinger.

Alexander, S. (1999). Recruiting big as a small shop. *ComputerWorld*, *33*, 55.

Arnold, S. J., Handelman, J., & Tigert, D. J. (1996). Organizational Legitimacy and Retail Store Patronage. *Journal of Business Research*, *35*, 229–239.

Arthur Anderson & National Small Business United (2000). *Survey of small and mid-sized businesses: Trends for 2000.*

Baker, T., & Aldrich, H. E. (1994). Friends and strangers: Early hiring practices and idiosyncratic jobs. *Proceedings of the Fourteenth Annual Entrepreneurship Research Conference*, 75–87.

Barber, A. E. (1998). *Recruiting employees: Individual and organizational perspectives*. Thousand Oaks, CA, Sage Publications, Inc.

Barber, A. E., & Roehling, M. V. (1993). Job postings and the decision to interview: A verbal protocol analysis. *Journal of Applied Psychology*, *78*, 845–856.

Barber, A., Wesson, M. J., Roberson, Q. M., & Taylor, M. S. (1999). A tale of two job markets: Organizational size and its effects on hiring practices and job search behavior. *Personnel Psychology 52*, 841–867.

Bartram, D., Lindley, P. A., Marshall, L., & Foster, J. (1995). The recruitment and selection of young people by small businesses. *Journal of Occupational and Organizational Psychology*, *68*, 339–358.

Baum, J. A., & Oliver, C. 1991. Institutional linkages and organizational mortality. *Administrative Science Quarterly*, *36*, 187–218.

Brass, D. J. (1995). A social network perspective on human resources management. In: K. M. Rowland & G. R. Ferris (Eds), *Research in Personnel and Human Resources Management* (Vol. 13, pp. 39–79). Greenwich. CT: JAI Press.

Brown, C., Hamilton, J., & Medoff, J. (1990). *Employers large and small*. Cambridge, MA: Harvard University Press.

Cable, D. M., & Graham, M. (2000). The Determinants of Organizational Reputation: A Job Search Perspective. *Journal of Organizational Behavior*, *21*, 929–947.

Cable, D. M., Mulvey, P., Aiman-Smith, L., & Edwards, J. R. (2000). The sources and accuracy of job seekers' organizational culture beliefs. *Academy of Management Journal*, *43*, 1076–1085.

Cable, D., & Judge, T. A. (1996). Person-organization fit, job choice decisions, and organizational entry. *Organizational Behavior and Human Decision Processes, 67*, 294–311.

Carton, B. (1995). Small Business; Help wanted. *The Wall Street Journal*, May 22, R10.

Colarelli, S. M. (1996). Establishment and job context influences on the use of hiring practices. *Applied Psychology: An International Review, 45*, 153–176.

D'Aunno, T., Sutton, R. I., & Price, R. H. (1991). Isomorphism and external support in conflicting institutional environments: A study of drug abuse treatment units. *Academy of Management Journal, 34*, 636–661.

DiMaggio, P. J., & Powell, W. W. (1983). The iron cage revisited: Institutional isomorphism and collective rationality in organizational fields. *American Sociological Review, 48*, 147–160.

Deephouse, D. L. (1999). To be different, or to be the same? It's a question (and a theory) of strategic balance. *Strategic Management Journal, 20*, 147–166.

Deephouse, D. L. (1996). Does Isomorphism legitimate? *Academy of Management Journal, 39*, 1024–1039.

Elsbach, K. D., & Sutton, R. I. (1992). Acquiring organizational legitimacy through illegitimate actions: A marriage of institutional and impression management theories. *Academy of Management Journal, 35*, 699–738.

Engler, N. (1999). Small emerging enterprises are using unique methods in order to attract IT talent and retain those employees. *Information Week*, February 8, 164.

Evans, D. S., & Leighton, L. S. (1989). Why do small firms pay less? *The Journal of Human Resources, 24*, 299–318.

Fisher, C. D., Ilgen, D. R., & Hoyer, W. D. (1979). Source credibility, information favorability, and job offer acceptance. *Academy of Management Journal, 22*, 94–103.

Freeman, J. H. (1982). Organizational life cycles and natural selection processes. In: B. Staw & L. Cummings (Eds), *Research in Organizational Behavior* (Vol. 4, pp. 1–32). Greenwich, CT: JAI Press.

Gatewood, R. D., Gowen, M. A., & Lautenschlager, D. J. (1993). Corporate image, recruitment image, and initial job choice decisions. *Academy of Management Journal, 36*, 414–427.

Goodstein, J. D. (1994). Institutional pressures and strategic responsiveness: Employer involvement in work-family issues. *Academy of Management Journal, 37*, 350–382.

Glynn, M. A., Barr, P. S., & Dacin, M. T. (2000). Pluralism and the problem of variety. *Academy of Management Review, 25*.

Guthrie, J. P., & Olian, J. D. (1991). Does context affect staffing decisions? The case of general managers. *Personnel Psychology, 44*, 263–292.

Hannan, M. T., & Freeman, J. (1984). Structural inertia and organizational change. *American Sociological Review, 49*, 149–164.

Haveman, H. A. (1993). Following the leader: Mimetic isomorphism and entry into new markets. *Administrative Science Quarterly, 38*, 593–627.

Honeycutt, T. L., & Rosen, B. (1997). Family friendly human resource policies, salary levels, and salient identity as predictors of organizational attraction. *Journal of Vocational Behavior, 50*, 271–290.

Internetweek (2000). Allbusines.com (dot.com) perks attract talent. April, 24, 16.

Keller, K. L. (1993). Conceptualizing, measuring, and managing customer-based brand equity. *Journal of Marketing, 57*, 1–22.

Kristof, A. L. (1996). Person-organization fit: An integrative review of its conceptualizations, measurement, and implications. *Personnel Psychology, 49*, 1–49.

Martin, S. L., & Klimoski, R. J. (1990). Use of verbal protocols to trace cognitions with self- and supervisor evaluations of performance. *Organizational Behavior and Human Decision Processes*, *46*, 135–145.

Meyer, J. W., & Rowan, B. (1977). Institutional organizations: Formal structure as myth and ceremony, *American Journal of Sociology*, *80*, 340–363.

Meyer, J. W., & Scott, W. R. (1983). Centralization and the legitimacy problems of local governments. In: J. W. Meyer & W. R. Scott (Eds), *Organizational Environments: Ritual and Rationality* (pp. 199–215). Beverly Hills, CA: Sage.

MacInnis, D. J., Moorman, C., & Jaworski, B. J. (1991). Enhancing and measuring consumers' motivation, opportunity, and ability to process brand information from ads. *Journal of Marketing*, *55*, 1–23.

Milliken, F. J., Martins, L. L., & Morgan, H. (1998). Explaining organizational responsiveness to work-family issues: The role of human resource executives as issue interpreters. *Academy of Management Journal*, *41*, 580–592.

Mosely, A. (1998). www.recruiting. *Business & Economic Review*, (Oct.–Dec.), 23–25.

Muson, H. (2001). The people problem. *Across the Board*, *38*, 87–88.

Oliver, C. (1991). Strategic responses to institutional processes. *Academy of Management Review*, *16*, 145–179.

Parsons, T. (1960). *Structure and process in modern societies*. Glencoe, Il: Free Press

Petty, R. E., & Cacioppo, J. T. (1986). The elaboration likelihood model of persuasion. In: L. Berkowitz (Ed.), *Advances in Experimental Social Psychology* (pp. 123–205). Academic Press.

Pfeffer, J., & Salancik, G. R. (1978). *The external control of organizations*. New York: Harper & Row.

Podolny, J. M. (1994). Market uncertainty and the social character of economic exchange. *Administrative Science Quarterly*, *39*, 458–483.

Podolny, J. M., & Stuart, T. E. (1995). A role-based ecology of technological change. *American Journal of Sociology*, *100*, 1224–1260.

Power, D. J., & Aldag, R. J. (1985). Soelberg's job search and choice model: A clarification, review, and critique. *Academy of Management Review*, *10*, 48–58.

Rao, H. (1994). The social construction of reputation: Certification contests, legitimation, and the survival of organizations in the American automobile industry: 1895–1912. *Strategic Management Journal*, *15*, 29–44.

Roberts, J. H., & Lattin, J. M. (1997). Consideration: Review of Research and Prospects for Future Insights. *Journal of Marketing Research*, *34*, 406–410.

Rynes, S. L. (1991). Recruitment, job choice, and post-hire consequences: A call for new research directions. In: M. Dunnette & L. Hough (Eds), *Handbook of Industrial/Organizational Psychology* (Vol. 2, pp. 399–444). Palo Alto, CA: Consulting Psychologists Press.

Rynes, S. L., & Boudreau, J. W. (1986). College recruiting in large organizations: Practice, evaluation, and research implications. *Personnel Psychology*, *39*, 729–757.

Rynes, S. L., Bretz, R. D., & Gerhart, B. (1991). The importance of recruitment in job choice: A different way of looking. *Personnel Psychology*, *44*, 487–521.

Salancik, G. R., & Pfeffer, J. (1978). A social information processing approach to job attitudes and task design. *Administrative Science Quarterly*, *23*, 224–253.

SBA (1999a). Small Business answer card 1998. [On-line] Available: (http://www.sba.gov.size/Guide-Entire.html).

SBA. (1999b). *Guide to SBA's definitions of a small business*. [On-line]. Available: (http://www.sba.gov.size/Guide-Entire.html).

Schwab, D. P., Rynes, S. L., & Aldag, R. J. (1987). Theories and research on job search and choice. In: K. M. Rowland & G. R. Ferris (Eds), *Research in Personnel and Human Resources Management* (Vol. 5, pp. 126–166). Greenwich, CT: JAI Press.

Scott, W. R. (1998). *Organizations: rational, natural, and open systems.* Upper Saddle River, NJ: Prentice-Hall, Inc.

Small Business Economic Trends (2001). NFIB Education Foundation Small Business Economic Survey. April, 1–16.

Sorenson, J. E., Rhode, J. G., & Lawler, E. E. (1973). The generation gap in public accounting. *Journal of Accountancy, 136,* 42–50.

Stinchcombe, A. L. (1965). Organizations and social structure. In: J. G. March (Ed.), *Handbook of Organizations* (pp. 153–193). Chicago: Rand McNally.

Stuart, T. E., Hoang, H., & Hybels, R. C. (1999). Interorganizational endorsements and the performance of entrepreneurial ventures. *Administrative Science Quarterly, 44,* 315–349.

Suchman, M. C. (1995). Managing legitimacy: Strategic and institutional approaches. *Academy of Management Review, 20,* 571–610.

Thomas, R. J. (1989). Blue-collar career: Meaning and choice in a world of constraints. In: M. B. Arthur, D. T. Hall & B. S. Lawrence (Eds), *Handbook of Career Theory* (pp. 354–379). New York: Cambridge University Press.

Turban, D. B., & Keon, T. L. (1993). Organizational attractiveness: An interactionist perspective. *Journal of Applied Psychology, 78,* 184–193.

Welbourne, T. M., & Cyr, L. A. (1999). The human resource executive effect in initial public offering firms. *Academy of Management Journal, 42,* 616–629.

Westphal, J. D., Gulait, R., & Shortell, S. M. (1997). Customization or conformity? An institutional and network perspective on the content and consequences of TQM adoption. *Administrative Science Quarterly, 42,* 366–394.

Williams, M. L., & Dreher, G. F. (1992). Compensation system attributes and applicant pool characteristics. *Academy of Management Journal, 35,* 571–595.

Williamson, I. O. (2000). Employer legitimacy and recruitment success in small businesses. *Entrepreneurship, Theory, and Practice, 25,* 27–42.

Windolf, P. (1986). Recruitment, Selection, and Internal Labour Markets in Britain and Germany. *Organization Studies, 7,* 235–254.

5. STOCK-RELATED REWARDS, SOCIAL IDENTITY, AND THE ATTRACTION AND RETENTION OF EMPLOYEES IN ENTREPRENEURIAL SMEs

Mary E. Graham, Brian Murray and Linda Amuso

INTRODUCTION

Entrepreneurial firms faced perhaps unprecedented pressures to attract and retain high-skilled employees through the early 2000s, and firms went to great lengths to meet staffing demands. For example, edocs Inc., a provider of online account management software, put together a recruitment team larger in size than its marketing function, and out of necessity, CEO Kevin Laracey is integrally involved in recruitment efforts (Lublin, 1999). However, despite such staffing pressures and recent research on rewards and staffing linkages (e.g. Barber & Bretz, 2000), there remains a dearth of rewards research in the area of attraction and retention in entrepreneurial firms.

To begin, we lack conclusive information on whether entrepreneurial firms employ different rewards strategies than traditional firms in their attempts to recruit and retain workers. There is a need for information on the results of rewards/staffing relationships as well. In short, it is unclear whether existing rewards research is relevant to entrepreneurial firms or whether entrepreneurial firms are so different that new, unique theories are needed. We examine this

Managing People in Entrepreneurial Organizations, Volume 5, pages 107–145.
Copyright © 2002 by Elsevier Science Ltd.
All rights of reproduction in any form reserved.
ISBN: 0-7623-0877-X

question in the context of firms' efforts to attract and retain workers, and as such, *employees* rather than owners are the focus of this chapter.

There are preliminary indications that entrepreneurial firms and their rewards practices differ in important ways from traditional firms. Entrepreneurial firms' lower survival rates and shorter life cycles (e.g. Katz, Aldrich, Welbourne & Williams, 2000) may translate into different reward strategies and outcomes for entrepreneurial as compared to other firms (Heneman, Tansky & Camp, 2000). On the other hand, the characteristics of entrepreneurial firms (e.g. business risk, product life stage, forms of funding and governance, and entrepreneur-founder characteristics) operationalize important contingencies found in widely studied theories and contemporary streams of compensation research, suggesting that existing rewards knowledge may transfer easily to entrepreneurial firms.

Absent a common definition of entrepreneurial firm, we direct our inquiry toward organizations of enterprising individuals who intensively discover, evaluate, and exploit opportunities to create future goods and services (Kirzner, 1973; Shane & Venkataraman, 2000) through the commitment and management of resources (Stevenson, 2000). Further, we narrow our scope to small- and medium-sized entrepreneurial firms which are more sensitive to competitive and environmental pressures than established firms due to their tighter resources, small size, and relatively young age (or life stage) (Heneman et al., 2000).

We write about stock-related rewards for several reasons. First, the popular press often highlights key differences in the way stock rewards are used by entrepreneurial versus more traditional firms (e.g. Tully, 2000). Converging with this view, there are initial research indications that those seeking jobs in high technology firms value stock options more highly than other workers (e.g. Ledford, Mulvey & LeBlanc, 2000). Second, the long bull market may have lulled some managers and owners into viewing stock options as a cost-effective panacea for staffing problems in entrepreneurial SMEs, and firms have only recently experienced the downsides of this approach, namely attraction and retention problems during a bear market (Tully, 2000). These issues raise obvious questions about stock rewards' long-term efficacy and viability. Finally, compared to research on other rewards such as cash incentives, stock rewards are relatively understudied in the organizational behavior literature, with the exception of employee stock ownership plans (ESOPs).

Our goal is to generate an agenda for future research. The chapter begins with a discussion of our decision to focus on social psychological rather than economic variables, followed by introduction of stock-related rewards alternatives. We then offer a description of the nature of work and the contexts in which entrepreneurial firms operate. As an organizing framework, we integrate social identity theory with three strategic or organizational theory perspectives used in current compensation research. Using this framework, we review and evaluate relevant research streams and suggest areas of future research.

A SOCIAL PSYCHOLOGICAL LOOK AT REWARDS AND STAFFING

In the chapter we emphasize social psychological rather than economic determinants of attraction and retention outcomes, partly in response to a call for such research (Rynes & Gerhart, 2000). The unique characteristics of stock-related rewards, such as their relatively high risk and volatility, suggest the potentially heightened influence of psychological variables on worker and firm outcomes. Also, examination of psychological variables will help specify the underlying mechanisms driving compensation effects (Barber & Bretz, 2000).

Inconclusive results in the economic area suggest a need for more a more micro-level approach to studying rewards as well. Labor economic studies of supply and demand tend to focus on worker behavior relative to an equilibrium wage, and even in cases of imperfect information, the worker is able to estimate his or her future income (Ehrenberg & Smith, 2000). However, given the uncertain and volatile nature of stock-related rewards in entrepreneurial firms, it is less likely that individuals will be able to make reasonable estimates of future income streams. Exacerbating the difficulty in determining the expected value of the stock-related reward is the substantially larger risk, or variance, surrounding the expected value. Therefore, we expect to observe different worker responses to stock rewards than we would with typical salary compensation. A related driver of the chapter's focus on social psychological variables is the inability of relative compensation level to unequivocally tie pay to attraction and retention outcomes (Kim, 1999). We rely on the concept of individual differences, or the stable personality characteristics of individuals, to help explain worker reactions and firm outcomes of stock rewards. Of course, however, we acknowledge the influence of economic boundaries such as the reservation wage (Osborn, 1990; Rynes, Schwab & Heneman, 1983; Tromski & Subich, 1990).

For all of the above reasons, we focus our chapter on the promising area of research involving individual differences in social identity. Our aim is to illuminate worker responses to stock-related rewards alternatives.

STOCK-RELATED REWARDS ALTERNATIVES

Because much of the discussion in this chapter relies upon the technical details of various stock-related rewards alternatives, we briefly introduce the following rewards programs: stock options, stock grants, stock ownership and purchase plans, and stock-related cash incentives.

Stock options permit employees to purchase employer stock at a set price sometime in the future, regardless of the price at the time of the exercise. For example, if a firm provides 1000 stock options at $20/share to an employee, and two years later the employee exercises the option and sells the stock for $35/share, the employee would earn $15,000 ($35–$20 = $15 × 1000 shares = $15,000). Stock options are only valuable to the extent that the firm's stock price is above the "strike price" or the price at which the options can be exercised; stock values below the strike price are worthless at that point in time. Firms may further emphasize the long-term performance of the firm by instituting longer vesting requirements (period of time before employee can possess and exercise options) or by basing the right to exercise options on performance goals (Johanson, 2000).

There are two primary forms of stock options: nonqualified and qualified. Gains from the exercise and immediate sale of nonqualified options are taxable to employees at ordinary income rates, and provide a corresponding tax deduction for the employer. Qualified option gains are taxed at employees' capital gain rates, and employers receive no corresponding tax deduction. Among other restrictions, qualified options are limited to employees (i.e. not directors, consultants, or others), they must be granted under a written plan document, and employers are not permitted to discount the qualified option exercise prices (Johanson, 2000). Unlike nonqualified options, employers are *not* required to recognize an accounting expense for qualified options.

Stock grants, employee stock purchase plans (ESPPs), and employee stock ownership plans (ESOPs) are additional vehicles for stock ownership. Stock grants are incentive grants to employees, sometimes in lieu of cash bonuses. ESPPs assist employees in purchasing company stock, often by providing discounts on the purchase price. ESOPs differ somewhat from grants and ESPPs in that employee ownership often occurs through retirement accounts, and employees may not have access to their stock and stock returns for many years. Finally, phantom stock plans and stock appreciation rights (SARs), sometimes referred to as quasi-equity plans, direct employee behavior toward increasing stock value, but may not involve actual employee ownership of stock. Phantom stock plans are cash incentives that link bonus payouts to appreciation in the value of a particular business unit, firm, or stock price (Snarr, 2000). Stock appreciation rights (SARs) reward employees in the form of cash or stock, in the amount of any appreciation in stock value (Johanson, 2000).

Thus, stock-related reward alternatives range from stock ownership, to options to purchase stock, to cash incentives tied to stock prices. Not surprisingly, the reward forms differ in their implications for employees and employers. Some rewards such as ESOPs focus employee efforts on the very long-term, with employees receiving returns only when vesting requirements are met and employees leave the firm. Other rewards, such as phantom stock plans, may provide *cash* bonuses in the near term. Similarly, some rewards might encourage or support an ownership culture more strongly (e.g. stock options) than others (e.g. SARs). Table 1 introduces and summarizes these stock-related reward forms (For additional detail on stock-related rewards, see the Foundation for Enterprise Development, 1998).

MACRO-LEVEL THEORETICAL PERSPECTIVES ON REWARDS

To support the organization's competitiveness and viability, human resource initiatives must be responsive to the environmental pressures faced by the firm (Jackson & Schuler, 1995). Stock-related rewards play a salient role here because they not only directly reflect the environment's response to the firm through share value, but they also focus the attention of share participants on the organization's value in the environment. Contingency, agency and institutional theories offer distinct, valuable perspectives on the process by which ventures use various reward strategies to respond to competitive and environmental pressures. Firms' compensation practices, in turn, affect the attraction and retention of employees. We use these theoretical perspectives to explain the interaction between the organization and its environment. Because there is little if any empirical work on the application of macro-level theories to entrepreneurial SMEs, we elaborate multiple and sometimes competing predictions of the theories.

Contingency or strategic explanations focus on the fit of reward practices to the environment, resources, and life-stage of the organization. Agency theory addresses how the risk of the environment and the traits of the entrepreneur influence the reward contract characteristics. Institutional theory helps explain why firms may reward employees in ways that seem less grounded in economic rationality or business strategy, and more in stakeholder expectations.

Figure 1 illustrates the relationship between environmental pressures, firm pay policies and practices, and staffing outcomes. Included in the "Entrepreneurial Venture Environment and Resources" box are pressures identified by one or more of the three theories we consider. For example, environmental turbulence, or risk, is most closely associated with agency problems and strategic fit issues. Firms use pay system choices such as the amount of risk in employees' pay, the extent to which pay rewards long-term accomplishments, and the bureaucracy associated with the compensation systems, to respond to environmental

Table 1. Stock-Related Rewards.

Type of Reward	Definition	Advantage to Employer	Employee Receives
Stock option	Right to purchase company stock at a stated price within a specific time period.	See below:	Difference between stock sale price and stock option exercise price. If hold stock, any corresponding gains.
Nonqualified stock option	Option not governed by Internal Revenue Code. It does not provide favorable tax treatment for the employee (i.e. sale gains are taxed at ordinary income rates).	Tax deduction for option gains. Focus employee efforts on the long-term.	Difference between stock sale price and exercise price. If hold stock, corresponding gains in stock price.
Qualified stock option (incentive stock option)	Option governed by Internal Revenue Code. It provides favorable tax treatment to employees (gains are usually taxed at capital gain rates), and employers get no corresponding tax deduction. Other restrictions apply.	Further focus employee efforts on the long-term since employee most hold stock for a period of time. Means to reduce the tax burden for high earners. No accounting expense required	Difference between stock sale price and exercise price. Corresponding gains in stock price.
Stock grant	Firm shares are given to employees for merit or other reasons.	Simple to administer. Tax deduction for employer.	Stock and stock gains.
Employee stock ownership plan (ESOP)	Firm shares earmarked for employees, which employees receive upon a certain events (e.g. death, retirement, vesting).	Focus employee efforts on the very long-term. Encourage ownership and participation in the firm. Reduce threat of hostile takeovers.	Stock and stock gains.

Table 1. Continued.

Type of Reward	Definition	Advantage to Employer	Employee Receives
Employee stock purchase plan (ESPP)	Employer permits employees to purchase firm stock at up to a 15% discount.	Focus employee efforts on the long-term. Encourage ownership and participation in the firm.	Discount on stock price and corresponding stock gains.
Phantom stock	Cash incentives based upon appreciation in the value of a business unit, firm, or stock price	Maintain ownership, while encouraging an ownership culture and long-term focus.	Cash bonuses.
Stock appreciation rights (SARs)	Cash or stock rewards based upon stock value appreciation.	If cash, maintain ownership. Focus employee efforts on the long-term. Encourage ownership and participation in the firm.	Cash or stock bonuses.

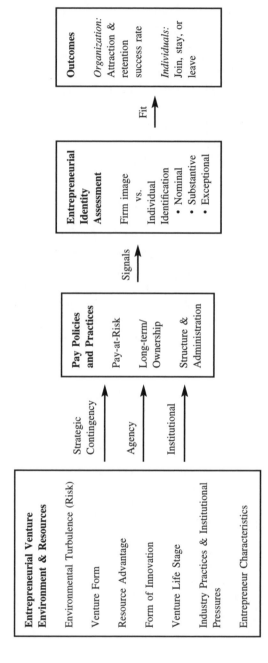

Fig. 1. Model of Reward Determination and Attraction and Retention Outcomes.

pressures. These pay system choices also communicate information about firm image or reputation to workers (Cable & Judge, 1994). Depending upon the degree of congruence between firm image with individuals' personalities and the contexts in which they live, workers may be more or less attracted or committed to particular firms. An underlying assumption is that firms act as both takers (i.e. firms' strategic options are constrained) and agents (firms are able to manage contingencies with chosen strategies) (see Oliver, 1991, for a discussion of this issue).

We rely upon social identity theory to illuminate the process by which rewards affect the attraction and retention of employees in entrepreneurial firms. The lower half of Table 2 considers which social identities might be reinforced by stock rewards choices that vary in terms of the characteristics of risk, ownership, and administrative flexibility. For example, firms facing strong stakeholder pressures may adopt pay strategies and forms that mirror industry standards and stakeholder expectations for more traditional firms, and therefore individuals seeking only a entrepreneurial appearance would be attracted. We posit that identities will vary with reward characteristics, and range as follows:

(1) Risk-taking: "I am a risk-taker" . . . "I look like a risk-taker"
(2) Ownership: "I am an owner" . . . "I look like an owner"
(3) Administration: "I fit here" . . . "I am an innovator" . . . "I am secure here"

The risk-taking and ownership components more readily translate into social identities than the administration component, but the latter is essential to an entrepreneurial identity. Flat, flexible, centralized pay forms would only attract and retain those who seek such a pay system, hence, fit is emphasized. In the case of agency problems, monitoring-based stock rewards systems, whose purpose is to manage risk sharing by eliminating employee discretion, would stifle the entrepreneur's preference to express risk-taking and individual choices. And the best practices approach associated with stakeholder expectations provides a more common and well-known reward package to employees, thereby communicating the message of security.

In the following sections, we further discuss implications for stock-related rewards and attraction-retention outcomes by elaborating on the three macro-level theories of firm behavior.

Strategic Contingency Theory

To be strategic in human resources, or specifically compensation, requires an integrated series of decisions that addresses contingencies in the internal and external environments, and that individually and together impact organizational

Table 2.   Theoretical Perspectives on Rewards in Entrepreneurial Firms.

Environmental Pressures on Entrepreneurial Firms	Multiple Contingencies	Agency Problems	Stakeholder Expectations
Theory	Contingency: firms match pay strategy to multiple contingencies such as environmental turbulence, source of capital, cash position, and employee preferences.	Agency: firms choose pay strategy to address mis-alignment of goals of principle and agent. Firms consider agent risk-aversion and cost of monitoring.	Institutional: firms implement pay strategies that conform to industry practices and stakeholder expectations.
Reward Characteristics			
Risk	Moderate – High; varies depending on types and levels of contingencies	High	Mirrors industry risk level
L. T. focus/Ownership	High	High	Mirrors industry ownership level
Structure/Administration	Flat	Monitoring-based	Intra-industry and intra-firm consistency
	Flexible		Adopt best practices
	Centralized		Perpetuate behaviors from incubators
Social identity reinforced	I am a risk-taker	I am a risk-taker	I look like a risk-taker
	I am an owner	I am an owner	I look like an owner
	I fit here	I am a rebel, innovator	I am secure here

Table 2. Continued.

	Multiple Contingencies	Agency Problems	Stakeholder Expectations
Environmental Pressures on Entrepreneurial Firms			
Who attracted and retained?[a]	Substantives and exceptionals	Substantives and exceptionals	Substantives and nominals
Caveats	Constant change may hurt retention of those who fit prior pay strategy	Sustained poor firm performance raises risks to employees	Merely symbolic efforts may hurt retention
		Over-sharing of risks lowers innovation	Consistency pressure precludes innovative rewards
		Ownership is more expensive than cash rewards	

[a] Nominals: Individuals with fairly low entrepreneurial orientations, who may seek entrepreneurial *appearances* primarily because of recent economic, social, and cultural influences.

Substantives: Individuals with moderate entrepreneurial orientations, who seek entrepreneurial *identities* because of their values and economic, social, and cultural influences.

Exceptionals: Individuals with high entrepreneurial orientations, who seek entrepreneurial *identities* almost regardless of contextual influences.

performance (cf. Gomez-Mejia & Welbourne, 1988; Milkovich, 1988). The compensation strategy literature affirms not only that important compensation decisions can differ across firms (Milkovich, 1988; Gerhart, 2000), but also that some combinations of pay systems and firm context may yield higher returns than others (Gerhart, Trevor & Graham, 1996).

Much research on human resource and compensation strategy has taken a contingency perspective that searches for the fit of compensation policies to organizational strategy and environment. Early research focused on typologies of corporate, product market, or human resource strategies on the product life cycle for identifying optimal compensation practices (see Gomez-Mejia & Balkin, 1992 for a review). More recently, focus has shifted from the content of typologies to the process for developing rewards strategies that fit key contingencies (e.g. resource based advantage, customer service focus, cost focus, global factors, and risk) (Milkovich & Newman, 2002; Tyson, 1997). Several frameworks define the processes and appropriate choice(s) for each contingency (Jackson & Schuler, 1995; Wright & McMahan, 1992).

For the entrepreneurial venture, contingency-based compensation strategy suggests that the form of the entrepreneurial innovation (e.g. cost advantage or differentiation advantage), market characteristics, venture life stage, and resource based advantage will determine the pattern of compensation practices that best address the contingencies. Thus, firms with appropriate supporting policies will realize greater organization performance. We discuss each of these contingencies in turn and consider the characteristics and implications specific to entrepreneurial ventures.

Form of Innovation
A foundational premise of entrepreneurship is that the venture relies on innovation and strategic management practices for organizational profit and viability (Carland, Hoy, Boulton & Carland, 1984; Stewart, Watson, Carland & Carland, 1998). Although there are a number of typologies of competitive strategies to encourage innovations, Porter's (1985, 1990) approach is especially instructive for the study of entrepreneurship. He defined generic strategies, including cost-leadership and differentiation. Ventures that innovate in the cost area are best supported by human resource practices that emphasize efficient use of resources and minimize the impact of labor costs. Reward practices that allow the firm to adjust the expense of labor with fluctuations in product price and demand (e.g. variable pay programs) could potentially support this contingency. Alternatively, companies may emphasize standard processes and technologies, thereby minimizing reliance on knowledge workers who may have more demanding risk/reward profiles.

The innovation of ventures with a differentiation advantage is best supported by reward practices that serve to maintain the source of differentiation. Firms adopting a differentiation strategy will choose rewards that maximize the firm's abilities to attract and retain the human capital necessary to support the differentiation. Therefore, such ventures should place greater emphasis on competitiveness in base pay and implement forms of pay, such as stock ownership, that motivate and reward longer-term commitment to the firm.

Market Characteristics
An important characteristic of the product market in which a venture competes is its volatility or environmental turbulence. Organizations that can adapt to fluctuation in their environments should be better able to compete. Reward systems that allow more flexibility in pay by sharing risk and de-emphasizing base pay should make it easier for firms to respond to volatile environments. Also, reward systems that create an ownership culture without transferring ownership preserve owner flexibility. Lincoln Electric is an example of a company that utilizes both types of flexibility. Lincoln Electric Company's annual profit-sharing bonus, which is tied to firm performance but does not transfer ownership to employees, has ranged historically from 50%–100% of base pay in the U.S., depending in part upon variations in firm profitability (O'Connell & Bartlett, 1998).

Pay systems in turbulent environments should also be characterized by flatter pay structures with less formalization of policies, and an emphasis on external competitiveness relative to internal consistency. As environments become more stable or predictable, organizations benefit from developing more formal mechanisms and structures for assessing and consistently responding to the environment. Therefore, they may be characterized by greater formalization of policies and hierarchy and a greater emphasis on internal consistency.

Venture Life Stage
It is likely that pay practices will differ over a firm's life cycle. As a venture advances from introduction, to growth, maturity, or in the case of some firms, toward an initial public offering; the necessary emphases in pay, ability to pay, and value and risk of different pay options change, as do the risk/reward profiles of employees (Nesheim, 2000). The absolute size of options granted earlier in the venture must be larger to recognize the risk of the new venture. Later in the cycle, cash compensation must rise to competitive market levels to retain employees, and following an IPO, stock performance is important to determining the effectiveness of options for attraction and retention (Wanderer, 2000).

Resource-based Advantage

Although a theoretical perspective in its own right (Barney, 1991, 2001), the source of a firm's resource-based advantage is an important contingency to consider in the reward system design. An organization possesses a competitive advantage when it produces value not being created by competitors, and it possesses sustained advantage when competitors do not attempt to, or are unable to, replicate the advantage (Barney, 1991; Barney & Wright, 1998).

Firms that identify their source of advantage (be it physical, human, or organizational; Barney, 1991) and design an integrated system of reward and other practices will better compete in their market. Because the essence of resource-based advantage is that it is organization-specific and inimitable, it defies the typical list of prescriptions that commonly accompanies contingency approaches. Although there has been little empirical research directly testing resource-based advantage in compensation or human resources, there is conceptual research drawing on a range of human resources studies supporting its tenets (e.g. Barney & Wright, 1998; Wright & McMahan, 1992).

Agency Theory

The second theoretical perspective, agency theory, explains the contracting terms between principals (owners) and agents (managers or employees) (see Eisenhardt, 1989; Fama & Jensen, 1983). The need for a contract is determined by the degree of (mis)alignment of goals held by the two parties, the asymmetry of information between them, and the cost of monitoring or obtaining information. Agency theory assumes that the goals of the principal and agent may differ, and that the agent will act in a rational and self-interested manner to achieve personal goals before, or in lieu of, the principal's goals. It also posits that the agent possesses greater information regarding personal behavior and ability, and that there is a cost for the principal to obtain this information. Finally, it proposes that the agent is effort- and risk-averse. The principal's objective, then, is to structure a contract that maximizes firm outcomes by aligning the goals of the two parties at a minimum cost of monitoring, incentives, or risk sharing.

When signals or information are not available, or monitoring is expensive, the principal can motivate the effort of the agent by creating favorable outcomes for the agent when the principal's goals are met (e.g. pay for performance, equity plans). Because entrepreneurial firms are likely to have less programmable and more fluid jobs, fewer resources with which to monitor worker performance, and employees with relatively short organizational tenures, we expect the greater use of performance-related incentives and stock-related rewards in entrepreneurial firms as compared to non-entrepreneurial firms. Reward systems structured in this way also affect the attraction of retention of employees, as discussed more fully later in the chapter.

A dilemma arising from agency theory is the relative risk born by firms versus employees. In using incentive pay, entrepreneurial firms must balance competing pressures in deciding how much risk to place on agents. In some instances, sharing risk is an appropriate substitute for monitoring. In other instances, however, tying pay to a variable outcome introduces significant risk into the relationship for which the risk-averse agent may demand a premium or decline the contract, or which may not yield the expected response from the agent (Beatty & Zajac, 1994; Bloom & Milkovich, 1998).

On the other hand, the potentially negative responses on the part of the agent are dependent on the assumption of the agent's risk aversion, but entrepreneurs may be less risk averse than other workers (Stewart et al., 1998). When the agent is risk-seeking, or risk-neutral, it is optimal for the principal to transfer risk to the agent (Baron & Kreps, 1999). In most entrepreneurial ventures, then, it is probably preferable to share some, if not all, of the performance risk with managers and employees, in the form of stock, options, or incentives based upon stock performance.

Institutional Theory

DiMaggio and Powell (1983; see also Meyer & Rowan, 1977; Oliver, 1991) developed an institutional theory perspective that is potentially useful for understanding compensation in entrepreneurial ventures. According to the theory, some forms of organizational behavior are a function of conformist pressures from firm stakeholders, such as investors and potential employees.

Institutional theory is useful for understanding the diffusion of reward forms across entrepreneurial firms, and there is evidence for institutional pressures as determinants of firm and pay structures (Eisenhardt, 1988; Staw & Epstein, 2000). Descriptive comparisons of the reward systems used by entrepreneurial and non-entrepreneurial firms support the operation of institutional pressures on entrepreneurial firms. For instance, entrepreneurial firms may emphasize stock options and stock-related rewards to a greater degree than established firms (iQuantic, 2000b). Conformity to the practices of other entrepreneurial firms signals not only that the firm is doing business in an acceptable manner, but also that it is a legitimate, entrepreneurial firm (Suchman, 1995). As entrepreneurial ventures mature, they may be rewarded by investors and other stakeholders for adopting more traditional, "legitimate" management practices.

The determinants identified in Fig. 1, ownership form (venture form), use of business development centers or other common or professional information sources (industry practices), and the background of the entrepreneur-founder (entrepreneur characteristics) may affect rewards through institutional pressures. In particular, corporate ventures are pressured to conform to existing pay systems to maintain perceptions of equity and facilitate the movement of people among organizational units (Sykes, 1992). The more similar to the established firm's products and the more tightly coupled the venture is to the traditional firm, the greater influence we expect the conformity pressure to exert on maintaining consistency in pay.

We likewise expect that venture capitalists (VC) will pressure venture managers to adopt particular management practices, especially those that the VC's have found to be successful in other firms or that facilitate the monitoring and evaluation of the venture by standardizing practices across VC holdings. We expect, therefore, to see greater homogeneity of compensation practices within a VC's portfolio of ventures than across different venture capitalists. We also anticipate that ventures that seek the assistance of small business development centers during their formation will exhibit greater conformity to industry or traditional pay practices, as they receive the same basic personnel advice and common referrals to experts in reward system design. Finally, entrepreneurs who gain experience in established firms or incubator environments bring to the venture beliefs regarding legitimate and useful business practices. To the extent that the entrepreneur sees similarity in environments, believes the learned management practices were effective, or is unaware of alternative practices, he or she will perpetuate the practices in the new venture.

REWARD PATTERN, SOCIAL IDENTITY, AND ATTRACTION-RETENTION

Although we cannot define a sole entrepreneurial pattern of pay, we can to a degree, posit that pay in entrepreneurial firms will include a greater sharing of risk and a significant ownership stake, and will arise from less formal and more flexible administration policies, as compared to the rewards in established firms (see Table 2 for a summary). Thus, rewards have potentially important implications for the attraction and retention of employees in the entrepreneurial firm because they can serve as vehicles for individuals to reinforce and express their entrepreneurial self-concepts. Social identity theory is an ideal perspective with which to examine how such characteristics influence individuals to join and remain with entrepreneurial firms.

Social Identity Theory

Social identity theory posits that individuals construct their self-concepts in part through associating with particular groups or organizations with which they feel comfortable and who affirm their self worth (Turner & Giles, 1981). While often used to explain conflict between groups (Tajfel, 1982), recent applications of social identity theory appear in employee staffing contexts as well (e.g. Turban & Greening, 1997). More specifically, there is growing evidence that individuals' identifications with the characteristics of organizations may influence whether they are attracted to or remain with them as employers (Frank, 1996; Gatewood, Gowan & Lautenschlager, 1993). There is even evidence that individuals may value the identity-congruent aspects of rewards as much or more than the economic incentives provided by these rewards (Cable & Judge, 1994). Thus, individuals may be drawn to entrepreneurial firms in order to reinforce the entrepreneurial social identities of risk-taker, owner, or innovator.

Entrepreneurially-inclined individuals enhance self-esteem and self-perceived social status by attributing favorable attributes to entrepreneurs and employees of entrepreneurial firms. The levels and types of rewards offered by firms help communicate firm reputation or desirable corporate images and cultures to job seekers as well as to current employees (Barber & Bretz, 2000). Particularly as of the 1990s to early 2000s, job seekers, employers, and society at large viewed entrepreneurship quite positively, largely due to economic boom in the U.S. the time, high profile start-ups of internet-related ventures, and stories of financial enrichment of regular employees from stock options (Fox, 1997). In fact, such shared images may have enticed to entrepreneurial ventures individuals who might not be expected to work in such firms based upon their personality traits alone (Shane & Venkataraman, 2000). It remains to be seen whether broadly favorable social constructions of entrepreneurship will persist, although the proliferation of entrepreneurship programs in U.S. colleges and universities (University of Southern California, 2001) suggests at least a somewhat stable favorable perception. Social identity theory would have it that positive images of entrepreneurs and entrepreneurship boost efforts to attract and retain employees. Conversely, in the context of unfavorable views of entrepreneurship, firms will be challenged to enhance job seekers' and employees' social identities in other ways or reward them more generously.

An Entrepreneurial Identity Heuristic

To discuss how firms can utilize social identity theory to attract and retain workers, we categorize individuals into three types: (1) *nominals*, or individuals with fairly low entrepreneurial orientations, who may seek entrepreneurial *appearances* primarily because of recent economic, social, and cultural influences, (2) *substantives*, or individuals with moderate entrepreneurial orientations, who seek entrepreneurial *identities* because of their values and economic, social, and cultural influences, and (3) *exceptionals*, or individuals with high entrepreneurial orientations who seek entrepreneurial *identities* almost regardless of contextual influences.

Since these categories recognize both trait and contextual influences on entrepreneurial orientations, they are necessarily fluid, similar to perspectives considering the interaction of the person and environment (e.g. Kristof, 1996). For example, in favorable economic climates we might expect a more obvious demonstration of entrepreneurial identities (e.g. more substantives and fewer nominals) than in poor economic times. Thus, unlike trait-based entrepreneurial orientations, our entrepreneurial identity heuristic provides a means to conceptualize shifting proportions of individuals seeking to work for entrepreneurial firms. We offer these categories as an initial heuristic for discussing what types of employees may be attracted to and retained by different reward strategies. We consider context in a broad sense, to encompass not only economic climate, but also societal views of entrepreneurship.

By considering context, we build on the literature on entrepreneurial traits. Traits interact with individuals' expectations of utility and with social norms to determine behavior (Ajzen, 1991; Ajzen & Fishbein, 1977, 1980). Our theoretical framework also considers the expected payoffs of demonstrating those behaviors and the social norms defining accepted behaviors.

Rewards and Identity

The rewards of employment with an entrepreneurial firm are multidimensional, including the risk and potential payoff from gambling on an innovation, invention, or business prospect. For employees, the risk-reward mechanism may be a long-term, variable pay system (e.g. stock options) with high potential payout if the venture succeeds, and no payout or a loss of pay if the venture fails. A second reward dimension is the satisfaction of ownership, the experienced responsibility that arises from having a tangible stake in the venture. One visible pay mechanism is the ownership of equity in the firm, or lacking that, incentives based upon firm performance or an ownership culture. A third reward dimension is the opportunity to work in an environment unencumbered by the traditional constraints of bureaucracy. In pay administration, this is observed as flexibility in pay setting and the offering of innovative benefits.

Reward dimensions form the basis for manifestations of the entrepreneurial identity as detailed in Table 2. Each of the identities (i.e. nominal, substantive, exceptional) draws on the owner-persona to define socially what it means to be an entrepreneur. Regarding risk/reward tradeoffs, we expect exceptionals and substantives to possess a different motivation for taking on the entrepreneurial identity than nominals. Either by trait or value, the exceptionals and substantives are risk tolerant or risk seeking. Therefore, they will seek an entrepreneurial identity as a social manifestation of themselves as risk-takers, and will believe themselves to be people who take risks in business opportunities. In contrast, nominals react to environmental pressures to look like risk-takers, but, in fact, nominals prefer greater security.

Similarly, we expect that different identities will realize "ownership" from different pay forms and in different ways. For example, exceptionals, and to some extent substantives, who possess a value system closely tied to *being* an entrepreneur will perceive strongly that they are an owner when provided equity. Nominals, on the other hand, value ownership because it enhances their entrepreneurial appearances.

Third, the focus on organizational outcomes, more so than on job behaviors, in a workplace will allow different perceptions related to the entrepreneurial identity. Exceptionals, who value being owners and the opportunities for personal risk, will see the equity-based reward system as an indicator that the organization is allowing him or her to express his or her idiosyncratic brand of being the owner. At the other end of the spectrum, nominals may view such ownership and risk opportunities as a threat to their economic security. If such rewards are within their risk tolerance limits, nominals will interpret contemporary, equity-based compensation as a legitimate approach to doing business, or one that is employed by firms that are more likely will be competitive in the long run.

Proposition 1: Reward systems that provide performance-based risk in reward systems, equity or equity-like stakes, and flexible pay systems, will evoke and reinforce *entrepreneurial* identities (i.e. risk-taker, owner, innovator) in exceptional and substantive identity individuals.

Proposition 2: Reward systems that offer *only symbolic* risk-based rewards, equity-related rewards, and flexible pay systems, will evoke and reinforce the entrepreneurial appearances of nominal identity individuals.

Personal and career development rewards, such as opportunities to work with thought leaders or with cutting edge technologies in particular industries, intersect the reward dimensions of risk, ownership, and flexibility. Employees may be willing to accept higher levels of risk to the extent they value the development opportunities and prestige of working for their firms. Individuals may also believe strongly in particular projects, thereby strengthening their ownership identities, even in the absence of actual equity. For example, those working for Celera Genomics Corporation, first to market the mapping of the human genome, receive career and intrinsic rewards that may rival other reward forms (Stipp, 2000). The young age of many entrepreneurial firms may also play into employees' reward perceptions in that greater career and income growth opportunities are perceived to be available at these firms. Finally, flexible, non-bureaucratic pay systems may represent a reward in its own right.

Social identity theory suggests that individuals who value an entrepreneurial identity may be more likely to work for firms that use performance-based incentives, including risk-sharing plans (i.e. previously guaranteed salary is now a performance-based bonus; Milkovich & Newman, 2002) and stock option plans. And the three complementary theories we consider – contingency theory, agency theory, and institutional theory – differ in their predictions of reward system characteristics, and ultimately, who will be most attracted and retained to entrepreneurial firms. That is, depending on where individuals fall on the entrepreneurial continuum described earlier, they may be more likely to identify with (and work for) firms with particular pay strategies.

We expect that individuals in the substantive and exceptional categories of our heuristic will be attracted to and retained by firms who incorporate significant risk into rewards, as well as firms that provide ownership opportunities and culture. In fact, individuals seeking a risk-taking identity may be attracted to firms specifically because of the downside and upside potential of their rewards packages. For example, many entrepreneurial firms face a situation where employees' stock options are worthless at a given point in time because stock prices fall below the option exercise price. Such stock options are referred to as "underwater" options (Larre, 1999). To a degree, "underwater" options or lean incentive years may actually serve as a "badge of honor" for individuals in the exceptional and substantive categories, retaining them because their risk-taking identities are reinforced. Similarly, individuals desiring flexible policies will seek out firms that provide this work environment.

Proposition 3: The attraction and retention of substantive and exceptional identity employees will be positively associated with the degree of *risk relative to reward* in firm pay systems, the degree of *ownership* opportunities in firm rewards, and the degree of *flexibility* in a firm's pay system.

On the other hand, social identity theory suggests that those nominally seeking an identity as an "entrepreneur" will also be attracted to firms that *appear* to use entrepreneurial rewards strategies. Firms embarking on this institutional rewards strategy may make primarily symbolic efforts at conformity, rather than actual or substantive efforts (Edelman, 1992). For example, firms may offer fewer or less valuable options than similar firms, yet preserve the recruitment and retention advantages of having a stock option program. While symbolic efforts are likely to promote the attraction of nominals and some substantives, they are less likely to retain substantives once the employees assess their rewards package against those of truly entrepreneurial firms. On the other hand, in a bear market, substantives may well remain at firms employing this strategy. Symbolic efforts may be most appealing to high quality, risk-averse employees who may seek the prestige of an entrepreneurial identity through nominal stock-related plans and an entrepreneurial work culture, but in fact prefer more traditional compensation systems.

Proposition 4: The attraction and retention of nominal identity employees will be positively related to reward programs that limit *risk* and *ownership* opportunities, and that utilize *bureaucratic* pay structures (i.e. symbolic reward programs).

Proposition 5: The *attraction* of substantive, exceptional, and nominal identity employees will be positively related to symbolic reward programs.

Proposition 6a: The *retention* of nominal identity employees will be positively related to symbolic reward programs.

Proposition 6b: The *retention* of substantives and exceptional identity employees will be negatively related to symbolic reward programs.

Caveats and Conclusions

The effects of each of the theoretical drivers on reward characteristics also suggest concerns for the ultimate attraction and retention of employees. Entrepreneurial ventures are typified by a dynamic existence, if for no other reason than their potentially quick progression through the early life cycle stages. As contingencies change, the venture changes its practices to respond to the new internal and external forces. The responsive changes in the reward system, especially as it changes its approach to risk, ownership, and administration, will attract different types of employees and may not serve to retain those who were initially attracted.

Second, while risk itself may be an attractive feature to entrepreneurial employees, rationality will motivate withdrawal from the venture if continued poor performance decreases the likelihood of acceptable returns. Sharing risk also comes at a cost to the firm of potentially lower innovation and the need to "pay" for the risk with large shares of ownership (Nesheim, 2000). However, the point at which employees from the three groups will exit ventures is unclear, since a substantial portion of employees' total rewards may in fact be the level of risk involved, as well as the "experience" of working for an entrepreneurial firm.

Third, because entrepreneurial ventures face the ongoing pressure of attracting resources, they must appear legitimate, or look like a good investment. Ironically, as firms balance the appearance of legitimacy with maintaining an entrepreneurial feel, they may drive away the type of employee that responds well to the true entrepreneurial environment as they obtain the capital necessary to remain an entrepreneurial venture.

Evidence Regarding Stock Rewards

To further consider the possibilities of social identity theory and the three organizational theories reviewed above, we next review and evaluate rewards research on entrepreneurial firms. Because our search yielded few studies of entrepreneurial SMEs, we summarize research on samples that are likely to include such firms, including descriptive data and research on stock-related rewards, as well as studies on initial public offering firms, high-growth firms, and firms operating in high technology industries, among others. As noted in the introduction, we focus on stock options and other stock-related rewards.

Basic Data, By Reward Type

Stock Options

We begin with the only economy-wide data on stock options, for purposes of providing a baseline for readers to evaluate subsequent information. These data contain entrepreneurial SMEs but it is not possible to isolate the data for entrepreneurial firms. In a data set of approximately 1,600 establishments (response rate 77%), the Bureau of Labor Statistics (BLS) found that 1.7% of private sector employees and 5.3% of employees in publicly held companies received stock options in 1999 (U.S. Department of Labor, 2000). This same survey indicated that higher-paid employees remain the primary (but not sole) recipients of stock options. Establishments with greater than 100 employees had a higher rate of stock option grants than establishments with fewer than 100 employees, and this size-related finding was more pronounced in privately held firms (U.S. Department of Labor, 2000). Based upon comparisons with 1994 BLS data, it appears that there is an overall upward trend in firms' use of stock options (Rosen, 2000).

One caveat about the BLS data is that it considers only the stock options of individuals who actually received them in 1999; those holding stock options from other years were excluded from the figures. In addition, the BLS adopts a more restrictive definition of small business (i.e. 100 employees or less) than the U.S. Small Business Administration, which most commonly uses a 500-employee cutoff (see *www.sba.gov* for definitions by industry). Also, finer size distinctions could yield somewhat different information as well. For example, Heneman and Berkley (1999), in a sample of 117 Wisconsin-based employers, found that 8.8% of firms with 50–99 employees utilized stock ownership plans, while only 0.1% of employers with less than 50 employees offered stock ownership plans. In any case, though, it appears that firm size, and perhaps other variables such as organization form, may be important covariates of the staffing and reward strategies of entrepreneurial firms.

Consulting firms also survey entrepreneurial firms on this topic, but their data are generally not in the public domain. By design, consultant surveys are often limited to particular industries and types of employers, and the attention to the representativeness of sampled firms tends to be informal, although consultant surveys are not the only ones facing this issue (e.g. Lebow, Sheiner, Slifman & Starr-McCluer, 1999). We present data from iQuantic, Inc., a consulting firm working with entrepreneurial firms in the high technology industry, by way of providing an example of the types of information available from consulting firms, and to highlight the fact that information from such sources is often more detailed than BLS data.

iQuantic (2000c) collected data on equity compensation in approximately 200 high technology firms, and like the BLS data, found an upward trend in the use of stock options. They also found that non-exempt employees were more likely to receive options in smaller firms, with larger firms favoring management and executives. In addition, particularly in smaller firms, stock option grants to employees at the time of hire (i.e. new-hire grants) have substantially increased, with new-hire grants at about 150–200% of the value of options given at periodic intervals to current employees (i.e. ongoing options) (iQuantic, 2000c). Stock options typically vest over a 4-year period (i.e. employee earns 25% of options per year) with a 10-year term (i.e. employee must exercise option, or purchase stock, within this window), but the study's authors noted a trend toward shorter vesting terms. Overall, the iQuantic surveys report information for 118 firms in 1998 and 201 firms in 1999, with approximately 1000 employees per firm on average. According to the principals of iQuantic, responses appear representative of high technology businesses, and many of the surveyed firms are entrepreneurial in nature (e.g. Amazon.com, Excite@Home).

To obtain the data, iQuantic contacted employers through multiple channels and only those interested in participating in the proprietary survey received it, with almost all firms requesting surveys completing them. Because this was a survey of paying clients, iQuantic does not have traditional response rate data to report. If such a response rate could be calculated, we expect that it would be relatively low by traditional research standards.

Besides consultant data, the National Center for Employee Ownership (NCEO), a private, nonprofit membership and research organization, provides valuable information on stock-related rewards. The NCEO collects information on firms' broad-based stock option plans, defined as plans in which most employees receive options (Weeden, 2000; Weeden, Rosen, Carberry & Rodrick, 2001). Targeting this type of firm, the NCEO reports a 10% response rate (5% response rate if only usable surveys are considered) for its most recent data, and notes difficulties with pinpointing the number of firms surveyed initially (Weeden et al., 2001). The NCEO also provides a useful summary of stock option studies by consulting firms (e.g. Hewitt Associates; Watson Wyatt) and other sources (Weeden, et al., 2001; see also Blasi, Kruse, Sesil & Kroumova, 2000). Although, once again, it is difficult to determine the proportion of these firms that are entrepreneurial, broad-based plans are consistent with the reward systems entrepreneurs might choose, namely programs that share risk with employees and that provide for flexible, discretionary distribution of some options.

Overall, the NCEO estimates that between 7 to 10 million employees receive stock options (Carberry, 2000). In 2000, the NCEO documented that 44% of the firms surveyed used nonqualified stock options only, and 35% of the firms used qualified stock options only, with the remainder using both types of options. By way of comparison, NCEO's 1998 survey found that 44% and 28% of firms using only nonqualified or qualified options, respectively (Weeden, 2000).

Both NCEO surveys documented that the majority of stock option plans for non-managers are ongoing (versus one-time grants), and are distributed at the discretion of managers, usually on the basis of merit or performance. The NCEO estimates that on average, 12%–20% of the annual pay of employees is in the form of exercisable stock options (Weeden, 2000). In addition, they find that 10 years is the most common term for stock options, 3.5 years the most typical vesting schedule, and the most common method of vesting is straight vesting (i.e. the same proportion of options become exercisable each year) (Weeden, 2000).

The NCEO documented that 86% and 58% of firms provided means for cashless exercise programs, in 1998 and 2000 respectively, the difference stemming in part from the greater proportion of private firms in the 2000 sample. Cashless programs involve firms providing employees the funds for a stock purchase and immediate sale, so employees do not have to have large amounts of cash to access option gains. While most employees exercise their options this way, substantial portions of both non-management employees (37%) and executives/directors (51%) hold their stock for at least a year (Weeden et al., 2001). The most recent NCEO survey documents an average overhang (the number of options outstanding as a proportion of total common shares outstanding) of 19.7% among their sample of primarily technology industry firms (Weeden et al., 2001). Relatedly, iQuantic (2000c) found that the median stock option overhang is 15.8% in high technology firms versus 4.3% for old economy firms.

However, the "costless" nature of stock options in the eyes of shareholders may be changing, as shareholders worry about the effects of dilution on stock price. Eleven percent of high tech firms surveyed by iQuantic reported that shareholders rejected requests for additional shares in 1999, as compared to 2% in 1998 (iQuantic, 2000c). In addition, we might expect a substantial reduction in the repricing of stock options in the future, since firms must now recognize an accounting expense for the increase in stock price from the date of the grant until options are exercised, forfeited, or expired (Fox & Hauder, 2001).

Employee Stock Purchase Plans (ESPPs)
There is less descriptive data available on other stock-related rewards, and no information on stock grants. The Bureau of Labor Statistics estimates that in 1999, 4.5% of private employers offered stock purchase plans (U.S. Department of Labor). The NCEO found that the majority of firms had an ESPP, with 44% of hourly employees and over 50% of other employee groups participating (Weeden et al., 2001). (NCEO targets firms thought to have broad-based stock options, which helps explain the relatively high rate of ESPP use reported.) iQuantic found that high-tech firms favor ESPPs over employee stock ownership plans (ESOPs); the former is offered by 83% of high tech firms surveyed, and the latter by 2% of firms in their sample. Of firms that offer the opportunity to participate in an ESPP, most offer their stock at 85% of fair market value to employees (iQuantic, 2000a; Weeden et al., 2001).

Employee Stock Ownership Plans (ESOPs)

Entrepreneurial firms may be less likely than other firms to use ESOPs due to the complexity of the plans, and ESOPs' inability to motivate performance and attract and retain employees to the same extent as other stock-related rewards (Foundation for Enterprise Development, 1998). However, two factors suggest that entrepreneurial SMEs may be considering ESOPs as a reward alternative (NCEO, 2001): (a) growth in the numbers of ESOPs appears to be concentrated in smaller firms, (b) ninety percent of ESOPs are implemented in privately-held firms (although ESOPs are used by only 1.1% of privately held employers (U.S. Department of Labor, 2000)). Unfortunately, more specific information pertaining to entrepreneurial SMEs is unavailable.

The NCEO estimates that as of 1997, there were approximately 11,000 ESOPs covering 8.5 million employees. These figures can be contrasted with estimates of approximately 4,000 plans covering about 7 million workers in the mid-1980s (Conte & Svejnar, 1990). The NCEO also documents higher proportions of employee ownership in private as compared to public companies, although this may in part reflect the greater value of publicly-traded shares. The BLS offers somewhat different estimates of the number of plans (approximately 8,500) and employees covered (7.4 million) by ESOPs in 1997 (U.S. Department of Labor, 2001).

Other Rewards

We located little information on phantom stock plans and stock appreciation rights (SARs). The Bureau of Labor Statistics estimates that 0.2% and 0.1% of privately-held establishments use phantom stock or SARs, respectively (U.S. Department of Labor, 2000). Some employers award phantom stock/SARs and stock options in tandem, so the returns from the former can help employees finance the latter (Johanson, 2000). As compared to stock option plans, both reward types have the advantage of not diluting ownership among current shareholders. This issue may be especially relevant to closely held firms that need mechanisms to attract and retain key people, but whose owners want to maintain ownership levels. Such concerns might be held by a substantial number of entrepreneurial SME owners who are awaiting returns on their investments.

Research

There are a number of empirical studies pertinent to stock rewards in entrepreneurial SMEs. In this section we highlight streams of research applicable to the model presented in Fig. 1, and provide example studies in each area. Again, in light of the difficulties of identifying samples of entrepreneurial SMEs, we focus on studies likely to contain at least a subset of these types of firms, or lacking that, research that might provide a starting point for research on entrepreneurial SMEs.

Firm Environment & Resources → Firm Pay Policies
One stream of research links environmental pressures to the types of incentives used by entrepreneurial firms. For example, small, growing high technology firms appear to place a greater emphasis on incentives (including stock options and stock grants) in employees' pay mix than other firms (Balkin & Gomez-Mejia, 1984). Additional studies confirm a greater emphasis on incentives by entrepreneurial versus other firms (Barringer, Jones & Lewis, 1998; Milkovich, Gerhart & Hannon, 1991), and these findings are consistent with both the contingency and agency perspectives displayed in Fig. 1. Yet on the other hand, multiple studies have documented a *lesser* emphasis on incentive pay for firms in turbulent or risky business environments (for a discussion of these studies see Bloom & Milkovich, 1998), in which entrepreneurial SMEs often operate. The apparent divergence in the two sets of findings emphasizes the challenges of fitting pay structures to environmental contingencies and in structuring productive contracts between principals and agents (Bloom & Milkovich, 1998). Several studies consider the relationship between reward choice and institutional pressures as well, although not directly in entrepreneurial SMEs (e.g. Barringer & Milkovich, 1998; Eisenhardt, 1988)

Firm Pay Policies → Social Identity Assessment → Firm Outcomes
There were no direct examinations of entrepreneurial firms' pay policies reinforcing individuals' social identity assessments, but such relationships might be inferred from several studies. Of all the stock-related rewards, we have the most information on ESOPs. ESOPs appear useful for promoting ownership cultures, and on the whole, studies document small, but significant returns in the form of enhanced firm performance and favorable employee attitudes from ESOPs, when combined with employee participation (Ben-Ner & Jones, 1995; Kruse & Blasi, 1997). Rosen, Klein and Young (1986) found a more direct link to retention in their examination of 37 relatively small firms: the greater the financial returns of the ESOP and the more opportunities for employee participation, the higher worker satisfaction and commitment levels, and the lower their intentions to leave the organization. On the other hand, workers responded less favorably to increasing percentage ownership of firm stock, voting rights, or increases in stock value. While ESOPs may be among the least utilized stock rewards to entrepreneurial SMEs, several studies find greater effects in smaller versus larger firms (Blasi, Conte & Kruse, 1996; Onaran,

1992; but see Tucker, Nock & Toscano, 1989). Perhaps suggesting a reverse causal order, Hochner and Granrose (1985) found that the entrepreneurial foci of employees such as willingness to take risks and desire for ownership, as well as individuals' collective orientations, predicted workers' willingness to participate in an employee buyout.

There is some initial evidence on the ability of stock options to reinforce individuals' entrepreneurial identities. Dunford, Boudreau and Boswell (2001) found that part of executives' motivation for shedding underwater stock options for more lucrative pay packages was their view of money as a reputation-enhancer or status symbol. Consistent with the nominals of our entrepreneurial identity heuristic, Keef's (1994) study of employees in a large firm found that even those who sell their stock maintain ownership attitudes similar to those of actual shareholders, and different from those who have never owned the firm's stock. Similarly, Ledford and colleagues (2000) found that a majority of employees of U.S. firms, including employees with few or low-value options, reported that they were satisfied with their options (at least in a favorable economic climate) and that the options reinforced an "ownership culture." They also found that stock options were more important to high technology workers, with 54% of high technology workers versus 32% of all workers agreeing that stock options were critical to choosing an employer.

Other studies find relationships between stock-related rewards and *firm* performance, which may possibly stem from social identity processes and attraction and retention effects. Balkin and Gomez-Mejia (1987) found that the use of incentives (including stock-related rewards) was reported by managers to enhance recruitment, but not retention efforts in high growth, small, and high tech firms. Welbourne and Andrews (1999) studied 136 relatively small initial public offering (IPO) firms in multiple industries. They found that firms that shared profits or provided stock options to managers and employees were more likely to be in business five years later than firms that did not offer these rewards. Similarly, Blasi, Kruse, Sesil and Kroumova (2000) documented greater productivity, shareholder returns, and growth rates for publicly-traded companies employing broad-based stock options. Again, though, it is necessary to infer attraction and retention effects from firm performance.

Evaluation of Evidence and A Suggested Research Agenda

Basic Data
Basic descriptive data on rewards in entrepreneurial firms is still needed, especially economy-wide evidence on stock options and other stock-related rewards. Through its National Compensation Survey (NCS), the U.S. Department

of Labor has begun to survey firms about stock options practices (see *http://www.bls.gov/ncs/* for information about the NCS). We encourage the Department of Labor to gather more specific information of employers regarding the types of stock option plans being offered, detailed firm-size categories, and firm-level data on growth rates and industrial sector. In addition, more information is needed on other rewards such as stock grants, stock purchase plans, stock appreciation rights, and phantom stock plans. Readily-accessible summary information on the stock-related rewards of publicly-held firms is also lacking. In short, there is a great need for basic data on trends in the use of stock options and other stock rewards at the national level. At a minimum, we encourage continued recognition of the limitations of initial data, while acknowledging the inherent difficulties in gathering it.

Research

In addition to the clear need for better descriptive data, we propose several future research directions, guided by Fig. 1. Our agenda emphasizes social-psychological, rather than economic perspectives, in part because rewards scholars have noted a need for compensation research in this tradition (Rynes & Gerhart, 2000), and because of the limited ability of economic approaches to illuminate the underlying psychological mechanisms that drive behavior.

Firm Environment & Resources → Firm Pay Policies
In the theoretical section of this chapter we detail environmental pressures and firm resources that could influence firm pay strategies and policies. For none of these factors is there substantial research on the effectiveness of various pay responses, in staffing contexts. A good starting point for future research may be typologies of strategic pay choices (e.g. Gomez-Mejia & Balkin, 1992; Milkovich, 1988). Strategic, agency, and institutional theories suggest that entrepreneurial firms will emphasize risk in pay systems to fit turbulent environments, to create efficient contracts with agents, or even to mirror industry trends; however, more research is needed to illuminate the benefits and limitations of these strategies. The theories also predict a range of firm strategic choices in the areas of employee ownership and reward system administration.

Contingency theories of strategy suggest that firms should alter pay strategies over firm life cycles as their business environments and resources (i.e. cash flow) change. Firm or venture type, as well as firm life stage, are also crucial determinants of reward system choice in entrepreneurial firms. Potentially useful comparisons include those between the reward practices of privately-held and publicly-traded firms, and between pre-IPO versus post-IPO firms. Further defining and categorizing types of entrepreneurial firms would simplify these comparisons. Strategic contingency perspectives would also suggest consideration of firms' resource based advantages, form of innovation, industry practices, and entrepreneurial traits, when designing pay systems. For example, research on how organizations identify entrepreneurial human capital (i.e. a resource-based advantage) would be quite useful, as would research on reward systems that exploit the entrepreneurs' talents, risk tolerance, and other characteristics, while retaining them.

Another important environmental influence on firms' pay system choices is the characteristics of individual workers. The success of stock-related rewards in attracting and retaining workers to entrepreneurial firms may depend upon shifting proportions of job applicants or employees who are seeking risk, ownership, or relief from bureaucracy. No research that we reviewed recognized the fluidity of these proportions. In response, we offer an entrepreneurial identity heuristic categorizing individuals into three groups according to their entrepreneurial tendencies or traits and the contexts in which they live and work: (1) *nominals*, (2) *substantives*, and (3) *exceptionals*. Future research considering both entrepreneurial traits and context in the tradition of person-organization fit literature (e.g. Kristof, 1996) is needed.

Entrepreneurial identity research could provide initial insights regarding the effectiveness of staffing strategies, particularly long-term retention approaches, during shifting economic and other contexts. For example, some entrepreneurial firms may find it ideal to "diversify" their workforces in order to ensure retention of enough quality employees in poor economic times, as nominals and some substantives leave for safer employment. In considering individuals' entrepreneurial identities, we suggest separate examination of managers, employees, and entrepreneurs because the risk factors, ownership opportunities, and administrative features of reward plans may operate quite differently for these three groups. Studies identifying the extent to which workers are similar to or different from the entrepreneur could guide the reward decisions of entrepreneurial firms, especially choices pertaining to congruence between entrepreneur and employee compensation components.

Firm Pay Policies → *Social Identity Assessment* → *Firm Outcomes*
We have some evidence that stock rewards may yield positive staffing outcomes for firms. However, we have no direct findings regarding the impact of stock rewards on the recruitment and retention of workers, the process by which rewards translate to staffing outcomes, nor do we have evidence of the operation of stock-related rewards specifically in entrepreneurial SMEs.

In Fig. 1 we posited that three characteristics of firms' stock rewards choices will signal entrepreneurial activity to employees and potential job seekers: pay-at-risk, long-term focus/ownership, and structure and administration. There is an interdisciplinary literature on pay risk that could provide a foundation for research on how individuals' identities as risk-takers are evoked or reinforced (for a thorough review of this literature as it relates to pay systems, see Wiseman, Gomez-Mejia & Fugate, 2000). An example combining psychology and economics is research by Heath, Huddart and Lang (1999) who found that employees do not necessarily maximize returns when exercising stock options, but instead establish reference points for stock prices and act relative to these reference prices. Beyond actual risk embedded in pay forms, *perceptions* of risk are particularly important in understanding entrepreneurial identities and resulting attraction and retention outcomes (Wiseman et al., 2000).

There are also intriguing research possibilities on the depth of ownership feelings generated by various stock-related rewards. Here too we draw on the dual concepts of actual versus perceived ownership. For example, to what extent do employees perceive differences between phantom stock and SARs and "real" stock options? Initial research on stock-related rewards supports a complex view of worker perceptions of such rewards (e.g. Rosen et al., 1986). In addition, research on ESOPs suggests that employee participation and other high performance work practices may be necessary to exploit the potential of employee ownership (Blasi et al., 1996). Similarly, desirable workplace rewards such as work-life balance, personal cash flow, career enhancement and development, and the opportunities for ownership may counterbalance or enhance the effects of stock-related rewards.

There is less literature on which to rely regarding worker reactions to the structure and administration of their stock-related rewards. Issues of organization hierarchy, bureaucracy, and centralization are central to consideration of this pay characteristic. Coombs and Gomez-Mejia (1991) raise fairness concerns about differentiating employee groups by their eligibility for stock-related rewards, and research on this topic is needed, particularly in organizations with flatter job structures. Another potential administrative issue surrounds the policies and procedures for awarding stock-related compensation. Research on how entrepreneurial SMEs balance firm goals of innovation and managerial discretion with the employees' fairness concerns is needed. And initial evidence suggests that entrepreneurial firms may be more likely to emphasize manager discretion in the determination of award eligibility and in award sizes than other firms (iQuantic, 2000a, b).

We found no studies that linked cognitive or affective processes to *firm* outcomes such as survival or profitability. Perhaps studies examining individual responses (e.g. Rosen et al., 1986) could be extended to firm outcomes. The studies on stock options and firm performance by Blasi and colleagues (2000) and Welbourne and colleagues (e.g. Welbourne & Andrews, 1996) are a promising start for firm-level research as well. Future research should improve upon conceptual and measurement problems such as the confounding of the effects of various reward types (e.g. Welbourne & Andrews, 1996).

We suggest drawing on a mix of additional theories of organizational behavior to understand worker judgments about entrepreneurial rewards, especially considering that the technical complexity of stock-related rewards makes worker reactions difficult to predict. We offer a discussion of two of these relevant theories: psychological contracts and organizational justice. Both literatures rely upon the important concepts of employee expectations regarding reward systems (Major, 1994) and the referents with which employees judge their rewards (Goodman, 1974).

Psychological contracts are employees' perceptions of the work agreements and relationships they have with their employers (Rousseau, 1995). Generally speaking, long-term rewards such as stock options should create relational contracts, such that the employees seeking ownership identities are more likely to be committed to that employer in the long term and vice versa. However, stock-related rewards that do not pay out as expected or do not exceed the total risk faced by employees, will probably elicit less favorable reactions. To the extent that the employees feel misled or unfairly treated by the reward system, they will judge that violations of the psychological contract have occurred, and be more susceptible to turnover. Complicating matters is rapid change in entrepreneurial firms, which may present sustained challenges to psychological contracts.

Organizational justice issues also abound with stock-related rewards (Folger, 1986; Greenberg, 1990). Outcome fairness issues in entrepreneurial firms may focus on extent to which workers blame top management of the firm versus themselves, for unfavorable returns on their stock-related rewards. There are also potential fairness issues surrounding employers' decisions about repricing or replacing underwater stock options. Both situations have direct implications for the retention of workers.

The tenets of justice theories also suggest the necessity of communicating stock-related compensation forms effectively to workers in order to maximize their returns for employers (Milkovich & Newman, 2002). We recommend that researchers borrow from the organizational communication literature (Tucker, Meyer & Westerman, 1996) to consider workers' understandings of their pay systems and subsequent staffing outcomes. For instance, employees may react differently when firms communicate the numbers of options rather than the value or potential value of the options, which can be two different figures (iQuantic, 2000c). Other communications topics warranting attention are the relative efficacy of various types and amounts of stock-related information provided to employees.

In summary, while initial work indirectly supports the propositions generated by an integration of organizational theories and social identity theory, we need better data and additional research on stock-related rewards in entrepreneurial SMEs. In addition to the potential usefulness of this information, entrepreneurial SMEs provide new and relevant settings in which to study existing theories of compensation strategy and micro-level employment processes.

Early in the chapter, we restricted our theory discussion the psychological, individual difference construct of social identity. As we emerge from this discussion, it is important to recognize the economic context within which social identity operates. As mentioned earlier, economic boundaries such as the reservation wage have been demonstrated to exist (Osborn, 1990; Rynes, Schwab & Heneman, 1983; Tromski & Subrich, 1990), and studies of social identity must at some point address this issue. For example, it is possible that exceptionals set lower non-compensatory cutoffs for the expected outcomes from stock-related rewards than do nominals. If true, this would serve as an additional explanation for why retention rate differences between these two groups might occur as the economic environment and expected value of stock-related rewards changes. In future work, we urge additional interdisciplinary work to capture these complexities.

CONCLUSION

Entrepreneurial SMEs face critical attraction and retention issues, including the securing of adequate numbers of employees in favorable economic times or high growth periods, as well hiring the right mix of talent for entrepreneurial activities. Similar to larger, more established firms, entrepreneurial firms experience strategic contingency, agency, and institutional pressures, and they must decide how to address these pressures within the constraints of their business environments. Firms rely upon various rewards strategies to "fit" the pressures at hand, address potential principal and agent conflicts, and satisfy stakeholder expectations. We considered three important reward choices for entrepreneurial firms: pay-at-risk, ownership and a long-term focus, and structure/administration. Rewards decisions in these areas have the potential to signal to job seekers and employees the extent to which firms are entrepreneurial; and individuals seeking entrepreneurial identities or appearances offered by these firms will be recruited and retained. In the chapter, we urged consideration not only of this process, but also the likely fluid populations of those with exceptional, substantive, and nominal entrepreneurial orientations in the workforce – a product of individuals' entrepreneurial traits and the worlds in which they live. Our framework complements existing rewards research, and is intended to help guide future work on stock-related rewards in entrepreneurial firms.

ACKNOWLEDGMENTS

The authors thank editors Jerry Katz and Theresa Welbourne for very helpful guidance and suggestions on the chapter. We also thank Kim Reifel for valuable research assistance.

REFERENCES

Ajzen, I. (1991). The theory of planned behavior. *Organizational Behavior and Human Decision Processes, 50,* 179–211.
Ajzen, I., & Fishbein, M. (1977). Attitude-behavior relations: A theoretical analysis and review of empirical research. *Psychological Bulletin, 84,* 888–918.
Ajzen, I., & Fishbein, M. (1980). *Understanding attitudes and predicting social behavior.* Englewood Cliffs, NJ: Prentice-Hall.
Balkin, D. B., & Gomez-Mejia, L. R. (1984). Determinants of R and D compensation strategies in the high tech industry. *Personnel Psychology, 37,* 635–650.
Balkin, D. B., & Gomez-Mejia, L. R. (1987). Toward a contingency theory of compensation strategy. *Strategic Management Journal, 8,* 169–182.
Barber, A. E., & Bretz, R. D., Jr. (2000). Compensation, attraction, and retention. In: S. L. Rynes & B. Gerhart (Eds), *Compensation in Organizations* (pp. 32–60). San Francisco: Jossey-Bass, Inc.
Barney, J. B. (1991). Firm resources and sustained competitive advantage. *Journal of Management, 17,* 99–120.
Barney, J. B. (2001). Is the resource-based 'view' a useful perspective for strategic management research? Yes. *Academy of Management Review, 26,* 41–56.
Barney, J. B., & Wright, P. M. (1998). On becoming a strategic partner: The role of human resources in gaining competitive advantage. *Human Resource Management Journal, 37,* 31–46.
Baron, J. N., & Kreps, D. M. (1999). *Strategic human resources: Frameworks for general managers.* New York NY: John Wiley & Sons.
Barringer, B. R., Jones, F. F., & Lewis, P. S. (1998). A qualitative study of the management practices of rapid-growth firms and how rapid-growth firms mitigate the managerial capacity problem. *Journal of Development Entrepreneurship, 3,* 97–122.
Barringer, M., & Milkovich, G. T. (1998). A theoretical exploration of the adoption and design of flexible benefit plans: A case of human resource innovation. *Academy of Management Review, 23,* 305–324.
Beatty, R. P., & Zajac, E. J. (1994). Managerial incentives, monitoring, and risk bearing: A study of executive compensation, ownership, and board structure in initial public offerings. *Administrative Science Quarterly, 39,* 313–335.

Ben-Ner, A., & Jones, D. C. (1995). Employee participation, ownership, and productivity: A theoretical framework. *Industrial Relations, 34*, 532–554.

Blasi, J., Conte, M., & Kruse, D. (1996). Employee stock ownership and corporate performance among public companies. *Industrial & Labor Relations Review, 50*, 60–79.

Blasi, J., Kruse, D., Sesil, J., & Kroumova, M. (2000). Broad-based stock options and company performance: What the research tells us. In: S. Riddick (Ed.), *Stock Options, Corporate Performance, and Organizational Change* (pp. 1–34). Oakland: National Center for Employee Ownership.

Bloom, M., & Milkovich, G. T. (1998). Relationships among risk, incentive pay, and organizational performance. *Academy of Management Journal, 41*, 283–297.

Cable, D. M., & Judge, T. A. (1994). Pay preferences and job search decisions: A person-organization fit perspective. *Personnel Psychology, 47*, 317–348.

Carberry, E. (2000). Introduction. In: S. Riddick (Ed.), *The Stock Options Book* (3rd ed., rev., pp. 1–21). Oakland: National Center for Employee Ownership.

Carland, J. W., Hoy, F., Boulton, W. R., & Carland, J. A. (1984). Differentiating entrepreneurs from small business owners: A conceptualization. *Academy of Management Review, 9*, 354–359.

Conte, M. A., & Svejnar, J. (1990). The performance effects of employee ownership plans. In: A. S. Blinder (Ed.), *Paying for Productivity: A Look at the Evidence*. Washington, D.C.: Brookings Institution.

Coombs, G. Jr., & Gomez-Mejia, L. R. (1991). Cross-functional pay strategies in high-technology firms. *Compensation and Benefits Review, 23*, 40–48.

DiMaggio, P. J., & Powell, W. W. (1983). The iron cage revisited: Institutional isomorphism and collective rationality in organizational fields. *American Sociological Review, 48*, 147–160.

Dunford, B. B., Boudreau, J. W., & Boswell, W. R. (2001). The dark side of stock options: Underwater options and employee separation. Paper presented at the 2001 Academy of Management Meetings, Washington, D.C.

Edelman, L. B. (1992). Legal ambiguity and symbolic structures: Organizational mediation of civil rights law. *American Journal of Sociology, 97*, 1531–1576.

Ehrenberg, R. G., & Smith, R. S. (2000). *Modern labor economics* (7th ed.). New York: Addison Wesley Longman.

Eisenhardt, K. M. (1988). Agency- and institutional-theory explanations: The case of retail sales compensation. *Academy of Management Journal, 31*, 488–511.

Eisenhardt, K. M. (1989). Agency theory: An assessment and review. *Academy of Management Review, 14*, 1, 57–74.

Fama, E. F., & Jensen, M. C. (1983). Separation of ownership and control. *Journal of Law and Economics, 26*, 301–324.

Folger, R. (1986). Rethinking equity theory: A referent cognitions model. In: H. W. Bierhoff, R. L. Cohen & J. Greenberg (Eds), *Justice in Social Relations* (pp. 145–162). New York: Plenum Press.

Foundation for Enterprise Development (1998). *The entrepreneur's guide to equity compensation* (2nd ed.). Washington, D.C.

Fox, J. (1997). The next best thing to free money. *Fortune, 136*(1)(July 7), 52–62.

Fox, R. D., & Hauder, E. A. (2001). Sending out an SOS. Methods for companies to resuscitate underwater stock options. *World at Work Journal, 10*(2), 92–96.

Frank, R. H. (1996). What price the moral high ground? *Southern Economic Journal, 63*, 1–17.

Gatewood, R. D., Gowan, M. A., & Lautenschlager, D. J. (1993). Corporate image, recruitment image, and initial job choice decisions. *Academy of Management Journal, 36*, 414–427.

Gerhart, B. (2000). Compensation strategy and organizational performance. In: S. L. Rynes & B. Gerhart (Eds), *Compensation in Organizations* (pp. 151–194). San Francisco: Jossey-Bass.

Gerhart, B., Trevor, C. O., & Graham, M. E. (1996). New directions in compensation research: Synergies, risk and survival. *Research in Personnel and Human Resources Management, 14*, 143–203. Greenwich, CT: JAI Press.

Gomez-Mejia, L. R., & Balkin, D. B. (1992). *Compensation, organizational strategy and firm performance*. Cinncinati, OH: South-Western College Publishing.

Gomez-Mejia L. R., & Welbourne, T. M. (1988). Compensation strategy: An overview and future steps. *Human Resource Planning, 11*, 173–189.

Goodman, P. S. (1974). An examination of referents used in the evaluation of pay. *Organizational Behavior and Human Performance, 12*, 170–195.

Greenberg, J. (1990). Organizational justice: Yesterday, today, and tomorrow. *Journal of Management, 16*, 399–432.

Heath, C., Huddart, S., & Lang, M. (1999). Psychological factors and stock option exercise. *The Quarterly Journal of Economics, 114*, 601–627.

Heneman, H. G., & Berkley, R. A. (1999). Applicant attraction practices and outcomes among small businesses. *Journal of Small Business Management, 37*, 53–74.

Heneman, R. L., Tansky, J. W., & Camp, S. M. (2000). Human resource management practices in small and medium-sized enterprises: Unanswered questions and future research perspectives. *Entrepreneurship Theory and Practice, 25*, 11–26.

Hochner, A., & Granrose, C. S. (1985). Sources of motivation to choose employee ownership as an alternative to job loss. *Academy of Management Journal, 28*, 860–875.

iQuantic (2000a). *Equity practices survey for the high technology industries*. San Francisco: iQuantic.

iQuantic (2000b). *Pre-IPO equity practices survey for the high technology industries*. San Francisco: iQuantic.

iQuantic (2000c). *Trends in equity compensation*. San Francisco: iQuantic.

Jackson, S. E., & Schuler, R. S. (1995). Understanding human resource management in the context of organizations and their environments. *Annual Review of Psychology, 46*, 237–264.

Johanson, D. R. (2000). Employee stock options and related equity incentives. In: S. Riddick (Ed.), *The Stock Options Book* (3rd ed., rev., pp. 23–62). Oakland: National Center for Employee Ownership.

Katz, J. A., Aldrich, H. E., Welbourne, T. M., & Williams, P. M. (2000). Guest editors' comments: Special issue on human resource management and the SME: Toward a new synthesis. *Entrepreneurship Theory and Practice, 25*(1), 7–10.

Keef, S. P. (1994). Employee share ownership and job attitudes: The effects of share sale. *Asia Pacific Journal of Management, 11*, 91–102.

Kim, M. (1999). Where the grass is greener: Voluntary turnover and wage premiums. *Industrial Relations, 38*, 584–603.

Kirzner, I. M. (1973). *Competition and entrepreneurship*. Chicago: University of Chicago Press.

Kristof, A. L. (1996). Person-organization fit: An integrative review of its conceptualizations, measurement, and implications. *Personnel Psychology, 49*, 1–49.

Kruse, D. L., & Blasi, J. R. (1997). Employee ownership, employee attitudes, and firm performance: A review of the evidence. In: D. Lewin, D. J. B. Mitchell & M. A. Zaidi (Eds), *The Human Resource Management Handbook* (Parts 1–3, pp. 113–151). Greenwich, CT: JAI Press.

Larre, E. C. (1999). Equity-based compensation at high-growth companies: Responding to long-term stock price declines. *Compensation and Benefits Review, 31*, 44–53.

Lebow, D., Sheiner, L., Slifman, L., & Starr-McCluer, M. (1999). *Recent trends in compensation practices.* Washington, D.C.: Federal Reserve.

Ledford, G., Mulvey, P., & LeBlanc, P. (2000). *The Rewards of Work.* Scottsdale, AZ: WorldatWork and Sibson & Company.

Lublin, J. S. (1999). An e-company CEO is also the Recruiter-in-Chief – Hiring becomes the boss's main job, as start-up aims to grow in a tight labor market. *Wall Street Journal,* November 9, B1–2.

Major, B. (1994). From social inequality to personal entitlement: The role of social comparisons, legitimacy appraisals, and group membership. *Advances in Experimental Social Psychology, 26*, 293–355.

Meyer, J. W., & Rowan, B. (1977). Institutionalized organizations: Formal structure as myth and ceremony. *American Journal of Sociology, 2*, 340–363.

Milkovich, G. T. (1988). A strategic perspective on compensation management. In: K. M. Rowland & G. R. Ferris (Eds), *Research in Personnel and Human Resource Management* (Vol. 6, pp. 263–288). Greenwich, CT: JAI Press.

Milkovich, G. T., Gerhart, B., & Hannon, J. (1991). The effects of research and development intensity on managerial compensation in large organizations. *The Journal of High Technology Management Research, 2*, 133–150.

Milkovich, G. T., & Newman, J. M. (2002). *Compensation* (7th ed.). New York: McGraw-Hill Irwin.

National Center for Employee Ownership (NCEO) (2001). *A statistical profile of employee ownership, http://nceo.org/library/eo_stat.html.* Oakland.

Nesheim, J. L. (2000). *High tech start up: Creating successful new high tech companies.* New York: Free Press.

O'Connell, J., & Bartlett, C. A. (1998). *Lincoln Electric: Venturing Abroad* (Harvard Business Review Case 9-398-095). Boston: Harvard Business School Publishing.

Oliver, C. (1991). Strategic responses to institutional processes. *Academy of Management Review, 16*, 145–179.

Onaran, Y. (1992). Workers as owners: An empirical comparison of intra-firm inequalities at employee-owned and conventional companies. *Human Relations, 45*, 1213–1235.

Osborn, D. P. (1990). A reexamination of the organizational choice process. *Journal of Vocational Behavior, 36*, 45–60.

Porter, M. E. (1985). *Competitive advantage.* New York: Free Press.

Porter, M. E. (1990). *Competitive advantage of nations.* New York: Free Press.

Rosen, C. (2000). New Bureau of Labor Statistics data on stock options. *Employee Ownership Update, http://nceo.org/columns/cr84.html.* Oakland: National Center for Employee Ownership.

Rosen, C. M., Klein, K. J., & Young, K. M. (1986). *Employee ownership in America: The equity solution.* Lexington, MA: Lexington Books.

Rousseau, D. M. (1995). *Psychological contracts in organizations: Understanding written and unwritten agreements.* Thousand Oaks, CA: Sage.

Rynes, S. L., & Gerhart, B. (2000). *Compensation in organizations.* New York: Jossey-Bass.

Rynes, S. L., Schwab, D. P., & Heneman, H. G., III. (1983). The role of pay and market pay variability in job application decisions. *Organizational Behavior and Human Performance, 31*, 353–364.

Shane, S., & Venkataraman, S. (2000). The promise of entrepreneurship as a field of research. *Academy of Management Journal, 25*, 217–226.

Snarr, B. B. (2000). Equity compensation in closely held companies. In: S. Riddick (Ed.), *The Stock Options Book* (3rd ed., rev., pp. 159–180). Oakland: National Center for Employee Ownership.

Staw, B. M., & Epstein, L. D. (2000). What bandwagons bring: Effects of popular management techniques on corporate performance, reputation, and CEO pay. *Administrative Science Quarterly, 45*, 523–556.

Stevenson, H. (2000). The six dimensions of entrepreneurship. In: S. Birley & D. F. Muzyka (Eds), *Mastering Entrepreneurship* (pp. 8–13). London: Financial Times/Prentice Hall.

Stewart, W. H., Watson, W. E., Carland, J. C., & Carland, J. W. (1998). A proclivity for entrepreneurship: A comparison of entrepreneurs, small business owners, and corporate managers. *Journal of Business Venturing, 14*, 189–214.

Stipp, D. (2000). Celera, the genome, and the fruit-fly lady. *Fortune, 142*(2), 148–151.

Suchman, M. C. (1995). Managing legitimacy: Strategic and institutional approaches. *Academy of Management Review, 20*, 571–610.

Sykes, H. B. (1992). Incentive compensation for corporate venture personnel. *Journal of Business Venturing, 7*, 253–265.

Tajfel, H. (1982). *Social identity and intergroup relations*. Cambridge, U.K.: Cambridge University Press.

Tromski, J. E., & Subich, L. M. (1990). College students' perceptions of the acceptability of below-average salary offers. *Journal of Vocational Behavior, 37*, 196–208.

Tucker, M. L., Meyer, G. D., & Westerman, J. W. (1996). Organizational communication: Development of internal strategic competitive advantage. *The Journal of Business Communication, 33*, 51–69.

Tucker, J., Nock, S. L., & Toscano, D. J. (1989). Employee ownership and perceptions of work. The Effect of an employee stock ownership plan. *Work and Occupations, 16*, 26–42.

Tully, S. (2000). The party's over. *Fortune, 142*(1)(June 26), 156–160.

Turban, D. B., & Greening, D. W. (1997). Corporate social performance and organizational attractiveness to prospective employees. *Academy of Management Journal, 40*, 658–672.

Turner, J. C., & Giles, H. (1981). *Intergroup behavior*. New York: Blackwell.

Tyson, S. (1997). Human resource strategy: A process for managing the contribution of HRM to organizational performance. *International Journal of Human Resource Management, 8*, 277–290.

U.S. Department of Labor (2000). Pilot survey on the incidence of stock options in private industry in 1999 (News Release, 10 October). Washington, D.C.: Bureau of Labor Statistics.

U.S. Department of Labor (2001). Abstract of 1997 Form 5500 Annual Reports, Table D12. *Private Pension Plan Bulletin No. 10*. Washington, D.C.: Pension and Welfare Benefits Administration.

University of Southern California (2001). *Compendium of entrepreneur programs*. 16 September, Website: www.marshall.usc.edu/entrepreneur/postoffice/compendium/Index.cfm.

Wanderer, M. (2000). Dot-comp: A 'traditional' pay plan with a cutting edge. *World at Work Journal, 9*, 15–24.

Weeden, R. (2000). The 1998 NCEO broad-based stock option survey. In: S. Riddick (Ed.), *The Stock Options Book* (3rd ed., rev., pp. 215–270). Oakland: National Center for Employee Ownership.

Weeden, R., Rosen, C., Carberry, E., & Rodrick, S. (2001). *Current practices in stock option plan design* (2nd ed.). Oakland: National Center for Employee Ownership.

Welbourne, T. M., & Andrews, A. O. (1996). Predicting the performance of initial public offerings: Should human resource management be in the equation? *Academy of Management Journal, 39*, 891–919.

Wiseman, R. M., Gomez-Mejia, L. R., & Fugate, M. (2000). Rethinking compensation risk. In: S. L. Rynes & B. Gerhart (Eds), *Compensation in Organizations* (pp. 311–347). San Francisco: Jossey-Bass.
Wright, P. M., & McMahan, G. C. (1992). Theoretical perspectives for strategic human resource management. *Journal of Management, 18*, 295–320.

6. PERFORMANCE AND GROWTH IN ENTREPRENEURIAL FIRMS: REVISITING THE UNION-PERFORMANCE RELATIONSHIP

Rosemary Batt and Theresa M. Welbourne

INTRODUCTION

A substantial body of research has examined the relationship between unions and firm performance. It generally has found a positive relationship between unions and productivity and a negative relationship between unions and financial performance (Freeman & Medoff, 1984; Addison & Hirsch, 1989; Belman, 1992; Freeman, 1992). The exit/voice model is most commonly used to explain this paradox (Freeman & Medoff, 1984). Freeman and Medoff argued that the "monopoly power" of unions leads to high union wages and restrictive work rules, both of which raise the costs of production and lower profit margins. The presence of unions, however, also lowers production costs by reducing turnover (exit) and providing incentives for employee effort through "collective voice." Thus, unionized workplaces may be at once more productive but less profitable because employees share in productivity gains through higher wages.

Managing People in Entrepreneurial Organizations, Volume 5, pages 147–174.
Copyright © 2002 by Elsevier Science Ltd.
All rights of reproduction in any form reserved.
ISBN: 0-7623-0877-X

There are a number of reasons, however, why the findings from prior research may not generalize to firms in the 1990s, particularly, high tech and entrepreneurial firms. First, under the exit/voice model, the relationship between unions and firm performance is an empirical question that depends on the net effect of opposing forces. Most of the empirical evidence on this topic, however, draws on data from U.S. manufacturing firms in the post-World War II period, when mass production models dominated the approach to organizing work, union power was at its height, and union-management relations were largely adversarial. In the 1990s, however, several forces have changed. First, U.S. firms, particularly high tech and entrepreneurial firms, have adopted much more flexible approaches to organizing work, such as "high performance work systems" (Appelbaum & Batt, 1994), which reduce status differences between workers and managers. Second, union power has dropped significantly, with union membership falling from 24% of the private sector workforce in 1973 to about 10% in 1995 (Bureau of Labor Statistics). Third, mutual gains and win-win approaches to bargaining (Walton & McKersie, 1965) have transformed union-management relationships in many instances, leading to greater co-operation and less zero-sum conflict.

For these reasons, we decided to revisit the question of the relationship between unions and firm performance by drawing on a unique set of 464 entrepreneurial firms at the time of their initial public offering (IPO) in 1993 and their subsequent financial performance through 1996. This is an important context to examine because entrepreneurial firms are a major source of economic growth in the U.S. They are known for their innovation and flexibility in responding to rapidly changing market demand. Unions are conventionally viewed as barriers to change and anathema to the type of flexibility and quick response needed to compete in entrepreneurial markets. Thus, it is important to know whether unions pose a negative threat to financial performance and economic growth in this important sector of the economy.

This is also an appropriate context for exploring the topic of unions and financial performance because most entrepreneurial firms are small and young. They are less likely to have the kind of "monopoly union power," conflictual labor management relations, or rigid work rules traditionally found in large U.S. mass production enterprises – the context of much prior research on unions and financial performance. In this context, firms and unions have more opportunity to adopt new forms of work organization and labor-management relations.

In this chapter, we first review the prior literature on this topic, including theoretical frameworks and the empirical evidence on the union-performance relationship. Then, we present our quantitative case study of unions and financial performance in entrepreneurial firms. In the final section, we consider our findings in the context of the prior literature and suggest avenues for future research.

PRIOR LITERATURE

Theoretical Perspectives

In the exit/voice framework, as applied to the employment relationship by Freeman and Medoff (1984), the relationship between unions and firm performance is the net result of opposing forces (see Fig. 1). On the one hand, the "monopoly power" of unions allows unions to negotiate wages and benefits that are above the market rate. In addition, unions may use their power to negotiate work rules that limit flexibility in the deployment of labor. In U.S. manufacturing firms, for example, many unions adopted a strategy of "job control" unionism in order to gain job security for members. That is, because there was no implicit or explicit employment security for workers, unions fought for seniority rights in layoff procedures and for job descriptions that prevented management from substituting supervisors for workers in direct production. These types of work rules tended to increase production costs.

On the other hand, high wages may attract a higher skilled and more productive workforce, and union presence may also reduce certain types of production costs, particularly the costs of recruitment, selection, and initial training related to employee turnover. In theory, workers in union settings quit less for two reasons: because their pay and benefits are higher than comparable non-union jobs and because they have opportunities for "collective voice," which allow them to express dissatisfaction and participate in correcting problems in the workplace rather than quitting.

Unionization institutionalizes the collective voice of employees with the support of labor law and creates a governance structure that replaces the unilateral authority of management. As a result, historically, union workplaces developed internal labor market rules that provided workers with some protection against external labor market competition (Jacoby, 1985; Doeringer & Piore, 1971). Union workers quit less and accrued more tenure than otherwise comparable non-union workers. In addition, with lower turnover, firms are more likely to invest in firm-specific training (Doeringer & Piore, 1971), which may raise productivity. Higher wages also may induce firms to take a higher productivity approach (Slichter, Healy & Livernash, 1960) or invest more in labor saving technology. Thus, union presence may contribute to higher productivity both by lowering production costs and by raising productivity.

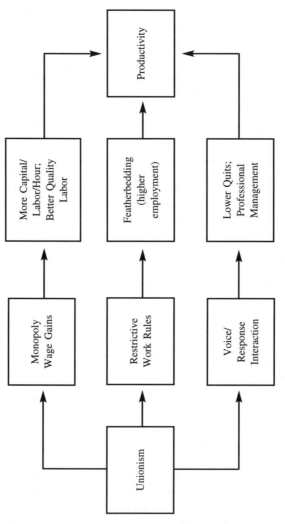

Fig. 1. Exit/Voice Model of Union-Performance Relationship.

Source: Freeman and Medoff (1984, p. 163).

Industrial relations theory provides a fuller explanation for the contingent relationship between unions and performance outcomes. In their seminal book on the transformation of U.S. industrial relations, Kochan, Katz and McKersie (1986) argued that union-management relations are contingent on many factors, including market and institutional factors, managerial and union strategy, the history of collective bargaining, and the level of trust and cooperation between management and labor (Fig. 2). First, external factors, such as the degree of competitiveness in the market and the state of existing union institutions, will affect union-management relations inside the firm. Second, Kochan, Katz and McKersie argued that the "strategic choices" of the actors play an independent role in shaping the degree of cooperation or adversarialism that exists in the union-management relationship, which in turn, influences firm-level outcomes. Third, they noted the importance of union and management strategies and actions at three levels of the relationship – at the level of business strategy, at the level of HR policies and collective bargaining, and at the level of the workplace. Thus, within certain constraints imposed by external market and institutional forces, the individual actors have considerable latitude to construct alternative approaches to solving problems, including those that maximize the benefits for all stakeholders involved. In keeping with this transformation thesis, industrial relations experts have developed "mutual gains" or win-win approaches to bargaining based on identifying the "integrative" issues in which both parties have mutual interests (Walton & McKersie, 1965). Mutual gains approaches tend to reduce labor-management conflict and create opportunities for union-management partnerships based on principles of shared governance.

Empirical Evidence

Both the exit/voice model of Freeman and Medoff and the transformation thesis of Kochan, Katz, and McKersie provide a contingency framework for understanding the relationship between unions and firm performance. However, empirical studies over the last two decades have demonstrated a consistent negative relationship between unions and financial performance and a consistent positive relationship between unions and productivity. If the effect of unions is context-specific, why have researchers consistently found these results? Under what conditions might unionization contribute positively to financial performance as well? To explore these questions, we next turn to a review and critique of the existing empirical evidence and discuss the ways in which prior research may be contingent on specific historical factors.

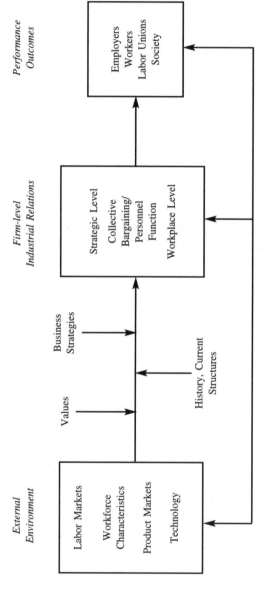

Fig. 2. Strategic Choice Model of Union-Performance Relationship.

Source: Kochan, Katz and McKersie (1986, p. 11).

Unions, Monopoly Power, and Financial Performance

Empirical studies that have found a significant negative relationship between unions and financial performance have used a variety of financial outcome measures, including price-cost margin, net revenues per unit of capital, Tobin's q, and stock market value. Addison and Hirsch's (1989) review of sixteen studies that used various methodologies and measures of profitability found a consistent large negative relationship between unions and financial performance. Freeman's review (1992) of studies in the U.K. and Belman's (1992) review of the literature reached similar conclusions. Bronars and Deere (1990) and Bronars, Deere and Stacey (1994) found that union elections were associated with significant declines in Tobin's q, the ratio of excess market value to sales, and the ratio of net operating income to sales.

Despite this seeming consistency, however, the empirical research also supports the argument that the relationship between unions and financial performance varies considerably by context. Hirsch (1991, 1992), for example, found a negative relationship between unions and profitability, but variation across industries. Allen (e.g. 1986, 1988) reported no negative relationship between unions and profits in the construction industry. Others have found that market conditions influence the extent to which unionized firms have lower profitability. One argument, that unions extract quasi-rents in monopoly markets with "abnormally high returns" (Freeman & Medoff, 1984), is supported by Karier (1985, 1988). He found that unions were associated with lower price-cost margins in industries with highly concentrated ownership structures (such as auto assembly) but had no such association in low concentration industries (such as construction). Hirsch and Connolly (1987), by contrast, found no variation in union effect by the degree of market concentration, but did find evidence that other market conditions such as the degree of foreign competition and a firm's market share were significant predictors of union rent-sharing.

Other researchers have found that the relationship between unions and financial outcomes varies over time. For example, Kendrick and Grossman (1980) reported a negative relationship between unions and productivity growth from 1948–1966, but a positive one between 1967 and 1978. Connerton, Freeman and Medoff (1983), cited in Belman (1992), found that union mines were 30% more productive than non-union mines in the 1960s, but only 15% more productive in the 1970s. This variation across industries and over time may be attributed to many factors including variation in union power, market conditions, and the changing strategies and relations between union and management.

A large literature also demonstrates that the relationship between unions and firm performance varies by the degree of labor-management conflict rather than union presence per se. Kendrick and Grossman (1980), for example, noted that when they included measures of strike activity, the positive relationship between unions and productivity between 1967 and 1978 was eliminated. Connerton et. al. (1983, cited in Belman (1992)) attributed the reduction in productivity in unionized mines in the 1970s to increased labor-management conflict and strike-related activity. Kochan, Katz and Gobielle (1983) found that a better industrial relations climate led to improvements in quality (but not output) is a study of eighteen General Motors plants in the mid-1970s. Similarly, Keefe (1992) reviewed empirical studies of unions and technological innovation and found that the outcomes were context specific. Martinello et al. (1995) conducted a study of the effects of union certification on expected financial performance of firms. They reported no strong negative reaction to certification in general, but found increased negative returns where the certification process was more conflictual.

Given the importance of industry and the labor-management context for firm performance, therefore, it is reasonable to examine whether there are certain contexts in which unions may be associated with better financial performance. The existing research on unions and financial performance, for example, may be limited because it is based on data from U.S. manufacturing in the 1960s through early 1980s (e.g. Addison & Hirsch, 1989; Belman, 1992; Becker & Olson, 1989, 1992; Hirsch, 1991, 1992). This represents a specific historical context in which oligopolistic markets and national bargaining agreements gave unions considerable monopoly leverage for extracting quasi-rents. At the same time, U.S. labor-management relations were highly adversarial and industrial unions engaged in "job control unionism". Under job control unionism, unions bargained wages for specific jobs and enforced adherence to job descriptions in order to increase job security in the absence of explicit security agreements. This approach resulted in arguably greater inflexibility in work organization, thus constraining productivity and process innovations (some empirical research has found that combining job classifications modestly improves economic performance, Keefe & Katz, 1990). In sum, much of the evidence showing a negative relationship between unions and financial performance may be understood as the result of oligopolistic markets, mass production approaches to work organization, and conflictual labor relations in a particular historical period.

In fact, more recent studies have found that the negative relationship between unions and firm performance fell in the 1980s. Menezes-Filho (1997), for example, analyzed data on unions and firm financial performance in the U.K. in the 1980s and demonstrated that the negative union effect declined sharply over the course of the decade. Hirsch and Morgan (1994) found an overall negative relationship between unions and shareholder rates of return between 1973 and 1987; but the differences in shareholder risk in union and nonunion firms were small and insignificant by the mid-1980s. Becker (1995) found that shareholders' average returns from takeover activity in the 1980s were higher for unionized target firms compared to non-union target firms, with unionized workers losing the equivalent of 50% of the wage premium normally associated with union coverage. The results of these studies could reflect declining union power and concession bargaining over wages and work rules, or changes in union-management relations and the introduction of new work systems. In either case, we would expect the patterns found in the 1980s to continue in the 1990s.

A perhaps more serious issue is whether unions are associated with lower economic growth or firm investment in research and development (R&D). Hirsch and Connolly (1987), among others, argue that measuring profitability in terms of price-cost margin (PCM), as is common in many studies, is a limited and static indicator. They argue that stock market valuations such as Tobin's q (the ratio of a firm's market value to replacement value) and investment in R&D are more important indicators of firm value and dynamic growth. A negative relationship between unionization and Tobin's q is interpreted to mean that unions negatively affect intangible rents. In this area, researchers have found mixed results as well. Some studies found that unionized firms in the U.S. have lower Tobin's q and lower R&D investment (e.g. Connolly, Hirsch & Hirschey, 1986; Hirsch & Connolly, 1987). By contrast, Wadhwani (1989) found no effect for British unions; and in a recent study, Menezes-Filho et al. (1998) found that a negative association between unions and R&D investment became statistically insignificant in the presence of controls for industry and cohort effects.

In sum, while researchers have found a consistent negative relationship between unions and financial performance, they have also found that the magnitude of the relationship depends on market and union institutional conditions. Moreover, some studies suggest that the magnitude and significance of the relationship have declined over the same time period that union power has been declining in North America and Britain.

Unions, Collective Voice, and High Performance Work Systems

The positive association between unions and productivity rests in part on studies of turnover, which consistently demonstrate that union facilities have lower turnover rates than non-union facilities, both in the United States and other countries (Cotton & Tuttle, 1986; Miller & Mulvey, 1991; Wilson & Peel, 1991; Lincoln & Kalleberg, 1996; Delery, Gupta, Shaw, Jenkins & Ganster, 2000;

Batt, Colvin & Keefe, 2002). Moreover, other studies suggest it is the collective voice of unions, rather than high wages alone, that account for lower quits among union members. For example, unionized workplaces have lower quit rates even after controlling for wages, (Freeman, 1980; Batt, Colvin & Keefe, 2002). In addition, due process (grievance and arbitration) procedures negotiated by unions significantly lower quit rates (Ichniowski and Lewin, 1987), with stronger procedures having stronger effects on quit rates (Rees, 1991).

The more controversial issue is whether the presence of unions also raises operational performance, based on the argument that long term employment relations induce firms to invest in firm-specific training and higher productivity work systems. Some research does support this view, with Norsworthy and Zabala (1986) finding a direct relationship between higher turnover and lower total factor productivity. After reviewing 30 studies investigating the union effects on productivity, Belman (1992) concluded that the majority of studies found that unions were associated with higher productivity. In a more recent study, Batt (2002) examined sales growth in a nationally representative sample of service and sales establishments and found that unions significantly lowered quit rates and that lower quit rates led to higher sales growth.

If union workplaces have lower turnover and higher productivity than their non-union counterparts, then under what conditions do these operational advantages translate into higher financial performance? In the exit/voice model, this might occur if competitive market conditions limit the extent to which unions are able to extract "monopoly rents" or if union institutions are too weak to extract monopoly wages.

The strategic choice model of industrial relations offers a different argument. By raising relative wages, unions provide incentives for firms to compete on the basis of quality and customization (Streeck, 1991), rather than cost alone. Because firm competitiveness in current markets rests significantly on the ability to compete on quality, customization, time-to-market, and innovation (Appelbaum & Batt, 1994), the presence of unions may induce firms to adopt a more effective approach to competing in current markets. To do so requires investment in new technologies and production systems, often defined as high performance work systems. These work systems provide employees with high relative skills and training, opportunities to participate in workplace decisions, and incentives to induce discretionary effort (e.g. Appelbaum et al. 2000). A classic example is GM's Saturn plant, which became a financial success through much of the 1990s due to its adoption of a high performance work system and joint labor-management governance structure (Kochan & Rubenstein, 2000). The union role in co-management of operations was a significant predictor of better quality and problem solving (Rubenstein, 2000).

Another example is Corning's Blacksburg plant, where the union and management negotiated a contract that reduced job classifications to 2 (eliminating job control unionism), created a self-managed team-based system of production, and linked pay to performance through a skill-based pay system and goalsharing (a combination of gainsharing and profit-sharing). The company and union then used Blacksburg as a model for union-management relations and high performance work systems at most other U.S. manufacturing plants (Batt, 1997).

A growing body of empirical research documents a significant positive relationship between high performance systems and firm performance, both in terms of organizational metrics such as productivity, quality, time-to-market, and sales growth (e.g. Appelbaum et al., 2000; Becker & Gerhart, 1996; Ichniowski et al., 1996; MacDuffie, 1995; Batt, 2002); and financial metrics (Baker, 1999) such as Tobin's q and the accounting measure, GRATE (Huselid, 1995; Huselid & Becker, 1996), and return on equity and return on assets (Delery & Doty, 1996; Snell & Youndt, 1995).

While many unions resisted these types of work innovations in the 1970s and early 1980s, unions have increasingly embraced such practices in the 1990s in order to save jobs. The AFL-CIO and many national unions have official policies supporting union-management partnerships, employee participation, and "high performance work practices" (e.g. AFL-CIO, 1994; International Brotherhood of Electrical Workers, 1993; Communications Workers of America, 1994).

In addition to influencing the *adoption* of high performance systems, unions may also make *implementation* of such systems more effective by mobilizing members to fully participate in workplace innovations. Union support for high performance systems often results in better and more sustainable implementation and greater acceptance of change on the part of workers (Eaton & Voos, 1992; Kochan & Osterman, 1994; Batt, 1997). This may occur, as in the Saturn and Blacksburg cases, because the union negotiates the terms and conditions for employee participation, including an employment security pledge that frees up employees to offer suggestions without worrying that their suggestions will lead to job loss. Thus the interactive effect of unions and high performance work systems may lead to gains over and above those produced by high performance systems alone. In a study of a nationally representative sample of establishments surveyed by the Census Bureau, for example, Black and Lynch (1998) found that the use of high performance work systems was associated with 10% higher productivity in non-union establishments, but 20% higher in unionized workplaces.

A more recent study provides evidence of a direct link between unions, operational performance, and financial performance in the U.S. airline industry between 1987 and 1999 (Gittell, Von Nordenflycht & Kochan, 2001). The authors found that unionization and shared union-management governance structures were significantly positively related to operational performance and financial outcomes, as measured by operating margins and return on assets (ROA). In addition, operational performance mediated the relationship between shared governance and unionization on the one hand, and financial performance on the other. Labor conflict, by contrast, was negatively associated with service quality, productivity, and financial outcomes.

In sum, there is a growing body of research that suggests that firms that compete on quality and customization and adopt high performance work systems will have better operational and financial performance, and that union support for adoption and implementation of these systems can lead to particularly positive outcomes.

UNIONS AND ENTREPRENEURIAL FIRMS: THE CURRENT STUDY

Prior research, therefore, supports the idea that the relationship between unions and firm financial performance is an empirical question that depends upon market and institutional context. In this study, we examine a set of privately held firms that have recently gone public. Thus, we essentially are exploring the financial results of privately held firms with unions, as well as what happens to them after they go public. We could find no prior research on unions and financial performance in this type of firm. However, we do know that on average privately held IPO firms differ from other publicly traded firms in that they are younger and smaller. For example, in our sample, the average firm at the time of its IPO was 4.79 years old. The median firm was 6 years old, and over 80% of the sample was less than 10 years old. The average firm in the sample employed 1,107 people, while the median firm had 190 employees.

These differences suggest a couple of ways in which unions may behave differently in IPOs compared to publicly traded companies more generally. First, because they are younger, they are less likely to have developed a system of job control unionism of the kind found in traditional U.S. mass production manufacturing. They are more likely to be in a position to adopt high performance work practices because they are not saddled with a legacy of traditional mass production systems or investment in outmoded technologies. Moreover, privately held firms do not have the pressure to meet the short-term financial expectations of investors, and they are not under the scrutiny of Wall Street. Thus, the union-management relationship has the potential to develop in a more cooperative vein because the firm is not under intense pressure from outside shareholders to meet financial expectations or risk a fall in stock price.

Second, as small independent enterprises, they are less likely to be part of national union contracts, or subject to industry-wide pattern bargaining. In enterprise bargaining, the monopoly power of unions is likely to be moderated. Third, unionization is likely to be a relatively recent phenomenon; and research shows that unions generally make modest economic gains in negotiating early contracts. Instead, the voice effects in early contracts are more important, including grievance and third party arbitration, seniority rights, and just cause and due process procedures (Freeman & Kleiner, 1990).

Our analysis of information in the corporate perspectus provided some support for these arguments. For those companies that provided information on labor management relations, for example, we found that only about 20% were organized by powerful national unions such as the United Steelworkers, the Teamsters, or the United Auto Workers. Other unions in the sample include: The United Brotherhood of Carpenters and Joiners of America, Graphic Communications Union, International Alliance of Theatrical Stage Employees, Association of Flight Attendants, Office and Professional Employees International Union, Amalgamated Clothing and Textile Workers Union, and the Moving Picture Machine Operators Union. For these unions, collective bargaining often occurred at the enterprise level, and many companies reported that they had never had a work stoppage.

Thus, the labor relations context in these privately owned firms appears to be one in which the monopoly power of unions is moderate and the labor relations climate is cooperative. In this environment, union wage gains are likely to be moderate, and union benefits for workers are likely to accrue in areas related to collective voice: employee participation in workplace decisions, procedural justice, and employment security. These collective voice benefits support the implementation of high performance work practices by helping to create an environment of trust and employment security that reduces worker resistance to process innovations. These contextual factors lead us to hypothesize that in this group of firms, unions will be positively associated with firm financial performance and growth.

Methods

Our research strategy involved selecting a specific cohort of IPO firms that went public in a given year and then tracking those same firms over time to study the effects of their early organization structure (whether unionized or not) on subsequent firm performance. We selected a sample of firms that went public in 1993 so that we could study performance over time after the IPO (e.g. performance from 1993 to year-end 1996). The number of firms that went public in 1993 and that produced a good or service (we excluded real estate trusts and financial groups with no employees) was 585; of those companies we were able to obtain the prospectuses (which are one of our primary data sources) for 535 firms. The sample was further reduced to 476 as a result of missing data. Fifty-nine firms no longer reported data for two of the dependent variables – stock price and earnings per share in (1996). Of these firms, we found that 50 had engaged in a merger or acquisition, two filed for bankruptcy, one went private, and six had no information available. In order to examine potential survival bias (the firms that dropped out were in some way inferior performers), we conducted an ANOVA to determine how those firms for which we did not have complete data (that dropped out of the sample) differed from the overall sample. We found that there were no significant differences in any of the variables used in the analyses for this research (e.g. risk factors at time of IPO, age of firm, size measured by sales and number of employees, and net profitability). The lack of significant differences, we speculate, is due to the fact that mergers may be conducted for healthy as well as financially troubled firms, and most of the firms for which we could no longer find data had engaged in a merger or acquisition. Our final sample was reduced to 464 due to missing data that were randomly distributed among the variables used in the analyses.

Data Collection and Coding

The primary data source was the prospectus of each firm. The prospectus is the document provided to the Securities and Exchange Commission (SEC) prior to the public offering, and it is also the document circulated by the underwriter to assess demand for the firm's stock. The SEC requires that firms follow strict guidelines in the format. In fact, the firm is legally liable for any information that might mislead investors (O'Flaherty, 1984). As noted by Beatty and Zajac (1994), top management is accountable to the SEC and to stockholders regarding the contents of the prospectus. The Securities Act of 1933 sets the requirements for the prospectus, thus assuring consistency in the type of information that is included in the document. The typical prospectus writing process involves at least three lawyers (one for the company and one for each of the investment bankers), two investment banking firms, and at least one certified public accountant. Each party has a vested interest in providing the public with an honest view of the company. Thus, we can be reasonably assured that the prospectus is a useful data source (Marino, Castaldi & Dollinger, 1989).

The coding strategy was developed and refined in earlier research (see method used by Welbourne and Andrews, 1996). Each coder received a coding handbook and attended an initial training session. A total of five coders worked on the data, and attended weekly meetings with the principal researchers to go over problems and/or inconsistencies in the prospectuses. Finally, we randomly cross-coded prospectuses (every 10th prospectus). For the variables used in this study, agreement was 90% or higher among the coders. Financial data were also obtained from COMPUSTAT, *Going Public: The IPO Reporter* (for financial data at the time of the IPO), and from a database obtained from the Securities Data Corporation.

Sample Characteristics
Table 1 provides the distribution of firms by industry and geographic location. For each industry and location, it also reports the percentage of firms that are unionized. The most striking observation is that IPO firms are located across a wide range of geographic locations and most major industrial sectors. They are not concentrated, for example, among high tech companies. The companies are located in all geographic areas within the United States with higher concentrations of firms in the Pacific (22%), South Atlantic (13%), Mid-Atlantic (11.7%), and Northeast (10.6%). In addition, 8% of the firms are based outside of the U.S. The sample firms are roughly equally divided between manufacturing (48.9%) and services (44.7%), with an additional 3.3% in extractive industries, and 2% in construction. Utilizing industry codes suggested by the U.S. Small Business Administration, we grouped firms into more detailed categories. The largest single category of firms was in apparel and accessory stores (26.9%), followed by industrial machinery (9.1%), utilities (8.7%), electronic equipment (8%), instruments and related products (6.5%) and chemicals and related products (6.5%).

A total of 95 firms (21%) reported having a union at the time of the IPO. This represents a higher rate of private sector unionization than the U.S. national average of 10% in 1995 (Bureau of Labor Statistics). This is due to the fact that 53% of the sample is the more unionized goods-producing sector, while in the economy as a whole, only 25% of employment is in this sector (U.S. DOL, 1999). The sample's rate of unionization varies widely from none in miscellaneous services to over 80% in stone, glass, and metal fabrication.

Measures of Variables
We coded union status from the company prospectuses. Because not all companies reported the percentage of employees that were unionized, we coded union status as a dummy variable, where one equals union presence, else zero. Of the 49 companies that did report more detailed information on unions, we found that on average 46.9% of employees were unionized. The median is 40.5% with a minimum of 1.5% and maximum of 100%.

Table 1.   Distribution of Sample Firms by Industry and Geographic Location.

Two-Digit SIC Industry	Percent of Total Sample	Percent Unionized
Metal, mining, oil and gas extraction	3.3	11.8
General building contractors and heavy construction	2.0	11.1
Food and kindred products, textile mills and apparel, and other textile products	6.0	16.7
Lumber, wood products, furniture, paper products	1.7	60.0
Printing and publishing	1.7	37.5
Chemical and allied products	6.5	11.8
Rubber, plastics, and leather products	2.2	36.4
Stone and glass – Metal, fabricated metal	4.8	82.6
Industrial machinery and equipment	9.1	20.0
Electronic and other electronic equipment	8.0	15.4
Transportation equipment	1.7	40.0
Instruments and related products	6.5	5.7
Miscellaneous manufacturing industries	2.4	8.3
Railroad and other transit	2.4	57.1
Communication	3.9	20.0
Electric, gas, and sanitary	1.1	33.3
Wholesale trade and building supplies	8.7	17.0
Apparel and accessory stores	26.9	12.9
Miscellaneous services	1.3	0.0

Geographic Location	Percent of Total Sample	Percent Unionized
Foreign country	8.0	57.9
Northeast	10.6	13.0
Middle Atlantic	11.7	19.4
East North Central	8.7	45.5
West North Central	6.7	13.2
South Atlantic	13.0	16.2
East South Central	2.8	31.3
West South Central	9.8	14.5
Mountain	5.4	10.7
Pacific	22.1	10.2

For dependent variables, we used three measures of financial performance: Tobin's q at the time of the IPO, growth in earnings, and growth in stock price. Tobin's q is the ratio of market value to book value (replacement value) at the initial public offering. Because book value is historic, it is not an exact approximation of replacement cost (which is what is intended in the calculation of

Tobin's q); but the IPO literature recommends stock price to book value as a measure of investor reaction to a firm (Smirlock, Gilligan & Marshall, 1984). Thus, Tobin's q indicates how investors value the firm, with a higher ratio indicative of higher value (Davis, 1991). At the time of the IPO, many factors influence Tobin's q, including information in the prospectus, how well the owners are able sell their company to investors (partly due to how many orders for stock are taken prior to the IPO), and how well the overall stock market is doing. Tobin's q is a good indicator of investors' assessment of the potential value of the firm.

Growth in earnings per share (EPS) is measured from the time of the IPO in 1993 to end-of-year 1996. EPS is a measure of internal performance that is often used by analysts and investors to assess future value of the firm. In the EPS analyses, we included earnings per share at the time of the IPO as a control variable. By conducting the analyses in this way, we eliminate measurement issues surrounding the use of change scores. However, we did run the analyses with change scores (percentage change from IPO to year-end 1996 as dependent variables), and the patterns of results (including significance levels) did not change.

Given that the primary reason investors choose to put money into an IPO is to make money when the firm's stock price increases over time, we also studied growth in stock price. Market-based measures represent the most prevalent and relevant firm performance measures in the IPO literature (for a review, see Ibbotson & Ritter, 1995). After controlling for initial stock price (adjusted for splits, buybacks, or any other events that affect unit price of the stock), our analysis reflects the increase in value of the firm in the first three years following the IPO.

We selected several control variables known to be correlated with unionization, including age, size, industry, and geographic location. Company age is based on the year the company was incorporated, as reported in the prospectus (calculated as 1993-date incorporated). Firm size is measured by the number of employees and by total sales at the time of IPO. For industry characteristics, we included nineteen (one omitted) dummy variables based on two-digit industry classifications as reported by the Small Business Administration. For location, we added nine geographic dummy codes (one omitted) (See Table 1 for industry and geographic categories used). We also used control variables suggested in studies of human resources and firm performance and the initial public offering literature (e.g. Welbourne & Andrews, 1996; Huselid, 1995; Beatty & Zajac, 1994). We included two measures of firm performance: total assets and net profit per share at the time of the IPO. For our analysis of stock price, we include an additional control for adjusted stock price (adjusted for splits, etc.) at the time of the IPO.

Although our sample of IPO firms consists of companies that are considered to be higher risk investments than companies currently in the public market (due to their having no prior stock price history), we expect that each firm will be subject to varying degrees of risk. Therefore, we added a measure of risk obtained from each prospectus. This measure is the number of paragraphs in the prospectus devoted to listing all risk factors faced by the firm. These risk factors must be disclosed to meet the requirements of the Securities and Exchange Commission. Prior research on initial public offering firms has found this measure to be a useful way to code risk (Beatty & Zajac, 1994; Rasheed & Datta, 1994).

Results

Table 2 provides the means and standard deviations for the entire sample, the means for the union and non-union sub-samples, and the results of one-way analysis of variance by union status. The results indicate that union and non-union firms are statistically significantly different on all dimensions except age. Compared to non-union firms, union firms are significantly larger (in sales and employees), have more assets and higher earnings per share at time of IPO, and have lower reported risk. Union firms also have significantly higher earnings per share and stock price in (1996). They have a lower value for Tobin's q, as anticipated, because Tobin's q reflects how investors value the firm, and investors typically interpret unionization as a signal that the firm will be less profitable.

Our examination of pairwise correlations (see Table 3) shows several expected correlations that are significant. Firms that are older and larger in size are viewed as "traditional" firms with lower growth potential, and therefore, have a negative correlation with Tobin's q (which reflects investors' assessment of a firm's potential for growth). Union firms are positively correlated with earnings per share and stock price in 1996.

Tests of Hypotheses

We tested the relationship between unions and financial performance by using ordinary least squares (OLS) regression equations in a two-step hierarchical model. In the first step we included all of the control variables. In the second step, we added the union variable to estimate the added significance of unionization for each of the three dependent variables. As noted earlier, the first measure of performance (Tobin's q) is at Time-1 (time of the IPO). The second two measures are longitudinal in nature, including controls for

Table 2. Means and Standard Deviations of Variables:
All Firms, Union Firms, and Non-union Firms Compared.

Variable	All Firms Mean (s.d.) ($N = 464$)	Non-Union Firms Mean (s.d.) ($N = 369$)	Union Firms Mean (s.d.) ($N = 95$)
Dependent Variables			
Tobin's Q at time of IPO	3.51 (9.13)	4.93*** (18.31)	−3.21 (51.41)
Earnings per share (1996)	−0.08 (1.56)	−0.24*** (1.54)	0.57 (1.48)
Stock price (1996)	12.04 (10.73)	10.87*** (10.35)	16.60 (10.86)
Independent and Control Variables			
Union Status	0.21 (0.40)		
Company age	4.79 (10.65)	4.35 (8.98)	5.13 (14.65)
Number of employees, time of IPO	1,107 (3,208)	674*** (2,394)	2,761 (4,791)
Sales at time of IPO	143,390,980 (335,243,460)	85,776,280*** (258,957,860)	368,887,000 (502,436,260)
Total assets at time of IPO	152,599,420 (446,778,780)	105,664,600*** (411,441,590)	344,661,540 (544,392,510)
Earnings per share at time of IPO	0.01 (1.70)	0.12*** (0.58)	0.41 (0.61)
Risk factors (total paragraphs in prospectus)	15.83 (4.88)	16.57*** (5.04)	13.38 (4.01)

Significant differences between union and non-union firms at $+ p < 0.10$; $* p < 0.05$; $** p < 0.01$; $*** p < 0.001$.

Table 3. Correlation Matrix.

	1	2	3	4	5	6	7	8	9
1. Tobin's Q (1993), Log	1.00								
2. Earnings/share, (1996)	-0.04	1.00							
3. Stock price, (1996)	-0.03	0.36	1.00						
4. Company age	-0.10	-0.09	-0.13	1.00					
5. Number of employees	-0.22	0.09	0.22	-0.01	1.00				
6. Sales, (1993)	-0.28	0.14	0.26	-0.07	0.75	1.00			
7. Total assets, (1993)	-0.14	0.12	0.17	-0.11	0.49	0.82	1.00		
8. Risk factors	0.08	-0.40	-0.37	-0.05	-0.20	-0.24	-0.17	1.00	
9. Initial stock price	-0.02	-0.04	-0.04	-0.04	0.16	0.17	0.13	-0.28	1.00
10. Union status (0/1)	-0.01	0.22	0.24	0.03	0.25	0.33	0.21	-0.26	0.24

Correlations above 0.07 are significant at the $p < 0.05$ level; correlations above 0.10 are significant at $p < 0.01$, and correlations above 0.12 are significant at $p < 0.001$. Industry and location dummies not shown.

Time-1 and predicting performance three years after the IPO (i.e. year-end 1996). These results are presented in Table 4.

For Tobin's q, the base case explains 18.6% of the variance. Once organizational characteristics are controlled for, unionization has a statistically significant positive and large relationship with Tobin's q. Unionized firms have a 15.2% higher Tobin's q than do non-union firms. The union variable increases the explanatory power of the equation by 1.3 percentage points. For the critical outcomes of earnings growth and growth in share price after three years, union presence is associated with 10.1% higher earnings per share and 17.1% higher stock price. The coefficient on the union is only marginally significant for growth in earnings per share. However, it is highly significant for growth in stock price, and raises the explanatory power of the model by 1.5 percentage points.

These outcomes control for important firm characteristics at Time-1, including size, age, industry, location, as well as assets, sales, level of risk, net income per share, and initial stock price adjusted for splits. Most control variables are statistically significant, indicating the importance of controlling for these factors. In most cases, they behave as expected. For example, assets are positively related to Tobin's q (investors' assessments of the potential long term value of the firm), but negatively related to stock price in 1996 (because larger firms tend to grow more slowly). Following a similar logic, initial stock price is negatively associated with stock price in 1996 – larger firms with higher assets and lower risk tend to have initial higher valuation in the stock market, but tend to grow more slowly. Earnings per share at Time-1 are positively

Table 4. Relationship Between Unions and Financial Performance
(standardized betas).

	(log) Tobin's q At IPO (1993)	Earnings Per Share (1996)	Stock Price (1996)
Step 1: Control Variables			
Company age	−0.122*	−0.072	−0.023
Number of employees	−0.005	0.076	0.097
Sales at time of IPO	−0.557***	−0.030	0.159*
Total assets	0.276***	0.066	−0.123*
Earnings per share at time of IPO	−0.128*	0.141**	0.166***
Risk factors	−0.062	−0.192***	−0.290***
Initial stock price			−0.234***
R^2 Step 1	0.186***	0.308***	0.337***
Union Status (0/1)	0.152**	0.101+	0.171**
Step 2: Change in R^2	0.013**	0.006+	0.015**
Total R^2	0.200***	0.314***	0.352***
Sample Size	444	434	460

Controls for industry and location not shown.
Significance: $+ p < 0.10$; $* p < 0.05$; $** p < 0.01$; $*** p < 0.001$.

associated with earnings and stock price growth. Higher risk firms have lower earnings per share and stock price in 1996.

In addition, in equations not shown, we controlled for other factors that we thought might be relevant, such as the percentage of the owner's compensation at risk, the percentage of the employees compensation at risk, and the presence of an HR department and statements concerning the value of human resources. Our findings above were robust to these alternate specifications (not shown).

Discussion

In this study we analyzed the relationship between unions and financial performance among entrepreneurial firms that conducted an IPO in 1993. After controlling for relevant organizational characteristics, we found a positive relationship between unions and Tobin's q at the IPO. We interpret this to mean that all things equal, analysts' often negative view of unions did not translate into a negative general assessment of the firm's potential to produce shareholder value. Consistent with our main hypothesis, we found a strong positive relationship between unionization and financial growth over time (especially growth in stock price). These results are contrary to most prior empirical studies on this topic, which have found that unionization is negatively associated with strong financial performance.

The strongest alternative hypothesis for these findings is selection bias. That is, arguably the better performing privately held firms became the target of unionization as unions perceived they would be better able to extract rents from the more profitable firms. We cannot completely discount this argument, but we believe that it is less plausible for the set of entrepreneurial firms for a number of reasons. First, the profitability of privately held firms is not publicly available, making it difficult for competitors and unions to know which firms to target. More importantly, we are encouraged by the longitudinal findings of better financial performance after three years. If unions do have a negative effect on financial performance after they organize a profitable firm, then we would expect that negative effect to show in later years. For example, we would expect the profitability of unionized firms' after IPO to become worse relative to non-union firms. In this case, however, we find that earnings per share and stock price of union firms three years after IPO is higher, after controlling for profitability at the time of the IPO. Whereas the average initial stock price of non-union firms was $10.32 and rose to $10.87 (a 5.4% increase), the average for union firms was $13.63 and rose to $16.60 (a rise of 21.8%). Thus, at the very least we can conclude that unions do not have a negative effect on these entrepreneurial firms. For these reasons, we find the selection-bias argument to be less applicable to this study.

In sum, this is the first study that we know of that examines the relationship between unions and financial performance in entrepreneurial firms. While our data present limitations, we believe that our findings are suggestive, particularly given our longitudinal measures of growth in earnings and stock price. Our research suggests that the role of unions in entrepreneurial firms is a subject deserving of further research.

CONCLUSIONS AND FUTURE RESEARCH

In this chapter, we have reviewed the theoretical frameworks and prior empirical research regarding the relationship between unions and firm performance. Prior reviews of the literature have presented this relationship as an open and shut case: unions increase productivity but reduce financial performance.

Our review of the literature, however, challenges that view. The relevant theoretical frameworks – both the exit/voice and the strategic industrial relations perspectives – provide a contingency perspective on the role of unions in firm performance. In addition, when we reviewed prior empirical studies, we found a much more nuanced story about the association between unions and financial performance. The union effect was contingent on market, industry, and institutional factors, and the negative relationship between unions and financial performance appeared to be declining in the 1980s. We also drew on more recent research on high performance work systems, which suggests that unions have an important role to play in fostering the adoption and implementation of such systems.

In the context of our reading of the literature, we then examined the role of unions in entrepreneurial firms, and found that compared to non-union firms, unionization had a significant positive relationship to Tobin's q at the point of IPO, to earnings per share in 1996, and to stock price in 1996. Our results provide initial support to challenge the prevailing view found in the literature and suggest that unionization does not inevitably reduce financial performance. Rather new forms of organizing work and union-management relations hold the promise of maximizing shareholder wealth as well as employee welfare. There is not an inevitable zero-sum trade-off.

Our study is limited in a number of ways, however. We had a limited number of measures of financial performance, were only able to study the presence or absence of union, and we were not able to disentangle alternative interpretations regarding why unionization is positively related to financial performance in these firms. Thus, we conclude by suggesting an agenda for future research.

First, future studies need to examine a broader range of operational and financial performance outcomes, and the relationships between intermediate and final outcomes. Second, future studies need to examine external factors that influence the union-performance relationship and to penetrate the black box of unions. Researchers need to examine how variation in union density and union strategy affects firm performance. Some initial research in this vein, for example, has found that the capability of union leaders and their ability to mobilize support among their members are important predictors of the process of restructuring and better outcomes for union members (Frost, 1999). Also, as indicated in our review, there is a healthy tradition in Industrial Relations of examining the quality of union-management relations, rather than union presence per se; but with the exception of a recent study (Hoffer et al., 2001), this stream of research has not examined financial outcomes.

Third, future research needs to examine the causal links that mediate the relationship between unionization and firm performance and the external contingencies that moderate this relationship. In this study, we have elaborated two major arguments as to why unions may be associated with better financial performance. On the one hand, the exit/voice framework suggests that in this case, the collective voice of unions is strong relative to union monopoly power. Thus firms gain from greater employee effort without paying higher wages. On the other hand, strategic choice theory in industrial relations suggests that the higher profitability is the result of more productive work systems, not lower wages. Entrepreneurial firms represent a new context that is more conducive to union-management partnerships and the use of high performance systems. In this view, unions may support high performance systems by supporting adoption and better implementation and sustainability of such systems.

In order to accomplish this research agenda, there are a number of methodological challenges. A first challenge is to link operational and financial measures of performance. Financial measures are typically available only at the firm unit of analysis, but most firms involve multi-divisional structures and a multitude of operational locations. Because within firm variation in human resource practices is great, most studies of high performance work systems and union-management relations have taken the establishment as the unit of analysis and have only been able to assess operational performance rather than financial outcomes. This is where the study of high tech and entrepreneurial firms provide an opportunity for researchers because these firms tend to be small and have few branch operations. Making the link between operational and financial performance indicators is more feasible.

A second challenge is to develop a much richer understanding of the role of context and contingency in organizational research. This is a particularly difficult challenge in the study of entrepreneurial firms because market conditions, innovation, and growth create such a dynamic environment. Nonetheless, one solution is to pay greater attention to qualitative research to inform quantitative analyses. To unpackage the black box of unions requires researchers to focus on unions as organizations and to interview local union leaders and stewards as well as managers and employees during field research. Frost's (1999) study of alternative union strategies and organizational capabilities in the steel industry provides a useful methodological model. This type of research will provide us with a more robust understanding of the boundary conditions for a positive relationship between unions and financial performance.

Third, there are major methodological challenges to examining the causal links between variation in unions and union-management relations, the adoption and implementation of high performance work systems, and organizational outcomes. Given the great variation in markets and institutional contexts, industry-specific studies provide a particularly useful research strategy. As indicated in our review, industry-specific qualitative and quantitative studies in autos, steel, apparel, semi-conductors, computers, telecommunications, and banking have provided some of the strongest and most rigorous research documenting the positive relationship between high performance work systems and organizational outcomes. These studies, however, have not done a sufficient job of unpackaging the black box of union strategies and union-management relations, and how variation along these dimensions interacts with the adoption and implementation of high performance work systems. The industry-specific approach combining qualitative and quantitative methods, however, provides a useful model for future research into these causal mechanisms.

Finally, this study of entrepreneurial firms has implications for research in human resource studies and industrial relations more generally. Much of the research in these fields has been conducted in large bureaucratic organizations. Our study shows the importance of questioning results of studies that have been conducted in the limited context of large organizations in highly institutionalized environments. Most prior research has focused on unions and firms with deeply institutionalized relationships that pose difficult barriers to change. Entrepreneurial firms provide a context in which to explore the role of unions without those embedded constraints. When we examined what was thought to be an 'accepted' conclusion – that unions have a negative effect on financial performance – in a sample that had not been studied before, we found different results. Lessons learned from research in these firms can supplement our current knowledge and create a richer understanding of labor management relations, the use of high performance work systems, and organizational outcomes across distinct contexts.

REFERENCES

Addison, J. T., & Hirsch, B. T. (1989). Union Effects on Productivity, Profits, and Growth: Has the Long Run Arrived? *Journal of Labor Economics, 7*(1), 72–105.

AFL-CIO (1994). Changing Work: A Union Guide to Workplace Change. Washington, D.C.: AFL-CIO Human Resources Development Institute.

Allen, S. G. (1986). Unionization and Productivity in Office Building and School Construction. *Industrial and Labor Relations Review, 39*(2)(January), 187–200.

Allen, S. G. (1988). Further Evidence on Union Efficiency in Construction. *Industrial Relations, 27*(2)(Spring), 232–240.

Appelbaum, E., & Batt, R. (1994). *The New American Workplace: Transforming Work Systems in the United States*. Ithaca, NY: Cornell ILR Press.

Appelbaum, E., Bailey, T., Berg, P., & Kalleberg, A. (2000). *Manufacturing Advantage*. Ithaca, NY: ILR Press, an imprint of Cornell University Press.

Baker, T. (1999). *Doing Well by Doing Good: The Bottom Line in Workplace Practices*. Washington, D.C.: Economic Policy Institute.

Batt, R. (1997). Reassessing Union-Management Partnerships: Lessons from Corning and the American Flint Glass Workers Union. January.

Batt, R. (2002). Managing Customer Services: Human Resource Practices, Quit Rates, and Sales Growth. *Academy of Management Journal, 45*(June), 3.

Batt, R., Colvin, A., & Keefe, J. (2002). Employee Voice, Human Resource Practices, and Quit Rates: Evidence from the Telecommunications Industry. *Industrial and Labor Relations Review*, (July).

Beatty, R. P., & Zajac, E. J. (1994). Managerial Incentives, Monitoring, and Risk Bearing: A Study of Executive Compensation, Ownership, and Board Structure in Initial Public Offerings. *Administrative Science Quarterly, 39*, 313–335.

Becker, B. E., & Olson, C. A. (1989). Unionization and Shareholder Interests. *Industrial and Labor Relations Review, 42*(2), 246–261.

Becker, B. E. (1995). Union Rents as a Source of Takeover Gains among Target Shareholders. *Industrial and Labor Relations Review, 49*(1), 3–19.

Becker, B. E., & Olson, C. A. (1992). Unions and Firm Profits. *Industrial Relations, 31*(3), 395–415.

Belman, D. (1992). Unions, the Quality of Labor Relations, and Firm Performance. In: L. Mishel & P. Voos (Eds), *Unions and Economic Competitiveness* (pp. 41–108). Armonk, NY: M. E. Sharpe.

Black, S., & Lynch, L. (1998). The New Workplace: What Does It Mean for Productivity? *Proceedings of the Fiftieth Annual Meeting of the IRRA*. Madison, WI: IRRA Association Series.

Bronars, S. G., & Deere, D. R. (1990). Union Representation Elections and Firm Profitability. *Industrial Relations, 29*(1)(Winter), 15–37.

Bronars, S. G., Deere, D. R., & Stacey, J. (1994). The Effects of Unions on Firm Behavior: An Empirical Analysis Using Firm-Level Data. *Industrial Relations, 33*(4)(October), 426–451.

Bureau of Labor Statistics (BLS). *http://stats/bls.gov*.

Communications Workers of America (1994). Executive Board Report on Union-Management Participation for the Telecommunications Industry. Washington, D.C.: Communications Workers of America.

Connolly, R. A., Hirsch, B. T., & Hirschey, M. (1986). Union Rent Seeking, Intangible Capital, and Market Value of the Firm. *Review of Economics and Statistics, 68*(4)(November), 567–577.

Davis, G. F. (1991). Agents Without Principals? The Spread of the Poison Pill Through the Intercorporate Network. *Administrative Science Quarterly, 36*, 583–613.

Delery, J., & Doty, H. (1996). Modes of Theorizing in Strategic Human Resource Management: Tests of Universalistic, Contingency, and Configurational Performance. *Academy of Management Journal, 39*(4), 802–835.

Delery, J., Gupta, N., Shaw, J., Jenkins, G. D., & Ganster, M. (2000). Unionization, Compensation, and Voice Effects on Quits and Retention. *Industrial Relations, 39*(4), 625–646.

Doeringer, P. B., & Piore, M. J. (1971). *Internal Labor Markets and Manpower Analysis*. Lexington, MA: Heath.

Eaton, A., & Voos, P. (1992). Unions and Contemporary Innovations in Work Organization, Compensation, and Employee Participation. In: L. Mishel & P. Voos (Eds), *Unions and Economic Competitiveness* (pp. 173–216). Armonk, NY: M. E. Sharpe.

Freeman, R. B. (1980). The Exit-Voice Tradeoff in the Labor Market: Unionism, Job Tenure, Quits, and Separations. *The Quarterly Journal of Economics, 94*(3), 643–673.

Freeman, R B. (1992). Is Declining Unionization of the U.S. Good, Bad, or Irrelevant? In: L. Mishel & P. Voos (Eds), *Unions and Economic Competitiveness* (pp. 143–172). Armonk, NY: M. E. Sharpe.

Freeman, R. B., & Medoff, J. (1984). *What Do Unions Do?* NY: Basic Books.

Freeman, R., B., & Kleiner, M. (1990). The Impact of New Unionization on Wages and Working Conditions. *Journal of Labor Economics*, January.

Frost, A. (2000). Explaining Variation in Workplace Restructuring: The Role of Local Union Capabilities. *Industrial and Labor Relations Review, 53*(4), 559–578.

Gittell, J. H., Von Nordenflycht, A., & Kochan, T. (2001). Mutual Gains or Zero Sum? Labor Relations and Stakeholder Outcomes in the Airline Industry. Manuscript.

Hirsch, B. T. (1991). Union Coverage and Profitability among U.S. Firms. *Review of Economics and Statistics, 73*(1)(February), 69–77.

Hirsch, B. T. (1992). Firm Investment Behavior and Collective Bargaining Strategy. *Industrial Relations, 31*(1)(Winter), 95–121.

Hirsch, B. T., & Morgan, B. A. (1994). Shareholder Risk and Returns in Union and Nonunion Firms. *Industrial and Labor Relations Review, 47*(2), 302–318.

Hirsch, B. T., & Connolly, R. A. (1987). Do Unions Capture Monopoly Profits? *Industrial and Labor Relations Review, 41*(1)(October), 118–136.

Huselid, M. A. (1995). The Impact of Human Resource Practices on Turnover, Productivity, and Corporate Financial Performance. *Academy of Management Journal, 38*(3), 635–672.

Huselid, M. A., & Becker, B. E. (1996). Methodological Issues in Cross-sectional and Panel Estimates of the Human Resource-Firm Performance Link. *Industrial Relations 35*(3), 400–422.

Ibbotson, R. G., & Ritter, J. R. (1995). Initial Public Offerings. In: R. A. Jarrow, V. Maksimovic & W. T. Ziemba (Eds), *Finance: North-Holland Handbooks in Operations Research and Management Science* (Vol. 9, pp. 993–1016).

Ichniowski, C., & Lewin, D. (1987). Grievance Procedures and Firm Performance. In: M. Kleiner (Ed.), *Human Resources and the Performance of the Firm* (pp. 159–194). Madison, WI: IRRA.

Ichniowski, C., Kochan, T., Levine, D., Olson, C., & Strauss, G. (1996). What Works at Work: Overview and Assessment. *Industrial Relations, 35*(3), 299–334.

International Brotherhood of Electrical Workers (1993). Employee Participation Programs: A Statement of Policy and guidelines for IBEW Local unions. Washington, D.C.: IBEW.

Jacoby, S. (1985). *Employing Bureaucracy.* New York: Columbia University Press.

Karier, T. (1985). Unions and Monopoly Profits. *Review of Economics and Statistics, 67*(1)(February), 34–42.

Karier, T. (1988). New Evidence on the Effect of Unions and Imports on Monopoly Power. *Journal of Post Keynesian Economics, 10*(3)(Spring), 414–427.

Katz, H. C., Kochan, T. A., & Gobeille, K. R. (1983). Industrial Relations Performance, Economic Performance, and QWL Programs: An Interplant Analysis. *Industrial and Labor Relations Review, 37*(1)(October), 3–17.

Keefe, J. (1992). Do Unions Hinder Technological Change? In: L. Mishel & P. Voos (Eds), *Unions and Economic Competitiveness* (pp. 109–142). Armonk, NY: M. E. Sharpe.

Keefe, J., & Katz, H. C. (1990). Job Classifications and Plant Performance. *Industrial Relations, 29*(1), 111–118.

Kendrick, J. W., & Grossman, E. S. (1980). *Productivity in the United States: Cycles and Trends.* Baltimore, MD: Johns Hopkins University Press.

Kochan, T. A., & Osterman, P. (1994). *The Mutual Gains Enterprise.* Boston, MA: Harvard Business School Press.

Kochan, T., & Rubenstein, S. (2000). Toward a Stakeholder Theory of the Firm: The Saturn Partnership. *Organization Science, 11*(4), 367–387.

MacDuffie, J. P. (1995). Human Resource Bundles and Manufacturing Performance: Organizational Logic and Flexible Production Systems in the World Auto Industry. *Industrial and Labor Relations Review, 48*, 197–221.

Marino, K. E., Castaldi, R. M., & Dollinger, M. J. (1989). Content Analysis in Entrepreneurship Research: The Case of Initial Public Offerings. *Entrepreneurship Theory and Practice*, (Fall), 51–66.

Martinello, F. et al. (1995). Union Certification in Ontario: Its Effect on the Value of the Firm. *Canadian Journal of Economics, 28*(4b)(November), 1077–1095.

Menezes-Filho, N. A. (1997). Unions and Profitability over the 1980s: Some Evidence on Union-Firm Bargaining in the United Kingdom. *Economic Journal, 107*(442)(May), 651–670.

Menezes-Filho, N. A., Ulph, D., & Van Reenen, J. (1998). R&D and Unionism: Comparative Evidence from British Companies and Establishments. *Industrial and Labor Relations Review, 52*(1), 45–63.

O'Flaherty, J. S. (1984). *Going Public: The Entrepreneur's Guide*. New York: John Wiley and Sons.

Rasheed, A., & Datta, D. K. (1994). Determinants of Price Premiums: A Study of Initial Public Offerings in the Medical Diagnostics Industry. Paper presented at the Academy of Management Annual Meeting, Dallas, TX.

Rees, D. (1991). Grievance Procedure Strength and Teacher Quits. *Industrial and Labor Relations Review, 45*(1)(October), 31–43.

Rubenstein, S. (2000). The Impact of Co-management on Quality Performance: The Case of the Saturn Corporation, *Industrial and Labor Relations Review, 531*, 197–220.

Slichter, S., Healy, J. J., & Livernash, E. R. (1960). *The Impact of Collective Bargaining on Management*. Washington: The Brookings Institution.

Snell, S. A., & Youndt, M. A. (1995). Human Resource Management and Firm Performance: Testing a Contingency Model of Executive Controls. *Journal of Management, 21*, 711–737.

Streeck, W. (1991). On the Institutional Conditions of Diversified Quality Production. In: E. Matzner & W. Streeck (Eds), *Beyond Keynesianism: The Socio-Economics of Production and Full Employment* (pp. 21–61). Brookfield, VT: Edward Elgar Publishing Company.

U.S. DOL, Bureau of Labor Statistics (1999). *Report on the American Workforce*. Washington, D.C.: Government Documents.

Walton, R., & McKersie, R. (1965). *A Behavioral Theory of Labor Negotiations*. New York: McGraw Hill.

Welbourne, T. M., & Andrews, A. O. (1996). Predicting Performance of Initial Public Offerings: Should Human Resource Management be in the Equation? *Academy of Management Journal, 39*(4), 891–919.

Wadhwani, S. (1989). The Effect of Unions on Productivity Growth, Investment, and Employment: A Report on Some Recent Work. Working Paper 356. Centre for Labour Economics, April.